THE SEXY, SOULFUL JOURNEY FROM BETRAYAL TO BLISS

THE *Kinky* VANILLA LOVE PROJECT

shhh...

LORD COLTRANE

The Kinky Vanilla Love Project: The Sexy, Soulful Journey from Betrayal to Bliss

First Edition. All rights reserved. No part of this book may be reproduced in any form without permission in writing from the author. Reviewers may quote brief passages in reviews.

Copyright © Lord Coltrane, 2019

DISCLAIMER

No part of this publication may be reproduced or transmitted in any form or by any means, mechanical or electronic, including photocopying or recording, or by any information storage and retrieval system, or transmitted by email without permission in writing from the author.

Neither the author nor the publisher assumes any responsibility for errors, omissions, or contrary interpretations of the subject matter herein. Any perceived slight of any individual or organization is purely unintentional. Some names have been changed for privacy.

Brand and product names are trademarks or registered trademarks of their respective owners.

The information, ideas, and recommendations contained in this book are not intended as a substitute for medical advice or treatment.

ISBN: 9781683092353

Difference Press

WWW.LORDCOLTRANE.COM

THE *Kinky* VANILLA LOVE PROJECT

The Sexy, Soulful Journey from Betrayal to Bliss

LORD COLTRANE

DIFFERENCE PRESS

TO ALL THE SOULS WHO HAVE
STRUGGLED IN LOVE,
BUT LOVE BOLDLY ANYWAY.

Table of Contents

The Shapeshifter's Journey

"You are the hero of your own journey"
—Joseph Campbell

Storytelling is a great way to heal the body from the pains and wounds that life and love sometimes bring to us. It is through the stories of others that we have an opportunity to feel through the five senses of our being to connect to the wisdom, inspiration, and healing that they have to offer. Narratives that are emotionally compelling allow our creative imaginations to tap into sections of the brain that connect to our feelings, so we are more engaged than if we read a set of facts. Our bodies respond as if we are going through those same experiences ourselves, and we learn more.

Sharing a personal journey is a brave act that offers readers a universal need; the call for adventure, the meeting of our demons and beasts along the way, the courage to traverse into the unknown, and ultimately the recognition of our destiny to transcend and transform.

Author and philosopher Joseph Campbell first coined the term "hero's journey," in his book *The Hero with a Thousand Faces*, where he writes about the archetypal hero of myths and legends. In essence, it is an epic tale where a normal person is living an ordinary life, then wham! something unexpected happens. The ordinary person is catapulted into the cave of the unknown, and forced to face many villains and obstacles along the way home to an extraordinary victory. It is the tale of Harry Potter, the Jedi Nights, and Wonder Woman.

A shapeshifter's journey is a journey within the depths of your multidimensional soul, where you find the allies and villains within yourself. And it is precisely this journey of meeting the many facets of the self, that you come to know the exquisite nature of your being. The book you are about to read is my shapeshifter's journey from betrayal to bliss, and my story is your story.

I've been in a relationship for over twenty years, and it has not always been easy. I've experienced moments of excruciating pain where the end of the partnership seemed like the only option. It takes so much courage to be in a long-term, monogamous relationship. It is a monumental task to be with the same person twenty-four/seven, to manage a twosome that often gets challenged by children, the threat of infidelity, the fear of being alone, the sadness of feeling completely misunderstood by the person you share a life with.

I am not a psychotherapist, marriage counselor, or licensed sex educator (though I have logged in many hours of research and experimentation that would suggest otherwise). I am a regular woman just like you, on a journey into healing with hopes and dreams and a deep desire to know what love feels like at its fullest expression. I have children. I do carpool. I go to P.T.A. meetings and soccer games. I have lunch with friends, walk my dog, and struggle with managing work and family. I have gratitude for the lifestyle I lead, and know my "champagne problems" of marital strife are nothing compared to the experiences of those without the basic human needs or the dignity that everyone deserves. Regardless, I yearn to feel whole, fulfilled, and intensely alive. I am hungry for the kind of passion that lives at the bottom of my soul and at the most tender spot of my heart. I want this. Don't you?

Throughout my marriage, I have often wondered if it is really possible to deepen our bonds, teach our partners how to be great lovers, truly enjoy sex with the same person after twenty, thirty, even forty years. What about communicating what we like or don't like without offending the other? What if we don't even know what we like or don't like? And how can we discover these answers without the reading material being so serious, or dare I say, so boring after a few chapters? For the most part, there aren't many self-help relationship books available that are playful, let alone sexy to read. As a certifiable self-help addict, I've searched high and low, and in the back alleys for the right message and tone that will lift my spirits, satisfy my heart, and tickle my groin.

To answer my own questions (and as a last ditch effort to save my marriage) I created The Kinky Vanilla Love Project, a thirty-day experiment as thirty different women with my husband. I stole ideas from polyamorous relationships, the intrigue of infidelity, the taboo B.D.S.M. lifestyle, and merged them with the ideals of monogamy, spirituality, conscious loving. I gave my husband an experience beyond any man's wildest dreams, which is not the point. I created this experiment because I wanted and deserved more.

I didn't know then that this experiment was going to awaken me to bliss, but it did. And that is when I began to really dig into the archetypal, psychological, and mystic worlds to back up what helped me transform. Unknowingly, I was conducting "grounded theory" research, which is the development of theories based on people's lived experiences rather than proving or disproving existing theories. Renowned research professor and storyteller Brené Brown uses grounded theory for her studies on shame and guilt. I was, and am, my own guinea pig.

I took a deeper dive into the teachings of Swiss psychoanalyst Carl Jung and his philosophies on the Collective Unconscious, archetypes, and the quest of the individual psyche to find wholeness. I continue to study the ancient wisdom of the Vedic scriptures where gods and goddesses are said to be expressing creatively through us. I've investigated the works of new thought leaders like Jean Houston, Carolyn Myss, and others to support what I found in my own experiment. I realized that I was taking ancient wisdom and transforming it into a modern concept that could help many failing partnerships that don't have the balance of good communication, support, equanimity, and sex. Sex might not be everything, but it (or lack of it) is usually the thing that couples fight about in long term relationships.

I should warn you now that this book might be a little racier that the normal "self-help" book that also suggests codes to awakening the soul. When I was looking for topics on love and sex, especially in monogamous relationships, at my local book store, the steamy and juicy parts seemed to be left out by our experts. I yearned for the phrases that made me blush. I wanted to be gripped with hungry attention, my animalistic urges exposed. I desperately wanted to set my inhibitions free.

I agree with popular ideas that we speak different love languages, that men and women might be from different planets, and our erotic nature may be caged by domesticity. All of these viewpoints get us closer to understanding the mystery of lasting love, but most academic relationship professionals, including those that cover intercourse and foreplay, tend to offer clinically dry descriptions. When I was reading books on how to touch the penis and the vagina, I was definitely learning the basics of how pleasure works, but I definitely was not getting turned-on by it.

I asked myself if it was wrong to awaken the erotic pulses that exist beyond socially accepted words while trying to learn more about intimacy and love. I mean that's the whole point right? I want to giggle with delight. I want my heart to throb and the place between my legs to quiver. I want my flesh to burn with desire. I want fantasy. I want to be captivated by the forbidden rituals of kinky play, or at least a healthy bite-size portion of it. Why can't we also explore that lustful urge to rip off our panties and just fuck? (Yikes, I just made myself blush!)

During my quest to unleash my undiscovered feminine powers, I found myself with an insatiable need to be inspired, tantalized, and turned-on by what I read, researched and experienced because that is precisely what was missing in my life and relationship. I know I'm not the only one who aches for variety and passion in the soft embrace of unconditional love. Over a 125 million copies of *50 Shades of Grey* have been sold worldwide although it is an erotically taboo read. Clearly, women around the globe aren't just looking for great literature. They also have a craving for the fantasy of intense romance, the mystery of the forbidden, and the naughtiness of porn without all the social complications. Wouldn't it be great to read a self-help book that inspires us to overcome shame and fear, enriches our sex lives (as well as normal lives), strengthens our relationships, and excites us like a trashy novel? It would be a best seller, a one-woman show, and maybe even a blockbuster movie! I declare the desperate need for a "sexy self-help" book!

I offer it to you now.

I share this story as an epic tale of love and healing, with profound lessons and how-tos along the way, so that you can dive into the journey of awakening the heart and soul, so you might *feel* awakened, or at least be inspired by it. I wrote this so you can get lost in a tale that shows how to merge the sacredness of being in love with the sensuality of making love. This real life story will show you, as it showed me, how to journey from betrayal to bliss.

1. Vanilla Lovers

A LOVE STORY

This is a love story, and it goes something like this:

My husband cheated on me.

With a hairdresser.

How cliché!

I hate clichés.

I know what you are thinking, "How can this be a love story?"

But it is, so read on.

LESSON: Not all love stories start off as fairytales.

CLUELESS

The night before the "big reveal," I was naked, in bed, waiting for my husband. I was going to do something really radical for me … initiate. Initiating sex was something I absolutely sucked at. In fact, I never did it. I always waited for his subtle signals, a soft touch on my arm, toesies under the covers, or him getting in bed naked.

So there I lay, waiting for him to finish with his bathroom routine. He was spending a lot of time in the bathroom these days. He got into bed with his underwear on, so I would have to figure out how to slip them off without being ridiculous about it.

He was looking really good, working out obsessively. I snuggled up against his strong body and wrapped my legs around his. He let out a little sigh. At the time, I thought it was a sigh of relief, his wife was finally getting it. It made my heart swell. "I could do this," I thought.

I started to rub my finger tips on his belly, and slowly up and down his chest. At times I'd pull at the hairs along the way. My thighs wandered aimlessly over his legs and rubbed against his sex, intending to cause an erection. He kept his eyes closed the entire time, deeply breathing it in.

I had secretly stashed a bottle of coconut oil beneath my pillow (how clever of me). I needed a lot of relaxation and foreplay in order for my body to surrender enough to become really stimulated. Since I was finally doing the initiating and I wasn't sure how relaxed I could get, a little "cheating" was warranted. While his eyes were closed, I put a little bit of oil between my legs and began to stroke him until I could feel his hard on.

I remember thinking how much easier it is for men to get turned on than women. I needed a bath, a little cuddle session, a little laughter, maybe even a back massage with warm scented oils before I ever wanted anyone on my private parts. Candles would be nice too. These things didn't happen with our busy lives. I was usually stressed out or exhausted by "mommy duty" to feel sexy. I often thought there was something wrong with me because I wasn't instantly as lustful as the women I'd seen in porn movies. I'll admit that I envied the women who got turned on by the hunky guy delivering a sausage pizza, and boom, they were on the dining room table in five different sex positions within minutes, she moaning with orgasmic ecstacy. I know that it's all fake, but if you are used to only vanilla sex, you never *really* know. We for sure never had wanton sex like that.

I took my thumb and started to pull off his underwear. I did it slowly, making sure he could feel my breath on his skin. His eyes were still closed, anticipating. Should I give him a blow job before I mounted him? Yes, that would be a good idea.

When I finally got on top and began rhythmically moving my hips up and down, I was relieved to see that his eyes were closed. I wasn't thrilled about my body at the time, and I wanted to focus on getting this whole initiating thing right, which meant making him orgasm. I was doing a pretty good job, if I do say so myself.

At one point, he opened his eyes and maneuvered our bodies to flip me over so he could get on top. I got so excited that he was excited enough to take what he needed to have his orgasm. I did have secret fantasies about being "taken" all the time.

He was on top of me, working hard I could tell, but he couldn't finish. He lay on top of me, quiet.

"Is everything okay?" I whispered.

"Yeah, just tired. I've had a long day and I'm just tired."

We lay there silent for a long time. I could tell he felt bad as he let another little sigh escape. He gave me a kiss on the cheek, rolled over, and fell asleep.

I didn't fall asleep of course. I sat up all night thinking: Was there something I wasn't doing? Was I asexual? Maybe I should work out more. Maybe we should send the kids off someplace. Maybe we should schedule in sex since he's so busy all the time. Maybe I would try again in the morning; he's always said he likes to have sex in the morning best. What did I do wrong?

At four thirty the following morning, I did try again. I knew he had to get up for work soon, so I started slowly. Lucky me – he already had his morning hard-on. I was too late though; the "do not disturb" function on his smart phone expired and all the texts and emails he received overnight started pinging him. He actually went to turn off the sound so we could finish. But some important text must have caught his eye; he grabbed his phone, turned it over, gave me a really big hug and said, "Sorry, I have to get ready for work." Then he got up, went to the bathroom and took his phone with him.

I fell back asleep.

LESSON: Sometimes the wrong questions leave us clueless.

OUCH

I woke up feeling like something was wrong. I guess I hadn't done a good job at initiating sex. We were too busy. *He* was too busy. His work was stressful; there were so many board meetings he had to attend to. I was caught in the monotony of doing the kid thing over and over and over again. The same routine: breakfast, drop off, pick up, carpools to afterschool activities, volunteering at the school ... I would fit in my work where I could. We were also finishing up a redo of our entire house.

I had to give it to my husband, he was doing something about relieving his stress by maniacally working out, playing mindless games on his phone (he was always on his phone these days), and leaving early on Saturday or Sunday mornings to drive his "mid-life crisis" Ferrari up and down the highway. I just sat home with the mundane chores and the lists after lists of things to do for other people. I wore my exercise clothes all day, hoping to take a yoga class or work out. I never did.

I was really glad it was "hair day." Going to the hairdresser for me was like driving to Target, where I could just sit in my car and listen to music for twenty-five minutes on the highway and have some time for myself. The shopping was cathartic. I knew that no matter what, I would spend at least three hundred dollars even if I was going just for toilet paper. It was the perfect predictable zone-out time that I needed. Going to my hairdresser was predictable too, only I had good looking hair when I left.

You already know the rest, but I will share with you the play by play, just to eke out any remnants of pain and shame there is left for me, and maybe you.

Kristine, my hairdresser, sat me in her usual chair. We always had great conversations about love and travel and the trashy novel I was starting to write. Clearly, I was just as frustrated as my husband and wanting to let out all my fantasies. I even took an online creative writing class hosted by Stanford University. One woman thought I shouldn't degrade myself by calling my novel "trashy," but I assured her that I *wanted* to write a trashy novel. It was going to be about this woman who was having an affair because she was stuck in a vanilla lifestyle. There would be travel, great sex scenes, love *and* passion in it.

I should have known then that I was psychic.

Kristine asked about my book, how the kids were, and then we decided I needed a few summer highlights. I had insisted on bangs in the winter, which I immediately hated after the first selfie. I clearly wanted a change, and hair was the easiest way to get there. Since my bangs had almost grown out, I figured highlights would spice things up for me. Kristine put the foils in, and colored the rest of my locks a nice chestnut brown.

Early that morning, I had grabbed my husband's old iPad so that I could search for furniture for our living room. The redo had been a disaster for us emotionally. Our architect wanted cold modern, I wanted eclectic textures and layers. We fought constantly about getting furniture. This morning, I'd decided that I was going to get a couch already.

As my hair processed, I opened up the old iPad and tons of texts popped up on the screen. I am not a nosey person; I was just going to close the page, but a photo caught my eye. There was a photo of three women in short dresses. I didn't know any of them. I looked closer. The text thread from my husband was asking one of the women to go meet him in N.Y.C. for a shopping spree. Which woman? I scrolled down to read more. She was a stewardess he met on the plane to a Miami conference. That explained the short, short dresses, tanned skin, and very distinct Miami photo op postures of arched backs, asses and boobs out. I scrolled down to find a set of different texts to a yoga instructor who was going to go to Bali to learn more about Buddhism. No pictures, but he complimented her on how cool she was to be doing that. Wait a minute, I thought, years ago I told him I was going to study Buddhism and he said I shouldn't freak out the parents at our kids' new conservative grade school. I was mesmerized; maybe in shock. I had to dig more.

Here's where it gets really good.

I must have looked like I had seen a ghost. Kristine asked if there was anything wrong. I told her that I thought I had just gotten my period and I ran to the bathroom with the iPad. I stayed in there for thirty minutes reading and rereading all these texts as I sat on the toilet, my highlights processing. The new texts that I found were way more intimate, and some really raunchy – porn-worthy raunchy. If it wasn't on my husband's iPad, I might think it was the Divine handing me some really good material for my trashy novel. There was enough evidence to say, without a shadow of a doubt, that my husband was currently having an affair – like right this very moment.

Ouch.

It was like a brick hit me in the forehead and a big-rig semi-truck, the kind with monster tires, ran over my heart. I almost threw up the smashed and broken pieces. I will admit, I also had an extremely shallow moment of feeling jealousy that she was way younger, obviously more sexually advanced, had huge fake boobs, and was clearly more desirable than me. And the worst part, she was a fucking hairdresser! I've already mentioned how much I hate clichés.

Fucker.

LESSON: A devastating blow to the head and heart is your wakeup call.

VANILLA LOVERS

And just like that, I'd been inducted into an inauspicious club — the dreaded twenty-two percent of married women who've been betrayed by their husbands because of a few rolls in the hay with Vidala Sassoon. I think the statistics are higher, it's just that people won't admit to it.

We all know that betrayal has been going on since the dawn of time. Brutus betrayed Caesar. Antony and Cleopatra betrayed each other. Judas betrayed Jesus. The Serpent betrayed Eve, who betrayed man. Lucifer betrayed God. And to top it all off, Jay-Z betrayed Beyoncé.

Lying, cheating, infidelity, treachery, silence, and disengagement breaks our hearts, destroys relationships, induces wars, and even changes history.

Infidelity sucks. It immediately takes you by the throat and thrusts you in front of the mirror. You look at your reflection to find all the flaws, each magnified by ten thousand. You notice every wrinkle. You hate the flabby belly (mothers know this best). Your boobs and ass are not perky enough. Your eyes and teeth are too yellow, and you need a haircut badly. Your wax is way overdue, and you realize you are wearing mommy GAP underwear. So you Google plastic surgery, you toss every single hideous nude colored bra and underwear in the garbage, and plan to hit Agent Provocateur in the next hour. You schedule a Brazilian.

Emotionally you are a train wreck, either losing or gaining weight depending on your unique mode of survival skills. Every single insecurity comes up: I'm not pretty enough. I'm definitely not sexy enough. I'm unworthy of love. I'm old. I'm going to die alone. I'm going to be a single mother. I'm a loser. Shame. Shame. Shame.

This is when you start to descend into the seven layers of Hell on a physical, psychological and emotional level. You, and the devil on your shoulder, take many deep steps into those dark spaces of the unknown to reveal truths about where you compromise, give up, close off, and how you love and how you don't love.

Psychologically, you become bat-crazy. You distrust all phone calls and texts that are not from you. You hover over his computer. You secretly follow him to work or after work. You do intense research trying to find everything you can about "the other woman." You read into every word or phrase. You are disgusted, needy, whiney, and desperate.

Betrayal sucks.

But there is also huge opportunity in betrayal. I only realized much, much later how I had brilliantly created this hellish scenario.

My husband did a terrible job at hiding his affair. I believe his subconscious desperately wanted him to get caught. In truth, this was the best thing that could have ever happened to me … seriously! Otherwise, we would still be vanilla lovers, void of passion, polarity, fun, and excitement. Too hopeful to leave and too scared to talk about it, our variety would continue to be a mixture of complacent happiness, dysfunctional fights, and boring false niceties. Our sex life would continue to be a chore.

Maybe, just maybe, betrayal is the very thing that wakes us up to another, more elevated, way of living and loving altogether.

LESSON: Betrayal sucks, but there is a silver lining. Promise!

2. Sleeping Beauty

INDIANA JONES FALLS INTO THE SNAKE PIT

"You were frozen, and I was left stranded in a desert island. What did you want me to do?" That was what came out of my husband's mouth during one of our therapy sessions with Dr. Bob, our therapist.

Bob was a very genteel, discreet, and brilliant clinical psychologist. He worked with the very "posh" couples in San Francisco who were most likely in the same position. He had to be the best because he was recommended by the "posh" medical concierge in the city, and I saw a few "posh" couples wearing dark glasses, walk out his office door, while I sat hiding in my car waiting for our appointment. Bob was great, I'd recommend him to anyone, but I was so traumatized, angry, sad, exhausted, and confused, that talk therapy just wasn't doing it for me.

"Um, have a conversation?" I growled like a rabid dog underneath my saccharine smile. "Or how about just *try*? Or how about coming home earlier? Or how about masturbate? Or how about a million other options than fucking a hairdresser in your fucking Ferrari?" I lost it. Why was it me who had to be the basket case every time we had an appointment? And how did my husband, all of a sudden, get to be the well-behaved A+ student? I hated therapy.

They both just looked at me as drips of venom escaped from my pursed lips and I tried to hold back tears.

"The one thing that I feared the most," I continued with a sigh of honest grief, "and for sure I thought could kill me was betrayal."

We all sat and chewed on that one for a long while.

Bob finally broke the silence and started talking about the movie *Raiders of the Lost Ark,* where Indiana Jones falls into the snake pit, his biggest fear being snakes. Bob explained that sometimes when we try so hard to avoid something in life, it is that very thing that comes to haunt us, providing us with the lessons we really need. I did not understand what he meant then, but I do now. He then asked me what I thought my role was to cause the affair.

What the fuck? My blood was boiling behind a sweet veneer. I had made a mental note to fire Bob right when we got home, because I couldn't do it to his face. I wasn't bold enough. And by the way, I never swore until after the affair. I have many distinct before and after affair moments, swearing like a truck driver, is one of them.

I disassociated from the rest of the conversation because they were ganging up on me, or at least I thought they were. As the two talked, I sat there thinking poetically that something in me had died, and I was now able to be reborn anew like the Phoenix in *Harry Potter.* I just needed to figure out exactly which parts of me have died so that

I could let them go, and which parts of me were simply wounded so I could heal.

I think I've already mentioned this, but betrayal sucks big time.

LESSON: Face your fears, or they face you.

GUCCI GOOGLE-ISH

This wasn't supposed to happen to me. My life seemed picture perfect up to that point, like a carbon copy of the high-class, hipster community portrayed in *Big Little Lies*, sans the murder scene (though both *Gone Girl* and *The Girl with the Dragon Tattoo* did cross my mind at times). I had been married for over fifteen years, lived in San Francisco, had two kids, a dog, two cats, and Pancetta the teacup pig. We were, what I affectionately call "Gucci Google-ish."

Neither of us had the best role models for a sexually satisfying, nurturing, *and* compatible relationship. His parents were the "let's sweep it under the rug" type, where formalities and suppression ruled. My parents were the dysfunctional and crazy ones, where explosions of emotions reigned. At a young age, I told myself that I would never be with a "cheater." My father did that to my mother, and she never recovered from it. Betrayal was *not* going to happen to me. I wasn't going to settle for Prince Charming, I was going to find Superman.

When I met my husband, I was thrilled that he was a protector and not a savior. He was masculine but not aggressive. He was charming but not a seducer. He was intelligent and not manipulative. He was generous, kind, honest, and loyal (he really was!). Never in my wildest dreams did I think he was capable of such a thing. Our relationship was better than the pristine, non-communicative, and unemotional household he was brought up in, and it was *way* better than the chaotic, deceitful, and hypocritical household I was brought up in. As far as I was concerned, our marriage woes were perfectly normal.

But after having the kids, I did get so deep into that role of being the perfect wife and mother, while my husband did get into that role of being the perfect provider. Carpools, soccer games, lunch duty, business meetings, travel, stress, and burning the late-night oil all added up I guess.

I can't really remember when we stopped having sex. I can't remember when I turned into a frozen, miserable, non-sexual robot. I can't remember when I started to fake everything – my true self, what I wanted out of a partnership, and, yup, my orgasms. There were times when I literally turned my back on him in bed, or pretended that I had my period so we didn't have to have sex. Now that I think of it, I might as well have shoved the hairdresser's big, fake boobs in his face.

Bob's words rang again in my ears: "What was your role in this?"

LESSON: I really, really hate to admit this, but it does take two to tango.

WAKE THE FUCK UP, BEAUTY

Do you remember the story of Sleeping Beauty, the princess predestined to be pricked by a spindle that would magically send Beauty into a slumber for 100 years? In the original story by Charles Perrault, seven good fairies were invited to bestow gifts upon the newborn princess. The gifts were beauty, wit, grace, dance, song, and kindness. But *oops*, the King forgot to invite the old dark fairy, which she gets pissed about. The angry fairy then gifts his daughter the curse of Spindle Death. Luckily, the seventh fairy hadn't given Beauty the gift of protection yet, so instead of death, she gifts the princess slumber instead.

After leaving the therapist's office that day, I decided to really think about how I might have been sexually sleep-walking through our marriage and wondered why. I started to look deeply into womanhood and reflect on women I knew and didn't know. I had to think about what was sexy and not sexy to me. I watched body language, how women used their voices, and if they appeared to be truly fulfilled and blissed out by life.

Sadly, I noticed that many powerful women keep their sensuality hidden, and sexy women are often dismissed as shallow. Aside from celebrities, it's hard to find both sexy *and* powerful in the everyday woman. The betrayed are not the only ones shut down and robotic. I feel like we are living in a world full of women who are asleep to their innate sexual powers.

Not to give men a bad rap or anything, but women have been suppressed for thousands of years by the patriarchy. Sleeping Beauty is just one metaphor. There's a great deal of literature on ancient matriarchal cultures like the Sumerians and Ancient Egyptians where women were both powerful *and* sexual. In fact, their power was their sexuality, and it was considered spiritual. But over time, this type of power was pushed underground, stoned, burnt at the stake, and shamed. This, by the way, still happens today in some cultures.

Can anyone really blame any woman who has fallen complacent and asleep to their feminine sexual wisdom with a history of betrayals like this? We have become the Sleeping Beauties waiting to be awakened by a kiss (or the election of an outrageous president). Unfortunately for some of us, that kiss is more like a sledgehammer to the face. Hello rupture!

One of my favorite mentors, psychotherapist Anne Davin, believes that our hardships are the greatest gifts our higher selves call in. These lessons help us awaken, rise, and reclaim our birthright as magnificent, feminine, divine creatures. The kiss of betrayal is our moment of awakening, or an activation to seek the mastery of ourselves.

Can our inner Sleeping Beauty actually be an opportunity to awaken from a deep, deep sexual and spiritual slumber, where the dominating culture of shame has pricked us to sleep?

Is it time now, Beauty, to wake the fuck up?

LESSON: Betrayal is the kiss asking us to wake up. It is time.

3. Soul Seeker in Stilettos

SELF-HELP ADDICT

So, now what?

We were doing pretty good for a while. We went to therapy, we pretended that everything was going great, and our friends had no idea that anything was wrong. I held in the pain because every time I let it out, we'd get into a fight, and my husband would ask why I just couldn't forgive him and get over it.

It was now the holiday season, which was really hard for me because this time last year, my husband gave this woman *Tiffany* earrings. Yes, you read that right. *Tiffany* fucking earrings! How do I know these things? Stalking, that's how. It is amazing how good we betrayed can be at deep investigation. So many women of infidelity tell me the same thing. We can all quit our day jobs if we need to; I was definitely a private eye in a past life.

When I was shopping for holiday gifts downtown, I couldn't help but look at the beautiful storefront with iconic blue boxes wrapped in white ribbon and sparkly diamonds in the windows. I wanted to burn it down. I went in to look for *the* pair. I couldn't find them. I wanted to know how much they cost. I was tempted to buy a ridiculously over-priced huge pair of earrings for myself, but decided that I'd have to boycott the brand, for a little while at least. Ask me if I own anything *Tiffany*. I don't.

My husband said that it meant nothing, and that the hairdresser asked for them specifically. He says he gave them to her because it was like paying a prostitute instead of having an "affair." I know that plenty of men buy plenty of things for their mistresses. I understand that some of these (I'm tempted to say gold diggers, but I won't) women are seduced by gifts into sticking around, but it still pisses me off!

Slowly, the reality of the whole thing began to seep deeply into my body. The hole in my shattered heart was starting to suck the air right out of the world. I was jealous of couples kissing passionately. When I saw a couple who appeared distant from each other, I was convinced there was an affair involved. I'd cry whenever I was alone, especially driving in the car listening to the Maroon 5 breakup songs I was obsessed with.

I felt too humiliated to share my experience with any of my friends because if our relationship worked out for the better, I didn't want to admit to having a blemish on our "perfect" marriage. At the same time, I continued to wonder if I should just leave him. Was I brave enough to really do that? I could not imagine myself signing up with an online dating service. Who would ever answer to "Unwanted and betrayable, single mother of two, who is not sexy and definitely not good in bed." My mind revolved around getting my sexy self back on and leaving him, castrating him, or forgiving him. I still couldn't decide which. I was afraid of the D word. "Divorcée" sounded so diminishing.

I was so alone.

I know, I know, I know already! You are still perplexed as to how this can be a love story as promised. Maybe you are even thinking why on earth I didn't get the hell out of there when I could. The Universe works in mysterious ways, and she had great things in store for me, and us. Stick with me.

I got on the computer and decided to ask Google some questions. Google knows everything. I first googled "How to stop being sick of yourself." Not much comes up except articles on vomiting, which made me laugh since I always felt like vomiting up my disappointment. Then I googled "How to be sexy." Please don't even bother watching the videos with the girls fake-flipping their hair and posing in contrived ways. Most of them end up offering hair, make-up, and wardrobes opinions "that men like," and are not authentic at all.

I knew better than that. I felt pretty confident up until I was betrayed. I already had a good sense of style and I wore my hair and make-up decently. Though all these things definitely helped me feel good about myself, I wanted to learn the deeper secret wisdom of sexy, not the superficial sexy.

I was getting even more depressed.

Then I remembered when a girlfriend threw me a birthday party at a pole dancing studio a couple of years back. I had jokingly threatened that I wanted to become a pole dancer someday, even though I do not have a dance background, to go along with my future trashy novelist persona. The woman who greeted us that evening was tall and heavy set, making me think she was just the receptionist. Yes, I shamelessly admit to my narrow idea of what a pole dancing teacher might look like. She brought us into the red lit room with four dance poles. The music started and she guided us in slow undulating movement that felt really good. The teacher took off her t-shirt and sweatpants to reveal a sports bra and short shorts. Her dark skin rolled into creases, but she had no body shame. I could not take my eyes off her. She had become the most exquisite, sexiest, most beautiful creature I have ever seen. I was blown away by her sensuality. It was incredible to watch. I had no idea how much power the body had when given permission to be set free like that. I wanted to sign up for classes after that experience, but I never got around to it. When I got home that night, I threatened to dance for my husband, but I chickened out. So he did a striptease for me instead, and we laughed about it for days afterward.

I tried looking up the pole studio again, but it was temporarily closed. There was a retreat coming up in two weeks and a link to a TED Talk featuring the founder. In it, she wore a cardigan sweater and a tame, flowy skirt. She danced beautifully and innocently around the pole to a deeply emotional love song. After, she talked about the truth of the feminine body. I could definitely do this, I thought. Everything she said resonated and my body knew that I absolutely must try this. So I signed up for the retreat without asking any questions.

That experience set off a chain of events where I became a self-help addict. After pole dancing at S-Factor, I signed up to walk on fire with Tony Robbins, smashed the patriarchy at The School of Womanly Arts, started meditating with Deepak Chopra, met an orgasm expert, learned sacred sexuality through Tantra, peeked into the kink dungeons, got acquainted with the Polyamory crowd (which was not my thing), and so much more. Once a month, yet another healing or growth opportunity presented itself to me, and I said yes to it all. That's what addicts do. Deepak Chopra would call these opportunities Divine synchrodestiny. Who am I to question the Divine?

Every experience and every teacher I sought out helped to reveal something new about myself. And bless my husband's heart, although he sometimes got annoyed by my new vocabulary and the non-stop regurgitation of my new wisdom, he never asked me to stop finding myself. My "PhD in me" research, however, just kept raising more questions.

What did I *really* want? No clue.

What did my husband want? What every man wants probably – variety.

How could I be everything he needed and still be my authentic self?

That last question led me to my "a-ha" moment.

LESSON: If you are going to be addicted to something, it might as well be to your growth.

SOUL SEEKER IN STILETTOS

Almost a year into my self-help addiction, I was in a much better space, but I was far from "over it." Healing is not that easy; I don't care what anyone says. I still had suspicions when my husband had to work late. I still worried that I would bump into the "other woman" on the street without any profound lesson or reprimand to offer her. I still didn't believe that I was "enough." Pandora's box had opened up, and now I was doing more than just healing betrayal. I was peeling off layers and layers of an undiscovered, tortured soul. The metaphor is perfect: onions make you cry, and the peeling never seems to end. At the same time, I was thoroughly enjoying the grit and grace that was my life. A typical addict's response. Many of the programs I chose to participate in were spiritual and motivating, but my favorites were the girly, glamorous events that that greeted us with pink feather boas. I started dressing up more, at the grocery store, at carpool pick up, anywhere I pleased. I wore nice lingerie no matter what I was doing. I had become an eager soul seeker in stilettos. I had to thank Bob once again for the comment I almost fired him for. I even said to my husband, "I will say this once, and only once … you did me the *biggest* favor, ever."

Even though I devoured every book on relationships, forgiveness, Consciousness, and had a plethora of wisdom to pull from, I was still missing something. Exactly *how* do we enter the conversation and communicate what's working, or not working, without the help of a counselor by our side at all times, twenty-four/seven to stop us from our inevitable missteps? Exactly *how* do we interact with honesty and authenticity, instead of practiced jargon we learned on "the couch"? Exactly *how* do we feel connected to the Divine?

We started going to a communications therapist, who advised us to use feeling words deeper than the emotions of anger, jealousy, and annoyance. I chose her because she was a woman, and I thought that we needed a woman's point of view. We ended up speaking to each other in robotic scripts eerily similar to Siri: "I feel hurt that you are late." "I don't feel loved when you criticize me." "I don't feel safe with x, y, and z." We both have type-A personalities, we both have a point-of-view, and we were still both in defense mode. The therapist asked us to try *not* saying "you" in conversation for a while. I dare you to try speaking without ever saying "you." It is impossible. We said things like, "I feel hurt when I have dinner on the table and there is one empty chair and our starving kids have to wait patiently for that chair to be filled before we eat dinner." Or, "I feel depressed when someone in the blue shirt still hasn't taken out the garbage when we agreed that it's blue shirt's job, and it's starting to stink in here." We became masters in the art of passive aggressive language. And if we goofed, our fights became comically ferocious.

"We are not supposed to use the word *you*, but *you* keep using *you*," I snapped.

"No I don't, *you* keep using *you*," he retaliated.

"I have been really working on not saying *you*. Plus, it's ridiculous to not say *you*, *you* have to say *you*.

"No, the therapist said don't say *you*. Let's get that one thing right."

I was exasperated. "She meant in accusation, *you* say it all the time I just don't point it out when *you* do it. *You. You. You!*"

"*You* get too emotional, so let's stop talking about this."

"Fine, I will stop talking to *you* about this."

I wanted to fire the communication therapist, too.

After the "you" conversation, I would randomly text my husband "YOU" just for fun. We started to make a joke out of it.

It's not that easy to jump into conscious communication properly, especially around intimacy, when you are still coming from the same wounded place. I don't think either of our therapists had been betrayed so they weren't getting what *I* was truly going through. Besides "getting over it," I still wanted to know what, *exactly*, do lovers need to keep them satisfied in a relationship. How *exactly* can we spice up our sex life after a wound so deep? *How* can we create mystery in our long-term relationships, especially when we haven't communicated our desires to change it? *How* do you, all of a sudden, add a little "kink" to a vanilla relationship when that is not your language, and you aren't sure you want it to be? I wanted to know the nitty, gritty *how*, especially the throbbing, steamy *how* so we could have fun again.

I was a little obsessed with the sex part because infidelity has a lot to do with sex, though I know it is not the only thing going on. We never really got to the "how" during couple's talk therapy. They weren't giving us the play-by-play in a sexy, juicy way, or telling us how to initiate the conversation when there was still the shame, blame, pain, and "you" cycle going on. I started to wonder if these therapists had really amazing sex lives that could stop affairs from happening in the first place, or if that was even such a thing. I was starting to get really fatigued by couple's therapy. We were offered sex therapy books, most too dry and mechanical for me to ever finish reading. I knew mechanical like the back of my hand already, it was the tension of desire that I wanted to learn, so I had to keep soul seeking … yes, now always in stilettos.

LESSON: Soul Seeking in Stilettos is way more fun than Couch Therapy.

THIRTY WOMEN IN THIRTY DAYS

"You have to be a maid in the living room, a cook in the kitchen, and a whore in the bedroom."

—Jerry Hall

I was attending a women's workshop in New York City, when I asked a question to the panel of men that were invited into class that day. The teacher was badass, Regena Thomashauer, creator of The School of Womanly Arts. This course was one of her smaller, more exclusive ones. "Men's day" wasn't a panel of professional relationship coaches or anything, just a group of men that the enrolled women invited. We were given permission to ask any question of them. The questions ranged from how to attract their attention, to flirting, to sex, to all of the above.

I was sitting in the back hiding. I was good at hiding in all these types of classes. But you can't hide from Regena, she keeps her eye on every one of her students. She scanned the room full of hands raised by richly dressed and empowered women, until her eyes landed on mine. Grrr, I didn't drop my gaze in time.

"What's your question?" she asked me, even though I didn't have my hand raised. I never raised my hand in class. I was completely intimidated by her, I don't like attention, and I was terrible at speaking in front of people. And now I had to try to speak with men in the room.

I wanted to ask why men cheated on women, even though I know the reasons vary and not every man or woman cheats on their partners. I was in a room full of women who had been betrayed, were betrayers, and were the "other woman." I didn't trust everyone in the room at that point, and that's why I kept my husband's affair secret. Even though I know this happens all the time, I googled the statistics on affairs and porn viewing. It's sadly a high number. But I felt like it only happened to me, or that I was the only one it wounded at the deepest part of my core. So instead of asking what I really wanted, I looked at each and every guy and asked, "How can we women be everything to you men?"

First there was silence, then confusion, then tons of speculation. One guy said it wasn't possible for women to be their sports buddies, and that men needed time alone with their dude friends. I told him that wasn't what I meant. Regena interrupted in her brilliant way, and tried to guide me toward more clarity. Because I still didn't want anyone to put two and two together and reveal that I had been cheated on, I asked it in a way that was even more confusing. I received only silence.

Finally, I blurted out, "Why do men cheat on women?"

Cheating was clearly a dicey topic. There were whisperings, uh-huh's, and a loud, angry "yeah" that I heard from someplace across the room. All of the women in class had some type of hard run in with oppression, aggression, and suppression by men. Their betrayals were not necessarily all from infidelity, but betrayals nonetheless. I guessed that Regena did not want anyone's actions to be "wronged." Part of what she teaches is to love where you are at in life, the good, the bad, and the ugly. I get that. My question was tabled, and we moved on.

After class, my friend Juicy J, who had been a student at The School of Womanly Arts for over ten years thought my question meant I wanted to be polyamorous. A male guest told me to read a book (title now forgotten) about men and what they needed. A couple invited me for a threesome. My question *was* really confusing. But there were plenty of other women who came up and whispered in my ear that they understood my question exactly.

It was the question that became the spark, the genius, the epiphany that would change everything for me. To answer my own question, I would participate in a challenge where I became thirty different women in thirty days for my husband. It was brilliant. I would find out for myself what men (or at least my man) wanted.

I posted portions of my shenanigans on the private group chatroom every day, along with some racy pictures. I took on the roles of these thirty different women from sun up to sun down, regardless if I had work to do, carpools to drive, or groceries to buy. The thirty days inspired many women in class, they were all rooting for me, and the rest is history.

The quote "You have to be a maid in the living room, a cook in the kitchen, and a whore in the bedroom," attributed to Jerry Hall, the famous model and former wife of Mick Jagger, was definitely on to something. I was just crazy enough to take it even further.

LESSON: Confusing questions can lead to the most creative solutions.

THE KINKY VANILLA
LOVE PROJECT

I would never recommend anyone trying to be thirty different women in thirty days, not because it isn't fun. It's so much fun! I wouldn't recommend it because it is *way* too exhausting. I would know; I did it!

For sure I would recommend unleashing, over time, the different personas that you already have within, as they are wildly excited to come out and play. And when they do, your life changes for the better. We are all soulful, sexy shapeshifters who just want to let our freak flag fly! Stick with me on this one; I promise it only gets better from here.

Yes, you are a multidimensional soul with a variety of roles to play, as crazy as this might sound. I am not trying to make excuses for what may seem like my burgeoning multiple personality disorder.

Psychoanalyst Carl Jung introduced the concept of archetypal energies being inborn tendencies influenced by the collective unconscious that play a role influencing our behaviors.

Many eastern religions teach that our multidimensional souls are the gods and goddesses of the archetypal realm actively creating and communicating through us, to become the individual expression from which Consciousness can experience itself. It is the goddess Shakti, the divine cosmic force that represents feminine power. She is known by many names and forms. She is the Creatrix, the Destroyer, and the one who restores balance.

The many ancient mystery schools that explore the essence of our true nature (a.k.a. spirituality) claim that there are many levels of higher consciousness, one being that we become our own witnessing awareness, experiencing the material reality (our 3D world of stuff and stuff to do) and the non-material reality (the world of dreams, energy, and magic) *at the same time.* At this cosmic level of consciousness, we realize that we often play different roles at different times in our lives. This is the quantum stuff that Deepak Chopra, Joe Dispenza, and other consciousness crusaders often talk about.

The reason I bring this up is because it is not a new concept. It is just new in the way we can use it to relate to each other intimately and in "real life." Real life meaning the day-to-day mundane tasks that often leave us wondering about life itself, "Is this really what it's all about?"

Through my profound experience, I will share how I learned to express these varying archetypes and personas in my partnership. I believe it was the answer to adding variety, depth, and great bonding for me and my husband. So please journey forward with me as I share with you my tried and true experiments of making my fantasies a reality, uncovering my deep longings buried someplace deep between rules and shame, and discovering the many personas that played a significant role in how I love and make love.

But beware all ye who enter here.

These are the confessions of my kinky vanilla love project. We will not be traveling in a linear fashion. You will see the naked truth about women, peek into taboo territory, and we might even travel through the gates of hell to meet the Devil herself. There will be sex, drugs, and rock & roll. You'll know the secrets to unleashing your soulful, sexy shapeshifter super powers.

You'll end up knowing me, and that I am you.

We are all in this together.

So let's do this. Let's go ahead and turn betrayal into bliss.

LESSON: We're all soulful, sexy shapeshifters. Let's let our freak flag fly!

4. The Desperate Housewife

WOMEN AREN'T SPORTS BUDDIES

Somehow this project that I got myself into allowed me to remove myself from being the victim of my own story and release the resentment of what happened *to* me, so I could really step into the creation of what happened *for* me.

I instantly forgave my husband and wasn't mad anymore. That's not exactly true – no one can instantly forgive someone and not be mad for such a violation. But the shift in how we started to relate to each other was so phenomenal, I felt like forgiveness could happen in an instant.

On the plane home from the weekend, I was emboldened by my project. I was so proud of my future self because I knew I would do a really great job at the dressing up part, and I definitely would have fun doing it. I had a closet full of costumes and wigs that rivaled any Hollywood set. Halloween is my favorite holiday. I'm not kidding. I had always made my entire family dress up in theme. We were the band Kiss, the Day of the Dead, Mythological Creatures, the *Wizard of Oz* complete with my dog Boomer who is a descendant of Toto, his breeder claims. We were bobble heads of significant Giant's baseball players after they won the World Series. My kids hated it at first, but after the first school award for best costume, they let me turn them into anything.

But this project was less about the external costume, and more about the internal sexy personas that I had to figure out how to let loose, and thirty of them! Inspiration would be tough. It wasn't like I was oozing sexy all the time.

I decided to call my first icon "The Cheeky Sports Bud," in honor of the knucklehead that said women aren't sports buddies. She was a cross between a racy cheerleader, the kind that could manage the entire football team, and the women who rode motorcycles in bikinis. A glorified porn star, since that is what many men *think* they want, and what many women *think* men want. I'd be that presentational bombshell that the media says we ought to be.

I wore nothing but a basketball jersey, while sitting on a basketball in our bedroom when my husband got home from work. Dinner was already on the table, but I decided to wait for him in the bedroom, knowing that he'd want to take off his sport coat and uncomfortable shoes.

So there I was, half naked sitting on a basketball, like it was just a normal thing I did. I had lost a lot of weight in the first few months after I found out about the affair, so I was looking pretty good and felt more confident about my body.

"What's this?" He smiled at me.

"I'll explain later," I replied, trying to be bold like the sexy women on all sports commercials, and a little naughty as if I were playing a role in a triple-x movie about a cheeky sports buddy nonchalantly sitting on a basketball. It was comforting to know that I could be a campy bad actress, since porn stars never win Academy Awards. I didn't need to be that convincing, I just needed to show a little more skin than I usually did. If you have ever kept your partner in the desert, as my husband once accused me of doing, then showing just a little more skin was like the Nile river making a miraculous detour, saving him from dehydration. It's that easy, I wish I knew this before.

"Let's go up and have dinner," I said as I slipped on a pair of dolphin shorts without putting on any underwear. I made sure he noticed that part. Before dinner, I had looked up the latest news on football and basketball, which I was not usually versed in. At dinner, I started a conversation about Colin Kaepernick and the 49ers and Stephen Curry and the Warriors moving to San Francisco. I brought up the Super Bowl and the soccer player Cristiano Ronaldo, just because he's a sexy stud and I might as well be as shallow as the role I was playing. I was cool mom for a change, and my husband was totally confused, yet pleasantly surprised.

At the end of the night, I crawled into bed with just the basketball jersey on, and guided my husband in a wild and raunchy sexcapade for the first time in forever. It was a great night of raw, uninhibited sex.

As he was falling asleep, I told him about my brilliant project, and that he'd better get physically ready for it. "Yes ma'am," he said playfully. I'm positive this was what he had been waiting a lifetime for, and I was going to overcome any of my own resistance, shame, fear or whatever else popped up during these next thirty days.

The Cheeky Sports Bud taught me that I could literally just put on a persona and go for it. I learned that I *do* have a little bit of that wild, uninhibited teenage dream girl inside me. And she's fun and sassy. I liked her.

According to the media, the sexy, girly glam scene was reserved for a select type of woman, like *Cosmopolitan Magazine* readers or the

Kardashians. If you have a secret desire to experience that type of beauty, there's an entire product line for it.

Maybe it was society telling me "no" I can't go there because I'm an intelligent woman and respectable mom, those days are over. But as I found out in an instant, the secret was to have that part of me come from the inside out. Now I knew that I could go there when I wanted, not for anyone else but for me. I was empowered. I was ready.

How was I going to come up with twenty-nine more personas? I did not think about which specific roles I was going to play, or in which order I would play them. The inspiration just came up spontaneously, as if the Cosmos really had a part in this love experiment with some higher level lessons to share.

LESSON: Forget the rules, women are better at being a sports bud than you think.

INSPIRED BY THE BAG LADY NEXT DOOR

I was doing the morning breakfast routine for my kids, when something out the window caught my eye.

There she was again, my neighbor walking the dog. I could watch her from my kitchen window without her noticing.

I was obsessed.

She was wearing flannel pajama bottoms, printed with thick black and white vertical stripes. She was like an eighties rock star groupie, except with baggy pants instead of the skin tight ones that the singer David Lee Roth wore. She was in her seventies. The terry cloth, maroon colored robe she wore was left open to reveal a pink sparkly top meant for a date night out.

It was seven a.m.

On her feet were white tube socks and a pair of Adidas slippers. Her hair was up in her signature pink sponge rollers, with a plastic Safeway bag over the curlers to protect her hair from the mist of the morning fog. I once (or twice) asked her why she wore a plastic bag on her head. She looked at me like I was completely nuts, as if to say, do you really expect me to expose my hair to the weather while my curls are setting?

I was inspired one Christmas to gift her a set of Conair hot rollers so she didn't have to worry about the rain or fog ruining her curls. Although my intentions were good, I especially wanted her to stop embarrassing herself in front of the rest of the neighbors.

I cared too much.

Every time I saw her, I had the grave sense of what to expect from women as they aged. Is this what happens to women when they are lonely, or worse, if they've been unhappily married for too long?

Lola, as we call her, preferred her old-school methods of styling. She never ended up opening the hot roller set. I received it back the next Christmas wrapped up in crinkled, recycled Holiday paper. She either did this on purpose, or forgot that I gave them to her in the first place.

Lola was swinging a long bamboo stick while a Cairn Terrier pulled her across the street where he wanted to go pee. The stick is irrelevant, but it stood out as something strange to do while walking a dog in curlers and a plastic bag on your head.

She perplexed me, and I was determined to understand her.

My own reflection in the window reminded me that I hadn't yet brushed my hair that morning, and I was still wearing a better version (I hoped) of flannel pajamas. I cringed at the thought that I might turn out just like her someday, maybe I already had.

Lola looked up and saw me at the window. She waved and started talking to me as if I could hear her through the glass.

I waved hello and goodbye at the same time, using my whole body to express that I couldn't hear her. She kept on talking, ignoring my gestures, so I opened up the window to the tail end of her high pitched voice screaming, "The street cleaners are coming today at nine a.m." It was very sweet that she reminded me of this event every single Friday.

I looked down at her with a heavy heart and a sigh, "Thanks, mom!" Then closed the window. We are always influenced by our mother's character, for better or for worse. My mother was the ultimate desperate housewife, and the perfect inspiration for the role I'd play next.

LESSON: Inspiration comes in many forms. And, you are not your mother!

PURITANS, PATRIARCHY, AND PORN

Let's press pause on that story, because now that I think about it, I had been playing by the same rules that kept my mother from understanding her own value and worth. Pre-affair, I was a real desperate housewife, I was totally bored, and I wanted my husband to feel sorry for me because it was the only way I could get his attention. I wanted his attention. I hadn't yet figured out that the simple flash of a boob would work best.

I had no idea at the time what I wanted, liked, or what gave me pleasure sexually, but I did want to be sexually charged. I just didn't know how to go about it; instead, I was a mommy martyr. A really good one.

I don't remember when I started wearing generic black yoga pants, frozen yogurt stained t-shirts, and Uggs all day long. What happened to the girl who used to sit in the sun topless at the beach studying with her college roommate? Yes, that was me once.

I had become a pleaser to everyone, not because it pleased me to serve, but because I got attention and admiration for being the good Samaritan in a monotonous lifestyle of my own making. No one told me I could be something more. I am throwing this out there to you now, you can and *must* be something more!

I complained about the monotony of doing laundry, going grocery shopping, the carpooling, making the same meals for dinner, and wearing the same yoga pants everyday with the other women who liked to complain about their lives too. We got a lot of attention for it, and we bonded over our misery. In between spit ups, changing diapers, that later turned into playdates, scraped knees and carpools, all I wanted was to be seen, heard, and acknowledged for the woman I used to be. The early years of child raising really put a wedge into our sex life, because the last thing I wanted was to offer up my nipples to a grown man. This was the start of the wedge that made it hard to reconcile the spark, and the space between us just got bigger and bigger over time. It's not always because you are "shut down"; life does get in the way sometimes.

Here's what I secretly really wanted at the time.

I wanted to be bad, really bad. I desired to break all the social rules. I wanted to go on a vacation solo. I wanted to be a sexy hot mess. Can you just hunt me down, pull my hair, and devour me already? Could I walk down the street with my hips sashaying from side to side and feel the freedom of my natural curves? Could I wear what made me feel sexy instead of what was appropriately acceptable to others once in a while? The answer was no for me. I was following some unspoken rules where mothers had one role to play and men got to watch porn.

I'm glad I found my Cheeky Sports Bud persona, because she gave me permission to express this, admittedly shallow, part of my psyche.

We all know that most men are hardwired for the quickie, it's a Darwinian survival of the species, alpha male wins sort of thing, my husband was no exception. And it's okay that they are. Porn for men is that quick arousal. But it's not okay for women to be the porn star. I didn't have enough confidence to feel sexually unihibited in the past, but I desperately wanted to be wantonly wanted, like I imagine my husband wanting *her*. The idea of a raw sexual impulse used to intrigue me and repulse me at the same time. I feared the truth of what I really wanted, and what we all really want, which is freedom to be who we really are. So I did what all of us do, hide behind conditioned, rule based perfection.

In ancient matriarchal cultures, women were revered for their sexuality *and* their powers. Somewhere down the line, this reverence was taken away. Today women are treated as secondary creatures to men; she does the cooking, the laundry, the mating, the mothering all for him. One of the good things about catching your husband fucking another woman, is the opportunity to rethink all rules, and dig into our birthrights as powerful *and* sexual women. I started asking the right questions like, "who took away our power and changed all the rules anyway?"

I had adopted the patriarchal codes of conduct that insist I play the role of "the good wife," and it took the sexy right out of me. These roles and rules are deeply ingrained into the psyche of men and women, and have been since way before Plymouth Rock. Women have been burnt, stoned, hung, and crucified into our modern limiting beliefs and tamed behaviors. Balancing a career and motherhood still makes us feel guilty, and we continue to feel torn if we have to choose between career or motherhood.

Unlike men, women have been compartmentalized. Men can be fathers, executives, sporty, intelligent, Sugar Daddies, and sex driven all at the same time and without judgment. Women are allowed to choose between mom, executive, or sex symbol, not all three at the same time. It's the continuation of the Madonna-Whore complex, with Wonder Woman thrown in, just to make it more complicated for us.

The Madonnas are the pure, untainted saints that raise the children and sacrifice their earthly desires for the greater good. Their sex is in service to the hardworking man who has to slay dragons to put food on the table, the dragons being their nine to five jobs. The Whores are the desired corrupt and shameless harlots that get a special throne in the heart of men's fantasies. It is hard for most men to reconcile these two parts of women, a Freudian concept that still clearly holds true. Both the Madonna and the Whore cannot exist in the same woman, or Goddess forbid, the balance of male power might shift back to women. What would the old patriarchy do then?

Now throw in the modern Wonder Woman, who is an intelligent woman seen to be equal to man, except she isn't. She is neither mother nor whore, she is a woman masking as a man in order to be accepted by an elite club of professional men. She's the ruthless Clair Underwood in

House of Cards. Her sex is her power, and I imagine her sex life having the same length and shallowness as the "wham, bam, thank you ma'am" that only the busy, high-powered man has time for. Imagine, for a second, if women were able to be beautiful, sexy, nurturing, independent, *and* powerful leaders all at once. Too good to be true, right? No wonder we've been shamed by the puritans, diminished by the patriarchy, and snubbed by the porn industry. Women would be ruling the world. And it would be a peaceful, joyous, and abundant world.

LESSON: Most of us were unknowingly forced into one role, which is not normal.

THE DESPERATE HOUSEWIFE IN A GARTER BELT

Back to my inspiration.

As my kids were eating breakfast, I made my way downstairs to search for the set of Velcro rollers I stole from my mom when I gave her the new set of hot rollers for Christmas. I wanted to take the pink sponge rollers she usually used because they were more embarrassing. She must have caught on to my sneaky ways and hid them from me.

Sometimes I would do this. I would go into her closet and remove the most embarrassing items, like the tie-dyed turtleneck sweater with fingers expressing the peace sign and the words "You Can Trip with Me" in bold letters. She has never smoked weed. And then there's the pink leopard print, MC Hammer pants. I have no idea where she found those. I took her most embarrassing items to the Salvation Army, where I planned to take the black and white striped flannels she had on that morning.

I started conjuring up a version of my mom by dividing my hair into sections so I could set my hair as my mom did. These Velcro's were bigger than the pink sponge rollers, and the look was very "behind the scenes" Hollywood glam. I liked it.

I felt sad for my mom. She had forgotten who she was at the deepest level. She had allowed the system to take her light and imagination. She became Cinderella interrupted, still stuck in the dungeon scrubbing the floors, and too proud to call on anyone for help. I have always believed that if she truly loved herself, she would have had the magic to call in a real Prince Charming. My dad was charming, but he was no prince.

My thoughts were cut short, "Are those my rollers?" Startled, I looked up to find my mother standing in the bathroom doorway.

For all the knowledge she did *not* share with me on sex, drugs, or rock and roll, she was fine walking into our home, making herself comfortable, and walking in on us naked, or on the toilet.

"Oh. Yeah. Sorry I borrowed them," I replied.

"You keep them," she pointed to the protective plastic bag on her head, "I have my sponge rollers. These work the best."

I could not help myself: "Is it raining outside? It looks like it'll get pretty sunny in no time."

"You never know." She touched the bag and giggled. "I'll go up and make sure the kids are eating," she left me to continue with my preparations.

"Okay, thanks, mom."

I was determined to turn the bag lady, the desperate housewife, the bored mother, the vanilla lover over onto their heads into something sexy, sassy, and seductive.

"Fuck you, Karma, I get it now!" I said to myself in the mirror. "This might go on for generations if I don't liberate myself from submission." Thank Goddess I have boys.

My liberation, I thought, would be my mother's liberation, and possibly mean freedom for every woman I know. I was going to change the desperate housewife into something desperately hot, and I was going to enjoy every ounce of this new kind of domesticity.

I decided on fifties inspired make-up with smoky eyes, cat eye liner on the top lid, and pink pale lips. I searched my new lingerie drawer for something soft and lacy. My drawer is not technically new, but as you recall, the first thing I did was throw out every single ugly cotton underwear and hideous nude bra that I had. It was a symbolic gesture to myself to get rid of the frumpy, dumpy and betrayable thing that I thought I was. If you are feeling inspired to throw out your old shit, do it now.

I chose a peach matching bra set that I got from Agent Provocateur. It was pricy as everything at Agent Provocateur is (but you are worth it!), and gave me a zing to know that I was wearing something sexy touching my skin. I wasn't going to wear regular clothes today. I was going to do what my mom does, wear a robe and rollers all day long, but I would add something special.

I put on the matching lace garter belt that came with the panties and bra. Agent Provocateur is brilliant that way. The ladies in the store wear these cute maid-like outfits with stockings held up with garters. Why, again, are movie stars and Agent Provocateur sales girls the only ones allowed to wear sexy clothes?

I drove my kids to school in my rollers and a robe that covered up my lingerie. I enjoyed the thought that I was wearing practically nothing underneath. My kids were clueless, and since they already knew of my costume fetish, they pretty much rolled their eyes and whatever'd me the whole time.

LESSON: You deserve to treat yourself to lingerie that makes you feel sexy. Wear it out always!

SEXTING: THE BEST THING SINCE SLICED BREAD

"If you are a man of note, found for yourself a household, and love your wife at home, as it beseems. Fill her belly, clothe her back ... But hold her back from getting the mastery. Remember that her eye is her stormwind, and her vulva and mouth are her strength."

—Ptah Hotep, 2000 B.C.

When I got back home after dropping the kids off to school, I enthusiastically started doing some chores. I felt like I was in a daytime soap opera where the mistress of the house fired her housekeeper for some silly, unknown reason. The mistress had to do an emergency tidy up of her home while in her Velcro rollers, lingerie, and high heeled shoes before her lover got there. Jason Derula's voice sang in the background, "Girl, you're the one I want to want me," as I danced with the vacuum cleaner. "There's nothing I wouldn't do, just to get up next to you." I imagined he was singing to someone like me. Yes, me! Who does chores in their skivvies? I do. At least now I do.

I would have never guessed that doing chores half naked would be the key to enjoying chores. I made a mental note to only do chores like this from now on. I haven't stopped since. (Full disclosure, I do have Bibi who comes in and helps me clean the house sometimes). I was on a roll, so I decide to clean up the cat hairs and my long hairs out of the bathroom and scrub the floor. I put on a pair of red rubber gloves and got to work. Try to imagine a woman on her hands and knees scrubbing the floor in full, glamorous fifties style make-up, complete with fake eye lashes, her hair in large rollers, wearing peach colored lingerie, with her high heels on. It was a good look.

I remembered a movie scene where a housewife was busy ironing her husband's clothes with a baby on her hip. She was on the phone having a conversation with a stranger as a phone sex operator. Now that would be fun I thought. So, I phoned my husband but he didn't pick up. Unlucky for him.

I decided to take a selfie and text him a picture with the caption, "Just doing some chores." Sexting is the new phone sex I decided, at least during the day when there might be other people around. If we are going to have technology in our lives, we might as well use it as foreplay. I know from experience that all people having affairs do it, why shouldn't couples?

An explosion of cute emojis fired back at me, and "Will you be in that when I get home?"

"I might have to take off a few layers, housework gets me pretty hot," I responded.

"Please." I could feel his joy from across the airwaves.

For those shy folks among us, sexting is the best thing since sliced bread! Technology, if used wisely, is great foreplay. You don't even have to say anything, you just have to send a suggestive picture and the rest can be left up to the imagination. Sending sexy shots to your partner can help you train your nervous system into accepting your budding sexuality. And since the male brain responds to visuals, this is a win-win.

That evening, I did open the door in my rollers, high heeled shoes, and robe. I let the robe slip open a bit for him to get a sneak peek. We had dinner, yes in my outfit. Later on, I took out the rollers and let fall some big hair. I felt very Zsa Zsa Gabór, the glamorous Hungarian movie star who had nine husbands and lived to almost 100 years old. Sexy might be the key to longevity.

LESSON: Sexting is foreplay, do it all day long.

5. Venus is a Luscious Lover

TELL ME THEN

Venus stands before me breathtaking and beautiful. She whispers in a voice that could melt iron, "Do you want to love and be loved? Do you want passion and depth, to be worshipped and adored? Do you want to know that you are safe and worthy of the most exquisite tenderness?" She paused, "You want devotion and to be left yearning for more. You want trust. You want passion. You want a love affair so abundant that it moves mountains, heals your soul, and satisfies your every earthly desire."

"Yes." Tears roll down my face.

"Tell me then, how much love are you capable of giving?"

I always wake up at this part.

LESSON: Our dreams guide us.

THE BIRTH OF VENUS

We were on our family spring break trip to Kauai. I woke up before dawn anticipating the day, my senses heightened. I listened for the frogs and roosters as they belted out their morning songs. I heard the wind whispering through the palm leaves, it sounded like rain. The ocean waves boomed in the background. Nature was singing.

We left the house in the dark, I could barely see the mountains or the plunging waterfalls that surrounded Hanalei Bay. There were no cars on the narrow bridge up to Princeville, the coiffed part of Kauai. We were headed for the magnificent fountain of Neptune that marks the entrance to pristine lawns, timeshares, and the St. Regis Hotel.

I had been obsessed with watching the dance of mist and light, and the eruptions of water that fall heavily in droplets onto the body of the fountain. But the water was silent, sleeping. A sign maybe? I stared at the massive bloomed shell quietly floating in the center of the water. A statue of Neptune stood keenly on top of the shell's swelled opening. He seemed to be waiting for the goddess' return.

I decided right then, that I would not let Neptune down. I would follow through with my plan to rise as the nude Venus in that humongous shell. She was the archetype I would embody that day to honor every woman who desired freedom to love and be loved fully. Crazy, I know.

When we got to the curb of the fountain, I boldly stripped away my clothes, and ran naked across the water toward the shell. I did have a little sense left in me to bring a sarong, just in case. I imagined myself running across the water in slow motion.

It wasn't exactly a Bo Derek moment; I had to hold my breasts from hitting my face, the water was freezing and deeper than I thought it would be. The bottom was too rough for my sensitive feet, and I had to lift my knees as if I were wearing rubber flippers just to get across. I climbed up to the rough shell, scraping my legs in the process. The sun was just beginning to share her light.

I finally stood at the center of the shell bare and exposed as the goddess Venus. I lost my sarong somewhere in between. I cupped my right arm across my breasts and used my left hand to cover the flesh between my legs. I could see strands of my hair catching the glowing light as they twirled in the wind. I silently absorbed every ounce of Venus' sensual beauty, and tried to fully embody the Botticelli image that was etched in my mind.

I felt proud and beautiful and free, even with the goose bumps.

I was glad it was early, because I didn't want to be arrested for indecent exposure. I looked over at my husband for an energetic "thumbs up." I could see him at the other end of the water, waving and calling my name.

How sweet, I thought.

He understood that my own nudity was still a challenge for me, something I deeply wanted to overcome. I willed him to call me by the name Venus, but he kept calling my real name and waved his arms frantically.

How supportive, I thought.

I didn't quite understand why he started yelling out, "Bust." Did he want me to flash him my boobs? I gave him a flash, but he kept on waving. I waved back. He kept on waving and pointing like he was saying, "You go, girl."

It seemed a little overkill until I thought I heard him say, "Bus" instead of "Bust." I looked toward the direction of his gesturing arms, and just turning the corner, heading straight for me, was a yellow school bus filled with children.

The things we do for love.

LESSON: Wildly bold acts of self-expression change the patterns that inhibit us.

THE LOVE TRINITY

The image of Venus that most of us have imprinted in our psyche is that of the beautiful nude goddess rising from the foamy sea in a large shell. She is the embodiment of innocence, purity, sensuality, and divinity. She is raw, naked love.

I know Venus. She has come to me in my dreams many times before. She tells me about love, sometimes on the back of Pegasus and sometimes as an image so bright I cannot see her beautiful face. But when I wake, I never really understand why she asks how much love I am capable of giving.

Before I continue with my journey of becoming Venus for a day, let me first tell you what I know about love.

Love.

Sigh.

It is so hard to define.

Love is ethereal, concrete, all-encompassing, and hard to grasp. It is full of pleasure and equally full of pain.

Love is known to be so big and vast it keeps growing. We don't know where it comes from or if it will end. It is a power we all know about, but we also know nothing about how to find it, keep it, or make it last.

We cannot hold its energy in our hand.

When we think about love, it is a beautiful mystery. There are brilliant stars, gravitational moons, and ecstatic explosions in love. But also in love, there are stars that suck the life right out of the people involved, rogue planets that don't play by the rules, and black holes that consume everything into oblivion.

Love to me, then, is the Universe.

Maybe you were expecting something more concrete, or something you could actually use, but allow me to get geeky on you for a moment.

The physicist Albert Einstein proposed his highly influential Theory of Relativity as energy equals matter multiplied by the speed of light (E=mc²), which helps us grasp (well, sort of) some concepts on the interaction of energy and matter across the physical universe.

I fully admit to *not* having the mindset of a physicist, so unless it's a "Cosmic Mathematical Universe for Dummies" version, Einstein's ideas and equations make my brain hurt. I have to simplify. This is how I understand it: energy equals everything, and everything equals energy, including Love.

It is said that Albert Einstein also philosophized on love. He wrote a letter to his daughter unveiling what he believed to be the most powerful universal force (and just to remind you, he's a genius).

In the letter, he instructed his daughter to guard the information he was about to share for decades if need be, for he did not believe society would understand this very important discovery. He wanted to wait until humankind was ready to receive it.

Einstein wrote:

> *"...There is an extremely powerful force that, so far, science has not found a formal explanation to. It is a force that includes and governs all others, and is even behind any phenomenon operating in the universe and has not yet been identified by us. This universal force is LOVE.*
>
> *When scientists looked for a unified theory of the universe they forgot the most powerful unseen force.*

Love is light that enlightens those who give and receive it.

Love is gravity, because it makes some people feel attracted to others.

Love is power, because it multiplies the best we have, and allows humanity not to be extinguished in their blind selfishness.

Love unfolds and reveals...."

He goes on and explains that instead of E=mc², we should consider that healing energy can be manifested by love multiplied by the speed of light squared. Which means that love is the most powerful force there is.

I knew it!

I knew it before I googled E=mc². I knew it as a child. I knew it despite my first heartbreak, maybe even because of it. I knew it when I first heard the Beatles sing *All You Need Is Love.* I knew it when I got married. I knew it when I had my children. We all know it in our hearts, but we're taught a narrowly focused definition of love that is conditional, and the conditions differ from person to person.

Full disclosure, there is no real proof that Einstein wrote this letter; I came across it surfing the internet one night. But somebody thoughtful wrote it, and I'm choosing to believe that someone is a genius who knows something about love. Many people think love means romance. Others only understand the love they have for their children, forgetting the love with their partners. Some people only experience plutonic love, like for their dogs or friends. Very rarely is there a person who knows what self-love means. No wonder it's so hard to conjure a life partner who can be equipped to fulfill all our needs and desires, be they emotional, psychological, or physical.

The Greeks put love into seven different categories.

1. Eros, the sexual passionate kind of love. This really needs no explanation, but it's the kind of attraction that makes you want to rip off your clothes and merge skin to sweaty skin, to surrender to the erotic moment until you are both pulsing in ecstatic pleasure.

2. Philia, the deep friendship kind of love. But in a long-term relationship, the key to keeping it exciting is definitely *not* the friendship part. If you have been having "roommate sex" with your spouse for years, one of you is going to start imagining fucking the workout coach, the latest porn star, or in my case the hairdresser.

3. Storge, which reserves love for parents and their children. No need to go into the Electra or Oedipus complex here, let's just all agree that we all want to give and receive nurturing and protection.

4. Ludus is flirtation. It is the pleasure of being playfully alive at the present moment, being curious about the person in front of you, allowing for delight to be expressed wildly, like spontaneous laughter, without worrying about what anyone is thinking because you aren't paying attention to anyone else. In my opinion, everyone should learn how to flirt, simply because it makes you and others feel good. It is honoring the joy in you, by giving joy to someone else. If you don't know how to be playful in this way, just watch babies or puppies. They are the best flirts on the planet. Their good nature, whimsy, and pure delight in everything can be very captivating. Couples rarely flirt with each other without the expectation of having sex, especially after years of being together.

5. Agape is universal love, or selfless love. We can extend this energy to all people and all living things.

6.   Pragma is longstanding love, or the love of long-term monogamous relationships. It is love over time. But sadly, many of us begin to lack passion or compatibility, and we start to do things separately. One of you golfs all day long, the other takes adventure trips with friends, someone heads to Burning Man without the other. You become strangers passing in the night, even though you really do love each other.

7.   Philautia, or self-love, not the narcissistic kind of self-obsession, but the self-love that teaches you to widen your capacity to receive and give love. This type of love might be the most important because it is the gateway to learning every other type of love.

There are many more types of love, like devotional love and sacrificial love. But I like to make things simple, so I created the Love Trinity. The Love Trinity consists of Self-Love, Unconditional Love, and Romantic Love. The Love Trinity helps us understand how to satiate our need for fulfillment, wholeness, and excitement.

To me, Self-Love is honoring the self on a physical, emotional, psychological, intellectual, and spiritual level. It involves forgiveness and learning from our past. It is about knowing that you are *more than enough,* so you have overflowing amounts of love to share. It is abundance mentality. It is beauty. It is truth. It is power. This love teaches us that the source of love is from within. This love is embodied.

Unconditional Love is the love of life, all that life has to offer, and All That Is. It exists at the physical, emotional, energetic and astral planes. Through unconditional love we learn that we are always surrounded by love and have the power to heal through love. This love is spiritual.

Romantic Love includes the flow and exchange of healthy passion and sex and emotions and desires, all at the same time. It requires partnership. In partnership, we see our own reflections, our deepest wounds and our highest emotions. This love helps us to know the deep bonds of true intimacy. This love is soulfully mindful.

In order for us to feel fulfilled in love, we must integrate each part of the Love Trinity. You won't find lasting romance if you don't love your whole self. It is impossible to love your whole self if you don't practice unconditional love. You can't test the resiliency of your self-love or your unconditional love without romantic love.

LESSON: Love is way *more powerful than you think.*

A REAL GODDESS WALKING DOWN THE BEACH

I did it! I did it! I did it!

Who tramps naked across a public fountain to pose like *The Birth of Venus*?

I do, that's who!

I was silently beaming inside as we made our way back to Hanalei Bay. We had to wait our five-car turn on the bridge this time, with all the farmers and surfers and tourists doing their thing. I noticed with great clarity, the sun illuminating the banana trees and the ripples on the winding river behind the Dolphin Restaurant.

The roosters had finally shut up.

So, what would Venus do now? I remembered my first introduction to a woman's Temple Circle at a small yoga studio in Berkeley years ago. We meditated on Lalitha, an aspect of Venus in the Hindu tradition. We recited the mantra "Ah-eem, Kle-eem So-ha, Ah-een, Kle-eem, So-ha" over and over again as our guru guided us to embody the goddess. Like Venus, she rules over sexual and spiritual love with imperial grace. She is the "Empress of Desire."

It was a tough guided meditation for me. Lalitha is about sixteen with ample breasts, rosy skin, four arms which hold a symbol of power in each, and sits on a bed with five gods supporting her, sometimes she is seen with lions at her feet. She is the essence of erotic bliss, spiritual sexuality, earthly pleasures, and all the ruling powers of the Universe. She is the unified feminine. I had to deeply tap into my imagination for this one.

I couldn't help but peek out from under my lashes now and then to see if anyone in the meditation circle actually transformed into this image of incomprehensible love. All I saw was a diverse group of women in lotus position, eyes closed and half smiles across their faces.

This idea that we could embody such a goddess stayed with me, and I've been obsessed with Lalitha ever since. This brings me back to Venus.

Inspired by the Lalitha mantra, I sat in our rented SUV silently breathing in my made-up incantation for Venus.

I am beautiful.

I am playful.

I am sensual.

I am powerful.

I am bliss.

I am love.

I said it over and over again hoping to become a love so empowered that I could see, hear, taste, smell, touch all the nectar love has to offer. It was only six forty-five a.m. and I realized that I had another twenty-three hours to go as this divine creature. I knew I could do it, I knew I must.

We stopped off at the coffee shop that has changed names several times since we started visiting Kauai. I still call it Java Kai. I ordered my favorite chai with coconut milk. The sun had finally risen and the typical balmy breeze fondled my skin. All of the California visitors were already in line for their macadamia nut flavored coffee and pineapple turnovers.

Maybe it was the sweet smell of waffles, baked goods, passionfruit jelly, and roasted coffee, but I felt radiant and delicious. Owning what I had just done, my powerful posture as Venus lingered in my body, and my gaze remained inviting and pure. For the first time, I noticed and accepted glances of admiration.

It was possible that people were staring at me because I forgot to put my bra and panties back on under my muumuu, but Hawaiians and their guests have seen more provocative bodies and outfits. I assumed the goddess was at work. Everyone was honoring the Venus in me, and I refused to adopt (as I usually did) that I was doing something wrong. I refused to dim my light. In fact, I was going to see how bright I could shine.

I am beautiful.

I am playful.

I am sensual.

I am powerful.

I am bliss.

I am love.

I kept the mantra going as I waited for my order and thought, what would Venus wear on the beach, besides her birthday suit?

The great thing about Kauai is the plethora of surf shops that sell bikinis, and the variety shops with no shortage of shell themed gifts. I decided to go shopping, and told my husband that I'd meet him on the beach later. I found a shell and coral headpiece, a rose-gold bikini, and some Maui Babe lotion to moisturize my skin and make me look luxuriously bronzed. I love Maui Babe.

I walked back to the house with my goodies and a second chai still chanting:

I am beautiful.

I am playful.

I am sensual.

I am powerful.

I am bliss.

I am love.

I found my boys entertaining themselves farther down the beach. I settled myself under the sun as a goddess would. I lounged on my back with both elbows propping up my torso. I had one leg stretched out and one knee bent up toward the sky. I arched my back from time to time and allowed my head to fall back so my hair touched the sand. I gazed out to sea, posing like a *Sports Illustrated* model, as if I was in deep mysterious thought.

Then I rolled over on my side with one hand holding the side of my head and the other hand resting on my hip. My bottom leg stretched out the full length of my body, while my top leg bent at the knee and folded over to touch the sand in front of me. This pose made my hips look curvy and my waist smaller than it really was. This, by the way, is the perfect goddess position for every type of body. Your leg covers the belly and lifts the hips to shrink the waist. And as an added bonus, your cleavage looks amazing at this angle.

Yep. I had goddess written all over me.

When the sun got too hot, I walked over to the edge of the sea and lay flat on my belly, propped up on my elbows (another cleavage enhancer and belly-hiding trick!) and let the waves surprise me with wet kisses.

It's possible that I looked like I was drugged out on ecstasy or some other mood-enhancing psychedelic. I stayed in my own world simply enjoying the rough sand that massaged the space between my toes, the heat of the sun that penetrated my body, and the warm breeze that licked my skin. I had the "Girl from Ipanema" tune in my head, and swayed rhythmically to a song that no one else could hear.

Is this what self-love feels like? Being drunk with the pleasures of your own body and grateful for the rapture of the present moment? I started to imagine a romantic evening with rose petals, oils, candles, and a decadent ceremony of goddess worship. Yes, I would concoct a love ritual where my lover (I decide to call my husband lover from there on out) would honor every ounce of my naked body.

I am beautiful.

I am playful.

I am sensual.

I am powerful.

I am bliss.

I am love.

I felt it. I felt pure joy and euphoria. I felt the power of my heart. I felt love.

Then I saw this blinding vision floating down the beach toward me. Her hair. Her body. Her radiant skin! She wore a white bikini that made my swimsuit look like grandma picked it out. She was thoroughly confident in her stature, her curves, especially her sex appeal. She was an illusion of luminous magic as she passed me. She flashed me the kindest, most beautiful smile, her teeth stunning me with white perfection.

"Aloha," she sang to me in her bewitching tone, and sashayed down the beach.

"Aloha," I half groaned in response, and shrunk back into a coiled shell that felt more comfortable to me. All of a sudden, I could see sweaty bronze streak marks on my body from my hurried application of Maui Babe. I noticed the jiggle of my inner thighs. I cursed my boys for the loose skin on my belly. I wasn't even going to think about the crown of shells on my head. Did everyone think I was crazy as I rolled around in the sand like a lunatic? What if the police were searching for me for indecent exposure, or worse, as a lewd predator?

I'm not beautiful.

I'm not sexy.

I'm not playful.

I'm not powerful.

I don't know what love is.

Ugh. I have a long, long way to go.

What was that woman's trick? How was she so confident? I can't even remember if she specifically had a perfect nose or eyes or lips or body. I am not sure how tall she was, or if her hair was thick and shiny as it seemed. All I really saw was radiance, confidence, sexuality, and a powerful energy that made me gasp. And it made me uncomfortable. Why?

Envy.

Pure envy slapped me back into reality when I saw a real goddess walking down the beach that day. The dialogue that went through my head was ferocious. I second-guessed everything. Who was I to think I could personify Venus when there are plenty of powerful, beautiful, and sexy women who grace the cover of magazines, billboards, movies, and anywhere that requires being in a swimsuit. It wasn't fair.

I fell back into my habit of self-conscious over thinking, which many of us do to keep from truly embodying our inner sexy love goddess, and from truly being seen. How easy things change with the intense mental chatter about how much we are *not*, rather than focusing on how much we *are*.

It is the lack of self-love, or Philautia as the Greeks called it, that allows us to slip back into self-criticism and ignore the source of our inner beauty. The secret to physical beauty I learned, is that it will only express itself outward if you let it.

It took me a long time to realize that self-actualized real goddesses spot out emerging goddesses, even if we aren't aware of it. Just like the woman on the beach did to me. They'll give us a wink, or a smile, or say hello. Too often, those of us who haven't quite awakened to our inner divineness, think they are reaching out to rub it in. This is an example of how we react from a lack of self-love.

I must remind myself, and you, that we are all goddesses just at different places of our metamorphosis.

LESSON: You are a real goddess just waiting to emerge.

THE BRAZILIAN BOMBSHELL HAD SELF-LOVE

Earlier in the day, while I was shopping for my Venus bikini, there was a Brazilian woman in the surf shop that kept choosing the same bikinis that I did. She was seriously gorgeous, a true Brazilian bombshell. She was a big-boned woman, not the media's standard of Giselle's supermodel perfection. She had hips, boobs, a soft belly, and a bit of cellulite on her bum. Her hair was thick and dark, her eyes a sea of green and brown with super thick (natural) lashes. Her skin *was* Maui Babe. Her lips were perfectly plump, the kind of lips that reality television stars try to inject, except Brazil Bombshell's lips were naturally good looking. The most intriguing part about her was her unapologetic confidence.

At one point, we tried on the same turquoise bikini at the same exact time. The tag said Brazilian cut, which meant the back only slightly covered more than a G-string. She must have been rubbing off on me. The bikini top had itty bitty matching triangles with tassels of gold and turquoise thread that decorated the ends of the spaghetti strings.

I never bought things this small to wear out in public, but what the heck, I was just standing naked in a fountain, I had to try it on. Through the corner of my eye, I watched Brazil Bombshell admire herself in the mirror. She adored her body, touching her hips, her belly button, the top part of her breasts and gave herself a slap on her own ass. She stepped out from behind the curtain and I realized how very skimpy this turquoise piece of cloth really was. She showed herself off to her male friend.

Am I really trying this on, too? I thought.

"Do you *love* it?" Brazil Bombshell didn't really ask her male friend, but told him in her sexy accent, "I *love* it." She praised her body again in the mirror.

"Don't you *love* it?" She looked at me, then immediately back at herself in the mirror, "I *love* it."

Satisfied, she turned and paid full attention to me. "Oh my God." She stood in front of my section of the dressing room. "You look amazing! You have to get it. It looks so good on you. Look at your ass." She physically turned me around to look at my ass. "Look at her ass in this," she encouraged her friend and opened the curtain on me.

Ahh! Was this a cultural thing? Blushing, I shut the curtain and said it looked better on her.

I didn't get the turquoise bikini; I got the rose-gold, comparatively grandma one instead. Brazilian Bombshell's confidence overpowered mine. I didn't really believe her compliments. I couldn't receive them at the time.

Brazilian Bombshell had self-love. Her attitude was not confused with narcissism, false pride, megalomania, or snobbishness; she was nothing but kind and supportive and generous with herself and her compliments for me.

The shadow side to self-love is masking deep insecurities, which turns self-love into self-absorption. We all know people who hoard their love and obsess about their own needs and desires. They are the takers, the ones who eventually suck us dry, and the ones that compete with us and try to rub their physical or intellectual gifts in. Then there are some of us who do not honor any part of the gifts we were given. We reject any form of compliment. We simply can't believe having any positive attributes, or if we do, we don't think they will last.

Love, like any other type of energy, needs to flow. It needs to be given out freely and received freely. It is an abundant, healing energy that never gets depleted. But somehow we still think there is not enough of it, or that we might not ever find it, or that we are not worthy enough to get the type of love we've always dreamed of. I know now that all other love comes to us through self-love, that we are our own source of love.

But how do we find it? How do we keep it? How do we step into it mind, body, soul?

I'm reminded of a quote by Hafiz that says, "Venus just leaned down and asked me to tell you a secret, to confess she's just a mirror who has been stealing your light and music for centuries." The Venus within holds the key to self-love. To always find yourself irresistible is the way toward disposing of the self-judgment, insecurities, and rules that no longer serve you. Owning your inner goddess allows you to experience pleasure in life, in your body, and in the union of your body with another body – without shame or judgment.

Self-love creates space not restriction. It gives freedom not imprisonment. It is the magnitude in which you are able to feel and express love at the center of your core *before* being able to share it with another.

Venus invokes admiration from others, a high level of worshipping without negative intent or greedy desire. It is the honoring of all women, the feminine energy that creates, gestates, and gives birth to new life on this planet. She vibrates with both power and awe. Your Venus within can be a subtle energy that lights up the sky, nourishes hearts, and inspires everyone you walk by. She can help us to look deeply within ourselves in order for us to see clearly the beauty others see in us. Even the slightest adjustment in knowing that you are perfectly "enough," allows you to respond to the cruelties of life with much more grace and forgiveness.

I know, easier said than done.

LESSON: Be in love with yourself and you will attract the love you deserve.

SHUT THE FUCK UP

I've already mentioned that I had googled "How to stop being sick of yourself." It was late in the evening. I probably threw in a few words like "feminine" or "sensuality" or "awakening," before I stumbled on that TED Talk done by Sheila Kelley on the feminine. It defied my memory of the strip club I had entered for a "research project" I was doing on feminism in college. Instead, what I watched was beautiful, moving, and emotional. As you recall, I signed up for the movement retreat without knowing what I was getting into.

The retreat packing list included clothing items like a white button down shirt, sexy shoes, and movement clothes that you "felt sexy in." Easy. I had done hot yoga before. I already owned the exercise booty shorts and a racer back yoga top that were popular in sweaty yoga classes. Outfit done.

I also had these killer stilettos that Carrie Bradshaw wore in *Sex and the City*. Shoes done.

I was ready.

When I got to the retreat in San Diego, there were women of every shape and size, all walking with a gracious and sexy flow. Some had sweatpants on, and some had sundresses on. All the teachers were in workout stretch pants and tank tops. I felt like I was at a Southern California -style health expo. I was glad that I brought all the right things.

But, as I looked more closely to what was going on, I started to feel much more intimidated. Imagine almost a hundred women from all over the world glowing with excitement as they greeted a "sister" they hadn't seen since the last retreat, giving each other hugs, admiring each other, loving each other, and supporting each other. They were all so stunning.

Even with every age and size and style, each woman was as magnificently unique as the next.

And then imagine one single woman, with her eyes bugging out of her head, clutching her Whole Foods canvas bag filled with yoga clothes, in it a white top, black booty shorts, a black tank, and some shoes. I must have missed something since everyone else had rolling suitcases full of clothes "to move in." I became so nervous, I didn't talk to anyone, and compared to everyone else, I stiffly lumbered down the hallway to the registration desk.

"This is feminine radiance," I heard a whisper in my ear. The voice was rich and buttery. I turned to see the most mesmerizing and exquisite creature, she correctly guessed this was my first time. This woman had the nurturing quality of mother earth, the primal energy of a panther, and the spirit of an angel. Her hair was cut so close to her scalp to show off a perfectly shaped skull. Her skin was the color of dark cinnamon, and the muscles of her body were sculpted to perfection.

I wanted to cry right then and there and tell her that I needed to go home, and to please show me the way out before anyone saw me. But instead I smiled and spontaneously blurted out, "You're a goddess of light." She knowingly smiled back at this. Her name was Bernadette, and she assured me that she'd watch over me. And she did.

The registration desk was also the register for the pop-up boutique in the back room. After signing in, I was asked if I needed anything from the boutique for the weekend, so I decided to take a look around. Displayed were stripper shoes, G-string underwear in gold, silver, hot pink, and black, there were body ties in all other neon, shiny colors on the table, mesh see through tops, sexy bras, fishnets, and nipple covers.

I think I was holding my breath and realized I made the biggest mistake by coming to this retreat. This was not what I expected from that

TED Talk video with the pretty woman in a cardigan sweater and a long skirt. I had my trusty Whole Foods bag with my yoga movement clothes that "I felt sexy in." This was beyond what I knew about being sexy.

Even the newcomers must have gotten a different set of instructions than mine, because everyone but me seemed prepared. Thank goodness they split up the advanced students from the newcomers. In the newbie group, we learned to move sensually, went to lectures, and came together as a whole to experience different workshops together. The retreat experience opened up so many repressed emotions that I was a basket case the entire time. I was way more sick of myself now than before I had started down this journey.

Toward the end of the retreat, Sheila came into each of our movement classes and watched us move individually. Talk about nervous wreck! This was such a stretch for me. I was not a trained dancer, nor could I touch my toes. I had never been comfortable doing anything in front of people, and this was my first time moving my body in this way. We danced in two groups. The first group danced together, and then my group danced. We were to get feedback afterward.

This was the beginning of a lot of really terrifying, yet valuable lessons for me. She was honest and generous in her feedback; one woman needed to linger in her movement longer, another needed to express more, yet another had an interesting need to be seen and unseen at the same time. Then it was my turn for comments.

I waited eagerly and humbly.

Sheila Kelley said to me softly, "All you really need to do …" She paused for a moment and then looked straight at me with so much love. "… is shut the fuck up."

Was I talking? No, of course I wasn't talking. Maybe my mouth was moving. How embarrassing. Do I say I'm sorry? Sorry for what? I was so confused. I finally looked into her eyes and understood her completely. She was referring to the constant chatter in my head:

"I'm going to go over to the wall and I'll do the frisk. Hands on the wall. Stick out your ass. Oooh, that feels really good on the hamstrings. Turn around and slide down the wall. Now what? Okay, just roll on the floor. I'll crawl to the pole. Ouch, bad idea, my knees hurt. Don't go to the pole. Crawl back to the wall. Ouch. Crawl up the wall. This cannot look good. Should I do a hip circle? I'll do a hip circle. How many hip circles should I do? How many have I done? Five? Six? Is that too much? I must have done enough. Should I slide down again and do a cat pounce? Yes. I'll do that. Great stretch ... I like the cat pounce. Wait what do we do after this? Oh, I could do the leg splay. Shoot, I'm not flexible enough to do the leg splay. My legs are shaking. It doesn't look good. I'm so not going to touch myself, or whatever they call it. I didn't do the kneeling hip pumps yet. What am I thinking? I must look like I'm constipated. Stop *now* they are way too hard! I'm just going to whip my head around. Ouch. Whip lash. I'm going back to the wall. I feel safer there ... Oh, thank God, the song is over."

Sheila *saw* this entire dialogue going on in my head, maybe everyone did. I would have appreciated it if someone would have just told me to stop and go home. But no one told me to stop and go home. No one told me I looked stupid. No one told me to stop trying. No one rolled their eyes at me. No one laughed at me.

They only encouraged me more. They understood me. They saw in me what they saw in themselves. They held me. We were all goddesses on the same journey of awakening. We wanted to express our truth. We wanted to be seen, truly seen, as our authentic selves. We wanted to fit in. We wanted a tribe that would support us, not hold us down. We wanted love.

It took me a long time to truly learn to shut the fuck up and trust my body, and I finally realized that the number one rule into finding our inner Venus is to quiet the mind, so we can listen to our bodies.

LESSON: Stop your critical mind and get into your body a.k.a. shut the fuck up.

BODY LOVE

As I watched the real goddess on the beach walk away, a big wave crashed into me and actually lifted me up and threw me onto my back. Sand ended up landing in my crotch and my left boob was dangling out from under my bathing suit top. Three seconds seemed like eternity. A wake up call.

"Shut the fuck up," I told myself and prepared for yet another embarrassing moment, "just shake it off". I was having one of those lucid daydreaming flashes when I could see the entire next scene play out in vivid technicolor before me. But, it was all happening so fast that I couldn't stop what was about to take place.

Thank you, Taylor Swift. I started singing out loud, whipping my head side-to-side, and jumping up and down on the beach. Dance breaks had become a new thing for me.

"'Cause the players gonna play, play, play, play, play
And the haters gonna hate, hate, hate, hate, hate
I'm just gonna shake, shake, shake, shake, shake
I shake it off, shake it off"

I sang the same verse over and over again because I never know the full lyrics to any song whatsoever. I couldn't stop myself from having what might have looked like a physical fit to everyone else, but a stress relieving dance break to me.

I secretly love making up my own verses to songs, I do it as unsolicited birthday gifts at parties that everyone can participate in (maybe that's why people avoid me). So while I whipped my hair from side-to-side and jumped up and down, I replaced the words (that I suddenly remembered), to the "Shake-It-Off" rap-ish part.

"My ex-brain has a new better brain

It's like "oh my God," I'm just going to shake it

Forget the goddess over there with the shiny long hair

I'm just gonna shut the fuck up, so I can shake, shake, shake"

I had officially gone mad, but it broke the spell that I was in and I settled down. I took a really deep breath.

I am beautiful.

I am playful.

I am sensual.

I am powerful.

I am bliss.

I am love.

Over and over I said to myself, I can do this, and I will.

Feeling better, I knelt down facing the ocean and closed my eyes. I listened to the sound of the waves, and the children playing, and the wind in the palm leaves. I felt energetically aligned with the earth and the cosmos so that I could hear the silent whispers of the universe.

Again, I felt the heat of the sun penetrating the skin on my shoulders and my upper thighs, while the wind softly caressed it. My senses came back alive to feel the tiny particles of rough sand in different places on my body, and to the smell and taste of the salty air. In my mind's eye, I recreated my response to the radiant woman on the beach.

Instead of recoiling into my shell, I stood and greeted her. We honored the beauty in each other, saw the reflection of ourselves in each other, and bowed internally to each other. "Namaste," I whispered out loud. "The divine in me bows to the divine in you." She slowly transformed into an ethereal being of glittering light, and I stepped right into her body.

I continued my meditation by focusing on my five senses until I relaxed and reconnected to the powerful force that my morning experience gave me. I was Venus again. I slowly stood to see where my kids were. They were boogie boarding. My husband, now lover, surfed. I headed back to the house, went straight into the bathroom where I stripped down to nothing.

I stared at myself in the mirror and decided to find myself adorable. I've heard this many times before, from many different inspirational speakers, and in many different forms; look in the mirror and love your entire body. So I looked.

I stared straight into my eyes, and for the first time noticed the clean patterns of my iris. There were streams of straight fibers radiating from the center of my pupils, and a dark circle cleanly bordering the whiteness of my sclera. I noticed there were no red veins at that moment, a beauty benefit of being offline I guessed.

I looked deeper into my eyes, trying to see my own soul. Tears began to run down my cheeks. This time I let them pour through me and out of me instead of holding them back. I cried for me and for no reason. I cried for everyone else and for every reason. I cried for all the wounded souls no matter how big or small the pain, because pain is pain. I cried for it all at the same time. I wasn't even on my period, I was just crying.

I realized I was never allowed to cry, ever. I was ashamed to cry. It was a sign of weakness that I could not afford to reveal. But this felt really good. I even let my tongue taste a tear. Salty.

I stepped back and started to look at my lips. They aren't so bad. My nose is tiny and kind of cute if I focus on its structure. My neck is sleek and collar bones defined. My breasts are full, and when positioned properly, I can appreciate that they have nourished my two babies. My shoulders are strong. My in-betweeny belly button was once attached to both of my children. How amazing is that? The flesh around my belly looked good when I stretched up my torso, and it revealed her hardship while stretching to allow me to carry my babies and give them life. I felt so grateful. My hips are narrow. My thighs are lean and longer than my height would suggest. I have a scar on my left knee, a college prank I'd like to forget. My ass isn't as taught as I'd like, but Brazilian Bombshell didn't seem to mind it.

I continued noticing parts of my body without judgment. And then I started thanking each body part for the role she played in my physical experience through life. The body, my body, is quite amazing actually. I was once a tiny egg penetrated by a tiny sperm, and without any written instructions, formed into this adult body. She tells me when I'm hungry and tired. My blood, my breath, my heartbeat flows, expands, and beats with precise regularity. Thank you feet for bearing the weight of my body as I walk along this earth. And there is so much more that my body has done to protect me.

I began to touch my body, to really feel her. I tenderly caressed my face. My nails softly grazed my right neck as I tipped it sideways. It felt so good. I let my fingers linger around my neck until they found the dip between my clavicles. From there, my fingers slowly caressed down the center of my body until I reach my pubic bone and delicately pull at my pubic hairs. I let my other hand feel around my breasts and nipples.

I realized how important it is to honor our own bodies. Mine has created life, carried life, birthed life. My body has nurtured life with her milk. My body has healed itself and healed others with a kind touch or warm embrace. My body has endured injuries, physical and emotional, yet still rises each morning for another miraculous day.

If I felt shame about my body, it showed up in how I stood, how I interacted, how I presented myself to another. If I felt shame, I would not open up fully, attract fully, or even love fully.

I had an epiphany.

The way to stop overthinking and listening to my inner critic was to experience full embodiment of an elevated emotion like self-love instead of fear, shame, guilt, or any other low vibrational feeling. I must be fully present in my surroundings and pay attention without judgment. I needed to know the needs and desires of my body at this very moment, at every present moment. I must learn to appreciate *my* body, as I'd like others to appreciate it. Whatever I see in the mirror is what others will see in me.

I needed my inner Venus to guide the way, so I could get out of my own way. I vowed to do this body love exercise every single morning. I decided to go find rose petals and candles for an evening ritual that was brewing in my imagination.

LESSON: Awaken your five senses. Love and be grateful for your body every day.

GOING CRAZY OR HAVING A SPIRITUAL AWAKENING?

Venus stands before me again, breathtaking and beautiful and whispers in a voice that could melt iron, "Do you want to love and be loved? Do you want passion and depth, to be worshipped and adored, to know that you are safe and worthy of the most exquisite tenderness? Do you want devotion and to be left yearning for more? You want trust. You want a love affair so abundant that it moves mountains, heals your soul, and satisfies your every earthly desire."

"Yes." Tears roll down my face.

"Tell me then, how much love are you capable of giving?"

At that moment, my chest pulled upward lifting my back into a deep arch. It was as if an invisible hand had reached into my ribs to rip out my heart. I feared excruciating rupture, shattering, and an explosion that would allow my blood to drip from my eyes, my nose, and my mouth. The mess would certainly terrify the poor soul who found my lifeless body, which would surely be my children. They'd be scarred for life and I hadn't set up therapy for them yet.

I waited for the burning, gripping pain to finally come and crush me. My eyes stayed shut and my hands clenched at the sheets beneath me. I held my breath. I waited. And I waited. And I waited. Finally, I surrendered to my inevitable death and let go of every fear, desire, hope, and dream. I was ready to die.

Then the most incredible thing happened. My lungs filled up with life-enhancing breath, far beyond what I thought them capable of. The air stretched into every cell of my body. It hurt and it felt good at the same time. It seemed as if I had been surviving underwater for centuries, that my body automatically swelled up and down as the waves of oxygen slammed into me.

Unworthiness came to mind.

Did I really think I was only worthy enough to take up as little air and space as possible? What a depressing thought, but somehow I knew that I was unconsciously living that truth. I never realized that I was holding my breath in the depths of an emotional sea that I refused and was refusing to acknowledge. The discomfort in my chest for all these years was not because of my fear of drowning; it was because of my fear of living and loving. Was I worthy of receiving love? I could easily give it out, but I secretly wondered if I would get real love in return, especially that kind I deeply desired. Did I truly believe that love could be safe, passionate, trustworthy, unconditional, monogamous, and exciting at the same time?

It was so much safer and easier for me to hide beneath the surface of the waters and float in between suffocating or coming up for air. I did this for years. How incredibly sobering it was to awaken to the thought that I've been living a partial life. The affection and love I was dolling out was hesitant and filled with expectations. How many times had I held back on initiating an affectionate moment with my husband for fear he'd want fast sex instead of the deeper intimacy I craved? Worse yet, how many times had I reacted out of fear for my children? Holding them back or guiding them onto a path that was not theirs to travel, because I feared they'd be hurt if I did not protect them with walls similar to the massive walls I had built to protect myself.

In addition to being lifeless with fear, I was anxious with the terrible boredom of being comatose. Floating in limbo between living and dying is truly boring and a tragic situation to be in. It's an invisible cage where you can see everyone else swimming in the water, flying in the air, or dancing on the earth while you sit motionless waiting for the sky to fall down on you.

Secretly, I cursed the heavens for it not happening already. During my bored states, I would create the drama that I expected from Armageddon. How shameful was the sudden realization that I instigated many mini wars just to *feel* something, anything.

How much love was I capable of giving? That question was so painful for me. It was not enough to let go of my fear, hopes, desires, and dreams, which only allowed me to breathe in the oxygen I needed to feel alive. I had to let my heart out of her protected iceberg that was trapped within a kryptonite cell, which was surrounded in glass, and wrapped in a pretty Tiffany's box with its white ribbon so no one could guess what was really going on. My heart needed to be set free to do her work; to love, to receive love, to support, to inspire, to start creating and to do everything that a heart desires to do.

It was not the blood of a broken heart that I felt on my face and body, it was the tears and sweat that have been corked up for too long and needed immediate release. I knew deep down that we have to truly open our hearts to fully love. There can be no barrier, no protection, no rules or conditions to our love. We must give it freely. But if we have ever been hurt, shamed, scarred or betrayed by those that are supposed to love us, how could we trust enough to open up to those we do love?

I decided to let go further and let my heart out, free to break, shatter, be crushed, and get messy and ugly (bye, bye Tiffany box!). If I died, I would die. If it hurt, let it hurt. I didn't care if I became the Tin Man without a heart...I was not very far from being rusty anyway. And then waiting for the end with closed eyes, there was the light. I was either crazy, which the day had already proven possible, or I was having a spiritual awakening. Maybe the two are the same thing. My heart lifted as never before. I felt a blissful opening to love that paled in comparison to the love we have for our babies. Pure joy and sensuality and magic coursed through my body. I was being lifted up to see Heaven on a winged horse. The feeling lasted forever, but really only a minute before the sensation trickled down my body and landed right between my legs.

Oh my.

LESSON: Pain is not from heartbreak, it's from the heart struggling to be set free.

GODDESS PUJA

I opened my eyes, knowing that I was willing to give every ounce of love I had within me. Hundreds of candles lit the bedroom, creating a beautiful warm glow. Quivers of light danced on the walls while the shadows chased after them. There was a light fragrance of jasmine that seduced my senses.

And there he was, kneeling at the end of the bed watching me. How lovely he looked in the candlelight. I sat naked in lotus position on the bed, fully exposed, feeling a heat at my core and a whisper of breath surrounding my skin. To be hot and chilled at the same time is the essence of erotic pleasure for me, a brand new feeling.

The ancient iceberg that had kept my heart captive was finally melting. I was finally melting. He didn't say a word, just picked up a pile of rose petals and set them right between my legs in worship. It was beautiful.

I watched as he held a single stemmed rose in his hand and began a journey of touch at my feet. With the petals of this deep red rose, he anointed every toe on my left foot and then twirled it at its arch before slowly trailing up my shins, my knees, and the inside of my legs. Then he ever so lightly brushed it in between my legs, lingering for the briefest of moments before continuing on to my right side. I noticed that my left inner thigh wanted much more, and quivered when he started on the right. He slowly teased me with only fleeting attention between my legs, which aroused a pulse that began to smolder toward all of my nerve endings.

The rose found its way back to my pubic bone and up the center of my belly. From there it found breasts and circled the outer part of my left nipple and then the right. He only gazed in my eyes once to make sure I was enjoying myself. Otherwise, he paid close attention to what he was doing. That intense focus on my body, and watching his enjoyment captivated me. The rose crawled up my throat and kissed me on the lips, stroked my cheeks, and tenderly explored my now closed eyelids. It even tickled the right side of my neck, which is one of my newly found secret spots of sensory pleasure. My entire body writhed involuntarily making me slither on the bed. Every part of me had been honored with attention and touch.

Keeping my eyes closed, I was suddenly surprised by a warm and slippery drip onto my chest, then a slow melting of the thick liquid downward to collect in my belly button. Moments later, he poured a more generous amount of warm potion over my pubic bone. It dribbled into the folds of my sex. I was swimming in a golden liquid dream of sweet almond oil and roses.

My mind took a nap, and my body awakened with thirsty greed.

Strong hands suddenly cupped the excess oil and rose petals between my legs, and a finger brushed my slit. I inhaled deeply as the tip of his finger entered and stroked upward. A hungry sigh escaped my mouth when he ignored my silent cry for more and went back to my feet. What torture.

My feet were pressed and squeezed and stroked. I wiggled my toes and let my hips squirm, inviting him to move upward please. He slowly massaged my legs and thighs and worked right in the crevasse where my thighs meet my pubic bone, so close to my craving groin. While straddling my right leg, he worked his way up my bodice to my breast, keeping his one knee close to my wet and oily center, which ached for attention. As he massaged around my breasts and pinched my nipples, I managed to sneak a pelvic grind around his strong thigh. A whispered groan escaped from the depths of my core.

Without warning, the warm and wet serum turned into a cool hard object that began to explore my body in similar ways as the rose did. My skin perked with the merging of warm oil and cool hardness. My eyes remained closed to fully experience the glossy touch that landed at the base of my throat and moved deliberately and slowly, too slowly, down to the tip of the opening between my legs. And there he paused and pressed.

I opened my eyes then, and locked mine with his. He was holding a colorful glass wand. As he fixed his gaze with mine, he slowly twisted the wand with intention and gently began to penetrate.

In and out.

In and out.

I could no longer control myself, and with our eyes still fixed on each other's, I allowed my entire body to explode in exquisite, pulsating release.

I woke up with my naked body wrapped around his naked body. I looked around to see only a few candles, a small bottle of massage oil, and the pikake petals that were the only flowers left at the Big Save Market when I went in search for roses. They smelled like jasmine.

I couldn't tell how much of my experience was real or a dream. I have never taught my husband how to do a proper Goddess Puja before. I made a mental note to do so. But it didn't matter. This was more freedom and feeling then I have ever allowed my vanilla love life to experience.

I looked at his sleeping face and knew I had deprived him of so much of the passion that was locked inside me. I touched his heart with my fingertip and felt my own swell up. It would take some time for me to really understand the blocks and forgive my past. But I knew I would and felt a sweet tingle in my groin. I gave thanks to Venus, she gave me courage and beauty and grace. She guided me to my heart.

I heard Venus whisper to me, "Remember, you are Venus. You are the source of love so powerful you are capable of anything." Then I fell back asleep.

LESSON: "The love you take is equal to the love you make."
– John Lennon

6. The Ingénue

FROM THE MOUTH OF BABES

My husband and I didn't have easy conversations about sex, we actually never talked about it, only around it. Raising kids may have taken the sex drive right out of me, but my husband wasn't exactly comfortable with talking about the subject either.

I made it a point to make sexuality and nudity an open, safe and transparent conversation with my children. I was making up for all the instructions I *didn't* get when I was a child. My boys weren't going to learn about sex from porn, their first encounter, or from someone else who might not know what they were talking about. I didn't ever want them to be ashamed about their bodies, or to shame anyone else's body, especially girls'. So, I walked around naked. A lot.

Once, when I was changing a tampon, my boys, two and four at the time, burst into the bathroom laughing after a game of chase. They stopped laughing immediately and stared at me on the toilet.

"What are you doing mommy?" asked my four-year old.

"Changing my tampon," I said frankly. I saw them peering into the toilet. "Don't worry, it's just blood from my period, and only girls get their periods."

"What's a period?"

Oh boy, I thought. I flushed the toilet and walked over to the sink. "It is when a woman sheds the lining in her uterus if there's no baby to nourish. It happens once a month."

"What's a uterus?"

"Where we carry the babies."

"What's that thing you put in your vagina?" My older son was advanced in the language of bodily parts.

"It's a tampon."

"What's it for?"

"To stop my period from staining my pants."

"Am I going to get my period?"

"No. You are boys; you won't get it."

"Good." He said relieved, and asked if he could see it.

"See what, the tampon?" I pulled out my box of O.B.'s as they both nodded their heads in excitement. I let them open a tampon each and showed them how it absorbed the water, while I explained more about the cycles of women and how their cousins will get it when they turned twelve or so. They weren't really listening; they just wanted to put the tampon under the sink water themselves, so I let them have fun with the process of watching the tampon expand under their little hands. Through some kind of little kid telepathy, they both decided to toss the wet tampons into the air at the same time, which stuck to the high ceiling. We all looked up and waited for them to fall back down. They didn't. We started howling with laughter. They wondered if the tampons might fall on their dad's head when he was brushing his teeth that evening. We decided to leave them up on the ceiling to see if that would happen.

A year later when we were visiting Hawaii (I clearly love the place), I was sitting near the pool and my three-year-old was wading in the shallow side with his "floaties" on his arms yelling, "Mommy, Mommy! Are you not coming into the swimming pool because of your pyramid?" Every parent around the pool looked up and gave him a really big smile. I blushed, but at least he remembered. Shortly after that trip, he barged in on me in the shower at home, and stared at me quizzically.

"Mommy, I have a discovery," he said in his baby voice.

"What is it?" I sounded really intrigued.

"*You* have a vagina. Me and Kai Kai" — that's what he called his brother — "have a *penis*. And daddy ..." he paused dramatically, "... has *both!*" Then he turned triumphantly around and left the bathroom.

I had to think about that for a second, truth from the mouth of babes, and then I started laughing. He was an observant kid. It was about four years later, when I remembered the tampons on the ceiling. There they still were, dried cotton blobs with strings dangling from them. I smiled and reminded myself to look up more often.

It is confirmation of our own comfort or discomfort levels around sex when we measure it against how we talk about it with our children. Kids are innocent and just want to learn without judgment. Childlike curiosity can help us discover how comfortable we are talking about sex with our partners. I needed to figure out how to add more innocent play and wonder into our relationship and how we communicated, and it was the funny things my kids did and said that would get me there.

LESSON: The seeds of innocence are being planted for you. Children are teachers too.

WONDERLAND

On Kauai, I also became Pocahontas the Trailblazer, as I guided my family through the twists and turns of the Kalalau Trail, all the way to the magnificent waterfall four miles into the jungle. I was the Easter Bunny, hiding candy in the tropical bushes by day, and morphing into a Playboy bunny by night. At the local variety gift shop, that also sold only one food item called spam wasubi (spam wrapped in rice and seaweed), I bought a plastic grass skirt and coconut shell bikini top. I was Aloha Babe. I made everyone take hula lessons from me and then doled out the spam wasubi, which became our favorite snack. Paniolo girl and Moon Goddess were the other two icons of that week. But it was Venus that rebirthed me from the sea foam of my unconscious sleep back into myself as a goddess-in-the-making.

I had so much more to explore, and I realized that I needed to up my self-love game. It was time to start diving into what these personas were trying to teach me, and if they could really teach me *how* to fall in love with myself.

In order for us to get to real self-love and then to the highest relationship we can have with our partners, it requires us to know our multidimensional soul. And in order for us to know our soul, we need to get into the wonderland of our innocence, the place before the first wound, the first sorrow, the first fear, or first conditioning. And then we need to feel. We need to feel everything.

Feelings are different from emotions. Emotions have a way of taking over our feelings, while feelings are sensations in the body that teach us things. If I feel the urge to eat, sleep, purge, release without any story attached to it, it simply means I need to have a meal, go to bed, go to the bathroom, or have sex. Feelings in our gut warn, while feelings in our heart attract.

If our emotions are out of control, one might withhold sex while the other might have an affair. I wish I knew this before. I'm sure I sucked at conscious communication because my emotions overpowered any sense of real feeling. Sadly, we were not grounded enough at the time, and we allowed our emotions to thwart the process of communicating in any civilized way.

Most adults are afraid to feel, while innocent children aren't. That is why we want to find our own kind of Wonderland, where we can go down the rabbit hole with curiosity and excitement. That is how Alice learned so much from the Red Queen, the Cheshire Cat, the Mad Hatter and the rest, with innocent curiosity. Dorothy also had innocent curiosity to meet her courage, her heart, her mind and her darkness.

The wonder, awe, curiosity, joy and pure innocence is where we need to go first on the pathway to our fullest potential not just as lovers, but as human beings.

LESSON: Tap into your inner magical child, she's in your heart somewhere.

LOLLIPOPS

After coming home from Hawaii, I was a little cranky. It was either the stark contrast from a warm and luscious paradise, with the return home to a cold and foggy San Francisco and our routine, or I was just about to get my period. It would have been a great day to be Jadis, the Ice Queen from *Narnia*, so I'd have an excuse to be cold and bitchy, and perhaps freeze everyone for 100 years while I got my act together without much more embarrassing moments.

My husband was starting to pay some real attention to me though. "You seem a little edgy today," he said. "I'll hold space for you tonight if you want to really let loose. You can go crazy, whatever you need." Yes, you read that right; his exact words included "hold space," which made all the difference in the world.

After a few workshops under my belt, I learned a great tool for venting. Instead of piling on my problems about kids, in-laws, psycho moms, or politics with my partner, I was to release strong energy and vent only with girlfriends who knew the language and could "hold space" for my venting. It was called Spring Cleaning, Bitch Fest, or Release depending on the teacher. All of them said, in one way or another, that men were not our hairy girlfriends. I learned to spare my husband the itty bitty details that his male brain could never understand. I became an expert in using this tool, calling my refined version The Purge.

After this generous gesture, my heart melted and I couldn't be Jadis. I wanted to give my husband something more appealing for being so observant of my needs. I chose to be a sweet, bashful, innocent ingénue who has never experienced anything hurtful, shameful, or demoralizing. She held no grudges, and got excited about every little thing that happened to her. I had put on white ruffled shorty short shorts, a St. Polly's Girl type cropped top, and white ruffled bobby socks. I learned my lesson on that first movement retreat and stocked up on sexy clothes of all kinds, you never know where you'll end up. I put on the bubble gum pink lipstick that looked amazing on the sales boy at the MAC counter one shopping spree day in my kitty cat outfit (stay tuned for that one). I put my hair in pigtails, a little mixture of Lolita, Betty Boop, and Marilyn Monroe. I found the jar of candy I had hidden from the kids from previous Halloweens, and having no idea if candy has an expiration date or not, I rummaged through the container and found a big round pinker-than-pink lollipop. I snapped a few selfies and sent them off with a few innocent questions like, "I wonder how long it would take to suck this lollipop all the way down to its juicy bubble gum core?" I added. "Could I golf in this?" My husband was golfing with a colleague that morning, so I fully expected that he wouldn't see the text until much later, but seconds later he replied back with a smile and heart emojis. He said, "Stop! I can't concentrate!"

I decided to put on a pair of stretchy wide pants over this outfit, mostly because it was cold, and went to my studio where I created custom outfits and photographed women. My work had always had a sexy element to it, most likely stemming from my repressed sexuality dying to escape. Now that I was getting deeper and deeper into what it meant to be soulfully sexy, that essence showed up even more in my work. One of my clients, a well-known fertility doctor who was considered to be the best in San Francisco, called me her "therapist" after I shared the story behind my pigtails. I confessed that my experiment was turning my relationship around, and that today I was learning to innocently flirt with life, which made everything flow so much easier for me. She wanted to learn how too.

LESSON: A little flirt goes a long way.

FLIRTING 101

"We all have a flirtatious and innocent side," I told Dr. Danielle Lane, in between sketches for a gown we were creating for the Opera, "and there are many more benefits to flirting than just looking for a relationship. We can use flirting techniques to talk to rogue colleagues to cut through the posturing and bullshit that is so popular with men these days. We can all use a dose of flirting with life itself!"

Flirting with life means enjoying life with more wonder and gratitude. When I use flirting in this way, I have an easier time with confrontational conversations. It's been especially beneficial when my husband gets grumpy and I need to diffuse tension and avoid the energy suck that sometimes happens with stress filled days. Flirting has helped me ask for what I want in a way that is easy to digest. Adding a little flirtation to my life has also helped me manifest desires easier.

This ingénue I tried on was a flirt that helped me gain more confidence, understand and strengthen my boundaries, gave me the experience of my own radiance, and then allowed me to share a piece of my sunshine with someone else. My flirty innocence became an act of kindness. I augmented conscious communication, which you know I sucked at, with flirtation and it made each step of that process sound lighter, natural, and more authentic. I felt more connected when I added a little flirt to my way of communicating, and the feedback was met with positive attention and acceptance. Flirtation has helped me "fill up my tank" with a soft feminine essence, so that I could share more of me without feeling depleted.

Many researchers who study flirtation have noticed that there are basic flirting techniques across cultures. These techniques are eye contact, smiles, and body confidence. The traits are more appealing to onlookers than physical beauty traits say the experts. BBC Science also says that flirting happens through physical cues more than spoken words, and that fifty-five percent of what makes a person attractive is their body language. What's the take away? We don't need to worry about being witty or "social media beautiful" when we are the flirtatious Ingénue.

Dr. Lane wasn't so sure about this whole flirtation thing for her professional life, but I assured her that there was a style of flirtation that she could incorporate with her serious persona too, and introduced her to the bashful, the playful, and the inviting ingénue.

The bashful ingénue is innocently curious about the world. She is the type that flirts with life, simply enjoying her senses and the joys her experiences bring. She is not seeking validation or attention. She is simply curious about the environment around her. She has an almost child-like quality to her presence. Like a breath of fresh air, she can change direction on a whim, experiencing every nook and cranny of life fully. She doesn't seek anything in return, but is generous with her radiant energy, like a butterfly who flits and flirts around, spreading her light and her joy. She is genuinely attractive for her simple innocence and purity.

It is a joy to serve the bashful ingénue because she is open and inquisitive, and that is why it's easy to manifest desires. She is opposite of the damsel in distress who seeks attention to fill a hole. The bashful ingénue is in exploration and joy mode. Her energy has zero neediness in it. She usually has people opening doors and offering her gifts without her ever needing to ask.

In social situations, the bashful ingénue's body language opens and closes. It is demure. She may use her eyelashes to think, or hold back tears of joy, or just because. This is *not* a contrived action, it happens naturally. In a professional setting or a confrontation, "the flirt" happens energetically to soften the hardness of cold conversations and direct people toward collaboration.

Then there's the playful ingénue who frolics in the second type of flirtation. She is the cute little puppy dog who wants interaction and attention, not necessarily needing or wanting intimacy. She acts like she has a lighthearted crush on everyone. I've become this type of flirt.

The difference between bashful and playful is interaction. Instead of being curious and observant with self and life in general, playful wants to interact more personally. She likes to safely taste test personalities to experience different energies. She doesn't have any desire to connect intimately, just play. Even in partnership, this is a fun way to interact and enliven life force energy.

We shouldn't ever feel guilty about flirting in this way. Every animal practices eye contact and uses body language to communicate. It is how we connect to others naturally. The playful ingénue understands her own boundaries and makes her boundaries energetically clear to her playmates. She makes eye contact and her body language is more open. Prolonged eye contact is known to release the hormone oxytocin, which helps in bonding, so playful is very attractive. She moves closer to other people in the room and assesses them with deeper interest.

The playful embodies casual confidence, we don't need to worry about what we look like or how we present ourselves, and we have lots of self-love and dignity, always paying attention to the self and to others in the present moment. When I flirt in this way, I'm negotiating interaction using my whole body expressively. I try to make everyone in the room feel like they are special, because they are. I'll mirror their pace, their tone and even their body language. I will face them so that they become the center of my Universe (for the moment at least). I remember to use their names, I'll smile, and I'll laugh when appropriate. I will choose to believe that they are the most interesting thing on the planet in that moment. Playful makes me feel good about myself, and everyone feels good about that. Feeling good is contagious.

An inviting ingénue is like a blossoming rose. She is spontaneous, and she is open to connecting intimately but only if it feels right to her. When I try this on, I make longer eye contact and my body language is more inviting, like I'm silently saying "come closer." I'm more demonstrative, touching an arm, a knee, maybe lean in and rub elbows.

Depending if you are trying to win over a stubborn child or rigid adult, flirting can be used as an energy to shift behavior. It is simply an exercise in enjoying life and a random act of kindness, like smiling at a stranger, sending anonymous flowers to a friend or lover, leaving beautiful quotes in the bathroom for someone to find. I like leaving rose petals where I've been. Maybe if we smile more at strangers and make eye contact a little longer than usual, we can spread a little more joy into this world. If we remember to flirt more with our partners, we won't project our issues on to them, and we won't be so affected by bad behavior toward us.

LESSON: There are lots of types of flirting that can brighten up any kind of day

THE BIG TEASE

That evening, we were going to a small birthday dinner that I couldn't wear my white ruffled shorty shorts to, the crowd was way too conservative for that. But I did keep the flirtatious ingénue in play. I took off the white and wore black ruffles out to dinner. The conservative environment challenged my creativity. I had to hide my discomfort with this particular group, they were a little uptight for my taste, the men spoke only of finance, while the women only of kids, schools, or the weather. I was really bad at small talk, and this crowd seemed to fear anything past that limited scope. I was already the "wild" one, which made me sad because I was really vanilla compared to the variety of worlds I was becoming exposed to. It wasn't that I didn't appreciate everyone, most were high achievers and very accomplished, we just didn't have deep conversations, and as I mentioned, I don't know how to do small talk.

To entertain myself, and keep in character of the innocent ingénue, I decided to buy a remote control vibrator at Good Vibrations in anticipation for a long night. I put the plastic vibrator in my panties, hoping it would not fall out.

When we all sat down to dinner, I quietly leaned over to my husband before we sat down, handed him the remote and whispered in his ear, "I wonder what this thing does?" and I pressed the button. I pressed my body close to his so that he could feel the vibrator buzz against his thigh. We both started laughing because it would horrify the group we were with. The group started laughing only because we were laughing, which made us laugh even more. Spontaneous laughter is a tool to liven up any situation.

During dinner, I felt the random buzz a few times at the most inconvenient moments, like trying to get a sip of wine, or reaching over for a piece of bread. Of course I would start laughing again, which would make my husband laugh and then we both could not stop laughing, and we could not tell anyone why. When I got up to go to the bathroom, my husband waited for me to walk a few steps away, and then pressed it full on – the intensity stopped me in my tracks and I had to maneuver slowly so that it wouldn't fall out. I laughed all the way to the bathroom.

We have never again been invited out to dinner with these conservative people, which was fine by me. Maybe they heard the buzz as I was walking to the bathroom and suspected a little naughty play which embarrassed them, or maybe peels of unsolicited laughter for no reason was not how "society" rolled. No matter, we had sexy playtime without having sex in public, and the memory and laughter stayed with us for months after. It cured my P.M.S., and I would randomly giggle at the memory in public. Someone even asked if they could be what I was on, and if I had any extra.

I enjoyed the innocent tease as much as my husband did. The ingénue was one of his favorite personas, which revealed a lot to me. I learned that his personality responds best in play. The ingénue was a fresh opposite to his typical serious work days and his more conservative friends, plus I think it brought us both back to our childhoods, the good parts. The ingénue created the soft friction and variety that we really needed.

Who knew that a little innocence and curiosity was a key to keep things fresh?

LESSON: Play and laughter cuts through negative vibrations.

INTO THE HEART OF PARADISE

The mythical Garden of Eden is the paradise of our heart. We can get back to this blissful paradise by having our hearts crack open, or maybe we can start of by imagining a lush inner life with sacred rivers, magic fairies, ancient trees, and perhaps our inner magical child that has no story to cling to, only wide eyed curiosity.

Einstein also said, "Imagination is more important than knowledge. For knowledge is limited, whereas imagination embraces the entire world." Imagination is a useful tool when navigating the world of personas in relationship to another.

Before we can learn to love another as deeply as we desire, we should know and love every aspect of our own self. This journey back home to self-love, takes us deep into the forests, where shadows and misunderstood creatures live. Before we can do that, we must remember the wisdom and safety and love in our hearts.

Every relationship in our lives does have something to teach us, especially our romantic partnerships. It seems like our most intense experiences, like betrayal, are our biggest opportunities to learn our old patterns. If we are brave enough to dive in and try to break those patterns, then we also have the opportunity to dissolve the karmic chords that hold us back from our highest potential to love and be loved.

Let's imagine that somewhere behind the power center of our abundant heart is the inner magical child eager and ready to explore her world. With a kind of reverence and awe for the unknown, maybe our inner magical child starts to walk over to a tree, perhaps *the* tree, where Eve took her first innocent bite of the forbidden fruit that awakened her. You know this story well I'm sure.

And let's imagine that you too would be as curious as Eve, curious to know the taste of the forbidden, curious to know how much power you truly have, curious to know how lovable you are, curious to know your fears and your desires, and maybe even curious to know the true nature of your relationships. Are you ready flirtatious, innocent one? Are you ready to dive deeper into the labyrinth of your soul?

It is now time to take your first bite.

LESSON: Imagination, curiosity, and the heart are your basic tools to navigate the soul

7. Don't Fuck with the Femme Fatale

HIGH FIVE

We are a motley crew, my siblings and I.

Although we have a deep bond that only an experience like ours can give, we live our lives separately, just trying to survive.

Survival is an instinct I've perfected. Not because I was raised by wolves, no. I was raised by something much more sinister than that.

Because of this, my need for safety had influenced my expectations of, and interactions with others. Whether in conversation, how I walked down the street, or my presence in social situations, I was on full alert and prepared for anything to go wrong. Sadly, my deepest darkest truth was that I felt most unsafe with intimacy … especially in my committed relationship.

Only now do I truly understand the enormity of how one's environment has a huge impact on the way we love and make love.

Whenever my siblings and I get together now, I'll raise my hand for a high five and joke, "We are so lucky we didn't turn out to be heroine-addicted prostitutes."

LESSON: There's a grain of truth in every joke.

UNFUCKABLE WITH

I glared into the mirror with razor blade eyes. I was ready to cut anything or anyone who got in my way. I smeared heavy eyeshadow and smudged black liner onto my eyes. I used way too much mascara, making my lashes thick and clumpy. I carefully applied oxblood lipstick that I bought years ago when my college boyfriend broke up with me, offering no reason. Jerk.

To finish the look, I drew a fake mole on the corner of my upper left lip, a la Cindy Crawford. Every dangerous woman should have a beauty mark, I thought. My hair was messy when I woke up, which worked perfectly for the day. It was an "I Don't Care What You Think" look. And thank you, it's true, I didn't give a hoot what anyone would think. I was a mixture of hot mess and raw, primal power.

"You are so lucky you're not here right now," I said to my husband in a deadly whisper.

He was on a business trip, but I knew he could hear my words echoing across the airwaves causing chills to run up and down his spine. I was really agitated from the articles I deliberately scrolled through while still in bed; another college campus rape, the "trash bin babies" of India and China, the legal stoning of woman in Saudi. And just to fuel the fire, I paused from my Femme Fatale makeover and picked up my phone to google more "injustices against women." The statistics are horrifying.

Things haven't gotten any better since that morning. It feels like things are getting worse, the atrocities against women are the highlight of today's news, yet the men who abuse their powers are getting away with it in broad daylight. What are we to do about the imbalance, the injustice and the brutality of male power that has surfaced so blatantly across the globe? This battle of the sexes is depressing. The #metoo movement has women coming out now with their truths about abuse, but it is still not easy for us. We are still fighting against a rabid Goliath ferociously defending a dying ideal that men are superior to women.

I always try to have "light" dinner conversations about the gender gap in the U.S., the lack of women leadership in government, in technology, in religion, or how medicine is male biased to the detriment of the female body. I have heard this exact response, "Well at least you live in the United States, you could be in a country where you were forced to wear a burka." The smoke of rageful frustration that seeped out of my nostrils went unnoticed by the commenter.

Today, the conversation is highlighted with men abusers, like the Olympic doctor Larry Nassar who was sentenced to prison for sexually assaulting too many young athletes; our current President Donald Trump who has twenty-two sexual misconduct allegations against him; the most recent sexual misconduct allegations of Supreme Court Judge Brett Kavanaugh, which did nothing to stop his appointment. Male oppression is all over the place and women are pissed. Actually, we've always been pissed, we just didn't know it. We remained compliant good little girls, hiding our truth.

I don't think the patriarchy can handle the truth. The truth about women. The truth about women's power. The truth that a woman's power is her sexuality. Why else would a huge rape culture exist, female genital mutilation be a practice, or laws that have some women completely hidden under layers of cloth enforced by death? Lilith, Adam's first wife, was banned from Eden for saying she wouldn't submit. Eve was blamed for the fall of man. Medusa was even immortalized as the beast who turned men into stone, when it was Poseidon who originally raped this beautiful girl in the Temple of Athena before she even became Medusa.

A note for you to pass on to all the good men out there: women are "shut down" because of the dangerous climate of patriarchal rule. It is safer for us to diminish our sexuality, than to express it. But not for long.

My thought tangents that morning lead me into sparks of fury. I wondered, as an American woman was I supposed to feel at ease because I was treated with subtle sexism instead of blatant sexism? Was I to continue to be a part of a culture that excused men who are accustomed to talking down to, diminishing, degrading, or raping women? Should I really be paid less than a man for the same job? As my male friend suggested, subtle sexism *might* be better than covering up an entire female body in public, legal stoning, murder, mutilation, and the slavery of woman, but am I really supposed to settle for conditions that are inferior to a man's just because the conditions here are better than conditions someplace else? Hell no.

"So I'm supposed to let it all slide because *you* don't feel like you have as much power and influence as ISIS men do?" I said to my absent husband, who at the moment represented all men. He had often suggested, in his annoying Harvard Business School way, that I give him statistics before making blanket statements, to change my tone so he could receive my words better, or to just look for the silver lining. My stacks of statistics were piling up.

Once I did try to change my tone and it came out something like this, "Does that mean I should be saccharin sweet (insert 'fatal attraction' smile) and neuter my emotions about atrocities that strike me at my very core because *you* (insert second V for vendetta smile), my testosterone-based love, *you* are a little uncomfortable? (Insert third fake innocent smile) *Really?*" Then I'd scowl righteously, "Welcome to my oppressed world, asshole." It wasn't my best moment.

Discomfort has been institutionalized for women since the onset of the agricultural revolution. And you wonder why we don't worship you, or want to hop into bed with you first thing! Think about it.

With renewed fire, I looked into my closet with the clear intention to find something badass to wear. I rummaged through hangers and drawers and picked out a black leather dress, fishnet stockings, and high heeled shoes that said "fuck you" instead of "fuck me." I decided it was a panty free day. I know it's dramatic, but I couldn't help myself.

To be transparent, the black leather dress, was really made of pleather, a.k.a. plastic. I bought it for an 80s karaoke party to be one of Robert Palmer's "Addicted to Love" girls. It still fit and I loved the 007 Bond Girl look it gave me.

I made breakfast for my kids in my sacred rebel get up, which ended up being so inconvenient because the fake leather didn't breathe, and I found myself dripping wet with sweat under the creases of my boobs and butt cheeks. I couldn't wipe it off unless I took off the dress completely.

Even though I looked like this really hot "rebel without a cause," I struggled between offering my kids Fruit Loops (which I store for emergency purposes only) or making them a real breakfast. Nurturing mom or anarchist? They are equally powerful. Mom won, so I stood by the smoke-filled stove frying bacon and eggs, sweating even more. My kids watched me, silently intrigued.

I did things a little differently that day. Instead of yelling at my boys to "hurry up and put on your shoes," "we're going to be late for school," or "eat more so your brains will work properly," I remained silent.

When it was time to leave, I told them I'd be waiting in the car. I didn't honk. I didn't yell out the window. I just started the car and turned up the music volume. I made a mental note to myself: remember this trick because it is so much easier than micromanaging every single move they make or don't make.

I was always in charge of the morning carpool. The two other boys in the neighborhood waited for my guys to come outside before they got into the car with me. The boys were completely oblivious to my *Girl with the Dragon Tattoo* demeanor. Perhaps my look kept them quiet for the entire car ride, maybe they were fascinated by my choice in music (an Eminem inspired playlist), or maybe they were waiting to see if I'd turn off the radio when the swearing part started.

"... His palms are sweaty, knees weak, arms are heavy
There's vomit on his sweater already: mom's spaghetti
He's nervous, but on the surface he looks calm and ready ..."

On the ride, I fantasized about instilling both fear and sex in anyone who made eye contact with me. I saw myself taking up as much space as I damn well pleased. When a man crossed my path, I wanted him to immediately fall onto his knees begging for mercy – for no reason and for every reason. I wanted him to know, with absolute certainty that I am unfuckable with.

I looked back through my rear view mirror. The boys were still quiet. I had this vision of them in the back seat with their elbows leaning on the open window sill with the wind blowing in their hair, heads bobbing up and down like little gangsters. My posse.

"... I've got to formulate a plot
Or I end up in jail or shot
Success is my only motherfuckin' option – failure's not
Mom, I love you but this trailer's got to go
I cannot grow old in Salem's lot ...."

I slowly drove into the carpool line at the overpriced private grade school my children attended. It was on the top of a hill in the fancy part of town. As protocol, the little kid on drop-off duty opened up the back door for my guys to get out. They all got out in silence and walked to the front door where the headmaster was greeting everyone with a morning handshake. The kid on drop-off duty completed his task perfectly with a sweet "have a nice day," before shutting the door.

For a second that lasted forever, the headmaster and I made eye contact. "Say hello to my little friend," I glared back at him. "Bring it on," I thought to myself while silently daring him to look away. He broke the stare-down first, which pleased me immensely. I noticed that he turned to smile and shake hands with a little kindergartner that arrived. Oops, the windows were still down and the loud pounding of the song was still blasting out of my open window.

> "... You better lose yourself in the music
> The moment, you own it, you better never let it go
> You only get one shot, do not miss your chance to blow
> This opportunity comes once in a lifetime, yo!
> You better ..."

I quickly drove away.

LESSON: Being unfuckable with has a look and a theme song. Use them wisely.

NAMASTE MOTHERFUCKER

I was working at home that day, and didn't have much to do but errands. This was a bummer because I looked really good and no one would see me. I decided to find a crowded Starbucks to use my new Femme Fatale super powers and try and track down any haters disguised as coffee drinkers. And, I wanted a venti chai latte with almond milk.

No one looked at me while I stood in line, even though I was trying to stare-down everyone. The only person who looked at me was this really cute baby in a stroller. His mom was on her phone, so I made googly eyes at him and telepathically told him he's ruining my cover. He laughed in response.

The Union Street Starbucks was great for people watching. There was a bus line right in front that drew in the downtown business crowd. The yoga studio across the street attracted mindful meditators. I assumed the many therapy offices in the neighborhood brought in people like me, who dressed up based on their mood. Our therapist Bob had an office on Union Street. I kept a look out for the easiest exit in case I spotted him. Sweaty athletic bodies came in from the nearby Soul Cycle and Crunch Gym. Glamor girls from the MAC make-up store were always the eye catchers. Every seat was taken by someone with a laptop.

The barista took my order and asked for my name. "Nikita," I responded. He looked at me under his brow. Maybe he remembered me from another time, I couldn't be sure. My eyes were ice picks back at him. Hmm, he seemed a worthy opponent.

"How do you spell it?" He continued to stare at me.

"N. I. K. I. T. A." I raise my eyebrows at him.

He writes it on my cup, "$4.45 please."

Was that sass I heard in his voice? I threw down a five-dollar bill slow motion style, and left the counter before he could give me any change. With my head held high, I walked slowly and deliberately through all the people waiting for their drinks. I cut through everyone and stood to the right in front of the counter. No one noticed me boldly staking my claim because all heads were looking down into their phones instead of me. Grrr.

Finally, there was a call for a Venti Chai, "for Nicky."

Nicky? I got up to the counter and read the name on the cup. "It says Nikita," I corrected him.

"Okay," he responded and continued working. "Grande Clover Sumatra for Charlie."

I clearly was not making the impact I expected, and I definitely was not getting the response I wanted from this place. On the walk back to my car, I saw a bumper sticker that read, "Namaste Motherfucker." I wanted to steal it.

I started to get more irritated as I drove back home sipping my chai. I'm not sure what I expected from these strangers, a street fight maybe? Suddenly I got a flurry of texts from my siblings that, yes, I read while driving:

"Mom says dad is coming to town"

"When?"

"Now I guess."

"He's here?"

"Yup mom just told me."

"He wants someone to pick him up at the airport."

"Why doesn't he take a cab?"

"Why is she telling us now?"

"He just told her."

"Mom wants someone to pick him up."

"Of course she does."

"So we just drop everything to pick him up?"

"Yes."

"You do it"

"No. Can't."

"I can't either."

"I'll do it."

"Sucker."

Once a year, around tax time, my father enters the country again. These visits usually come unannounced after a year of silence, save a birthday text. When he does arrive, we pretend that these once a year visits are completely normal, and the dysfunction in our family doesn't really exist. Denial has become a way of life for us.

Though I'm thrilled to complain about how ridiculously impaired my parents are, I had never really got down to the truth of my tumultuous childhood with anyone. Glossing over the impact of my experiences, was how I unknowingly fostered a debilitated adult life, which showed up in how I treated my partner. We all have the potential to project our parent's relationships onto our partners if we remain unconscious.

I immediately called my mother to berate her on her decision to continue this co-dependent and destructive relationship that was not even a relationship because they had been divorced for years. She didn't answer the phone.

I tried another outlet for my growing fury. I dialed my husband's number. No answer. I called again. No answer. I tried Face Timing. No answer. I texted.

"You there?"

(waited one minute)

"Hello?"

(waited two minutes)

"Tried Calling"

(waited thirty seconds)

"Call me"

(grumbled)

I'm a cell phone stalker. I knew my husband was in a meeting. I knew that he'd be in a car and on a plane back home in a couple of hours. I knew I'd see him that night. I knew he could tell when my texts had an irritated energy around them. I knew that he felt uncomfortable with a flurry of texts and phone calls with no real message attached because he never knew what to do about it. He was a fixer.

(fifteen minutes later)

"In a meeting. I'll call you in a bit."

I pretended I didn't see his text and continued on home.

LESSON: Projecting your fury onto your partner is not productive. No cell phone stalking.

THE THINGS I'VE SEEN AND HEARD

We still haven't completely answered why some couples lose interest in each other over time, grow apart, or just stop communicating.

Many long-term couples stop taking care of themselves, or only start working on themselves *after* an affair, divorce, or the threat of either. Many of us would say the lack of passion is to blame for their distance. And then some of us try to keep the passion going with constant bickering and drama. Some of us go to couple's therapy, some divorce, while others resign to being in loveless and sexless marriages.

Esther Perel, a renowned couple's therapists, is often given credit for saying, "Tell me how you were loved, and I'll tell you how you make love." Oh how I wish this weren't true for me. For the longest time, I just thought I was bad at sex and avoided it at all costs. After the affair, I began to deeply research what stopped me from being surrendered enough for my body, not my mind, to feel like having sex.

Per Esther Perel's advice, I took a good look at my upbringing *and* my husband's, we couldn't have more of a contrast. One of the things my inner Femme Fatale did for me was give me the courage to look deeper within myself, and to my past, for answers. Why did I increasingly become more and more distant in my relationship? What I found out wasn't so pretty.

It only takes one unresolved issue, like someone calling you fat, to start the process of building the walls that protect your heart from potential disintegration. The experience doesn't have to be gigantic to make an impact on how you might hold yourself back, maybe someone said something like, "girls don't do that." A simple continuous message from society also stops us from evolving emotionally, and can have a negative effect on how we see ourselves, which snow balls into how we treat our partnerships.

Here are just a few things that I've seen and heard.

****

When we were just toddlers, my father decided that the proper punishment for wetting your pants was to put you in the dark basement alone. He thought it was the perfect environment to think about why you couldn't control yourself.

My younger sister was the one who wet her pants. She was only four.

Where was my mom? Where was my older sister? Maybe they were in the house somewhere and didn't know what was going on? Could anyone else see the injustice of this punishment?

I decided that I had to be the brave warrioress that would make everything right in our house. I would be the savior. My first task was to sneak down the steep steps and save my sister from the darkness. I was five years old.

Although the basement door looked ordinary enough, I knew of the ominous space that lay behind it. I took a deep breath and quietly opened the door despite the fact that I was breaking every one of my father's rules.

And there she was, just a tiny little girl in a romper dress and white knee high socks. Her bangs were cut way too short in a jagged line, probably by me or my older sister.

My little sister sat on a small chair in the middle of the oppressive basement, pressing her hands on her knees to help her maintain an upright and perfect position. She stared straight ahead exactly as she was told to do. Although I had an incredible gift for silence and invisibility, she turned and looked at me with hopeful eyes, and I gazed back at her with unspoken reassurance.

That's when I heard my father yelling again. We could hear him all the way from the basement. I had to make a choice. Would I go in and hide with her to keep her company? Or would I pull her out of the basement and lead her outside to freedom? The front door was just two steps away.

We heard more screaming and heavy footsteps. We both looked up toward the ceiling. I can't remember even making the decision, I just kept my eyes on my sister for forever it seemed. She looking at me, I looking at her as we stared at each other until all I could see was a cheaply painted particle board surface. I had shut the door on her.

I quickly and silently locked it and ran out the front door as my father's screaming got louder. I was supposed to be the savior, but I had failed her and me. This was my first blow in thinking I could make a difference.

****

When I was six, my mother's family came to visit us for a long weekend. One early morning during their stay, I snuck into my mom's room to watch my aunt sleep, she must have stayed out all night because she was really tired. I was so obsessed with how pretty and funny my aunt was, that I wanted to be by her side right when she woke up. The curtains were drawn and my mom, a nurse at the time, hadn't come back from working the night shift yet. I didn't remember seeing my dad that whole weekend. I sat on the edge of the bed waiting for her to wake up. While I was staring at her sleeping, I could hear my grandfather calling her name from downstairs. I ran into the closet to hide so I wouldn't get into trouble for bothering her.

My grandfather and my two uncles came bursting into the room to wake her up. They weren't very gentle. They shoved her around and eventually pushed her out of bed. When she got up, they started beating her.

I hid behind my mom's dresses and could see through the crack of the sliding door as they scolded her while taking turns punching her in the face, and then in the stomach. She kept sobbing "No!" while she tried to cover her face and gut as she crouched down in fetal position. It was horrifying.

I don't know how long I stayed in that closet, but I do know that I held my breath until it was over and everyone had gone. It was a really long time.

Many years later, I found out that these men, my family members, wanted her to accept the courtship of a wealthy man. They chose to violently force and abuse a woman's body simply for the hope of money. A marriage was never guaranteed her, and no one could remember how much money the man actually had. My aunt ran away that night with her boyfriend. She was only nineteen. They've been happily married ever since.

Even now, I often catch myself holding my breath for no reason.

****

There was the time when my dad in a fit of rage, yelled at my mom in the front yard of our home, threatening to get his gun and shoot somebody. Attempting once again to adopt the role of savior, I ordered my younger sister and brother to find the gun and bury it in the backyard. In the meantime, I would make sure my mother was safe and the neighbors kept at bay. I'd also watch for the police. At some point, the neighbors would have had enough. I wondered why no adult ever came out to help us.

I was positive I could talk my way out of the police taking my father away. Even at an early age, I knew that it would equally kill my mother if my father was taken away from her. I was ten then.

I'm still haunted by my dangerous instructions to my siblings, but more by the truth that my mother's childhood wounds of abandonment were so powerful that she fell for the smallest act of kindness and tidbits of affection from my dad, and forgot the abuse.

****

My father has always had rage problems. But there was a time when he was deliriously drunk, something we had never really seen before. He threatened my mother with a cold, evil whisper, "Do you want me to kill you?" He had the barrel of his gun pressed under her chin.

At eleven, my brother could not take the abuse any longer. His fear was so great it turned into a wild plea to try and stop him. He punched all the walls his eleven-year old hands could find, telling my dad to leave our mother alone. This shocked both my parents awake to the potential fatal conclusion of this fucked up scene.

My mother, blinded by devotion for a flawed man, told my brother to apologize through the bathroom door, where my dad had eventually hidden himself.

****

I vividly remember the belt being wrapped around my father's big hands, ready to strike us if we were out of line. I also still hear my mother telling us how lucky we are that our father is not like other men. Hmm.

****

Then there were things I've seen and heard outside the walls of my family home. My first grade teacher asked me and two other kids to come up in front of the class. I jumped up obediently. We stood in front of the class while the rest of the students sat waiting. Then she told us to take off our shirts.

All I can remember was the shame and humiliation of this request, and knowing how wrong it was. The other girls had undershirts on, so they boldly stripped off their tops. I did not. I can't recall if I went through with the request or not. Each time I try to think back, all I can remember is trying to hide behind the teacher as my arms resisted pulling up my top. I still can't figure out why she asked this of us.

****

When I was twelve, my neighbor told me that her uncle made her sit on his lap while he bounced her up and down. One day he made her do it in front of me and it felt weird.

Another friend shared that her piano teacher made her sit on his hands.

A few friends have had penises shoved in their mouths at way too young an age.

Too many women have shared with me their personal affronts of rape by strangers, dates, parents, neighbors, even family members.

So many of us have been looked at with lecherous eyes. I'm sure I'm repressing something more.

Then again, there's the news.

****

I don't want any pity for this, but I do want to give it recognition. I have lived in denial because of shame and social norms, but denial kept me from a course of right action that might have helped me overcome my blocks in the first place.

I have come to know that it is a great privilege when someone shares a traumatic story that is so personal. It can be cathartic for them, while diminishing the shame associated with it for others. I am now honored when I get this kind of gift. It is not only a lesson in non-judgement, empathy, and compassion, it is a remarkable awareness of one's ability to hold a safe and sacred space for another human being.

From my own experience, when I kept my emotions repressed and unresolved, I instinctively froze up and put up barriers. It was protection from either physical, emotional, energetic abuse, or all of them. Over time, I shut down emotionally and then sexually. To share, to release, to move past is the key to healing and loving. To witness, to hold space, to support is the key to deep bonding.

LESSON: Your body is offended by the normalization of physical, emotional, psychological and energetic assaults – even if you don't know it yet.

RAGE AGAINST THE MACHINE

I knew exactly what I had to do after reliving childhood drama triggered by a few texts. I had to go home and release some rage, otherwise I'd keep phone stalking my husband and end up making it his fault that my parents were so irritating. So I ignored his other two texts and rushed home.

I parked my car in the driveway and went straight into the garage. I connected my music to my Bose speakers and turned up the volume. It was extremely loud. I placed two large exercise mats on the floor, and pulled Bob beside the mats along with a bat, a fake sword, and a few pillows.

Bob is a torso training bag for professional boxers, not to be confused with Bob our therapist. Boxing Bob had a life-like chest and head stuck on a polyethylene base filled with sand, so he wouldn't tip over no matter how hard he was hit. The only reason we had a Bob was because we couldn't think of a holiday gift for our boys one year. I thought they could punch and wield their fake swords at Bob instead of at each other. Bob was a hit, no pun intended.

I learned at a very early age, how to highlight all the good parts of my upbringing, even if I had to embellish them a little bit. Looking at the "bright side" (or denying any shadow) helped me stay armored and protected, so I wouldn't fall apart. This is a very advanced trick of survival. But I realized that if we don't allow our bodies to honor the painful memories and release them properly, we will explode or implode sooner or later.

My bright side memories included being excited for my dad to come home, on Christmas Eve after being absent for a few days, with colorful wrapped gifts. He'd then put fresh dollar bills on the tree for a healthy competition of money hording at the count of three. I thought it was so fun then, I was the tallest.

I remembered Neapolitan ice cream and having it cut into squares and served on a plate. There was always a variety of Lucerne ice cream, Sara Lee frozen cheesecake, and Cool Whip in the freezer. A dozen donuts and a special custard filled pastry greeted us every Sunday morning before church.

I remember my dad telling us to pull his finger, which made him fart. And sometimes he'd pull out his dentures to make us laugh. At the same time, we were told that crying made us look ugly, and laughing too loud was not lady like. So if something made me cry, I'd clench my stomach and wrap up the feeling in a little ball until it froze. If something made me laugh, I'd cover my face to stifle the sound and stiffen my body into perfect posture.

I was always on hyper alert of being wronged for something I *might* do. I constantly tried to please in order to avoid punishment. I constantly held my breath waiting. When every emotion finally froze into a single ice ball, I placed it in the stainless steel cage that was surrounded with Kryptonite barbed wire, covered in the turquoise Tiffany gift box complete with its satin white ribbon that I talked about earlier. I hid this precious part of me in the darkest, most secret place I could find. I tucked it far back behind the left corner of my cervix attached to the deepest part of my vaginal wall (more explanation on that later). Then I stood remarkably still in order to keep all the layers in place. The result was an emotional range of just on single note; a pretty smile.

The soul is supposed to live in the lush abundance of the heart center where our magical inner child plays, grown up she's the ingénue. Her very essence is the full expression of emotions; from fear to love, rage to passion, pain to pleasure, apathy to ecstasy, betrayal to bliss without judgment. In her whole state, the soul can take us from the material to the spiritual, the superficial to deep meaning, from lust to unconditional love and back again.

When the soul is disembodied, it goes into hiding, and we find ourselves living a half-life, a zombie life, just trying to get from A to B without meaning. We are left always wanting "more."

Even I had a rare emotional wave of yearning and choked up during the movie *Jerry McGuire* when Jerry (played by Tom Cruise) says to his girlfriend, Dorothy (played by Renée Zellweger), "you complete me." I deeply wanted to feel complete. I 1,000 percent believed that would happen through someone else's love for me. But contrary to what I thought and what many people think, another person cannot "complete you," to make you whole again. The soul needs to come out of hiding, the soul needs to feel safe, the soul needs the richness of the garden within your heart. The soul needs to remember that she is multifaceted. Only then will the soul find her true mate.

Becoming Lord Voldemort is one extreme outcome of cutting up your soul into many separate pieces and spreading them far and wide in order to find a false power that masks the intense pain of loneliness and fear. I didn't go that far, I just decided to freeze. I became so skilled at hiding my feelings, my thoughts, my voice, my whole being that I had developed the skill of invisibility, and keeping my truth and my emotions hidden for most of my life. I could disappear anytime I wanted. I learned how to pretend that everything was so perfect and so pretty and so right, that I had convinced myself for years that everything was so perfect and so pretty and so right. Until it wasn't.

The sound of an electric guitar that pierced the air also pierced my train of thought. Then I heard the bass guitar, and then something pounding on metal in a rhythmic sound of constraint and agitation. It was music by *Rage against the Machine*, how perfect. When the melodies merged, I shed off all of my clothing in a slow, ritualistic way, like I was going into an ancient battle. I was completely naked before the lyrics arrived.

"Killing in the Name of ..."

I dropped to my knees like an animal out for the hunt.

"Some of those that work forces, are the same that burn crosses ..."

I put my forehead down and began slapping one palm on the mat to the seething pulse, as I started rocking like a psychopath in a padded room.

"Killing in the Name of ..."

I slammed both hands down, now fisted, with epochal hammering that intensified with every pound.

"Now you do what they told ya ..."

And then I was in it. I was writhing and wielding and screaming and slamming myself into Boxing Bob. I took the baseball bat to him and tried to kill him with a sword. I started throwing pillows and jumping up and down like a mad woman being attacked by imaginary fire breathing dragons. It was not pretty.

I sobbed because I didn't like the rage. I wailed because I didn't like the hate. I growled because I didn't want to experience or witness injustice anymore. I erupted because I didn't want to be placed in a box. I broke down because all this has already happened. I wept because I was living and breathing the rage and hate and abuse stuck inside too small a box.

"Fuck you, I won't do what you tell me,"

I was maniacally half screaming, half crying the lyrics at the top of my lungs with snot coming out of my nose, black mascara running down my face, and my hair in a crazed hornet's nest. My head was thrashing, my arms were fighting, my legs were stomping, my body was convulsing.

"Mother Fucker!"

I finally collapsed in physical and emotional exhaustion even though it was only a five-minute and twelve-second song. The garage was in shambles, but Bob was still standing stoically as if nothing had happened. I loved Bob.

I laid on my back with my legs and arms splayed, palms up, and feet turned out, Davinci's Vitruvian man. I remember breathing heavily. Although my neck hurt from all the head whipping, I felt amazing. I felt raw. I felt alive. I felt like I healed the wound of betrayal for all women in my family, and maybe even for the collective.

This was my swamp, an unapologetic solo freak out session that helped me to release the rage I have against the machine that is not only my father, but the rules and conditions of a patriarchy that has dominated society for the last 4,000 years. I was exhausted by it.

I first learned how "to swamp" at Mama Gena's School of Womanly Arts. I thought I was going to be learning how to be an elegant and refined goddess who could float like an angel across the floor as Bernadette did at my first movement retreat a few months before. She was the one who whispered in my ear to "look up Mama Gena" during a live drumming session at sunset with barefoot women dancing in the sand. Images of voodoo magic came to mind, and I did have a mysterious attraction to the dark side.

When I googled Mama Gena, I wasn't impressed. At that time, the website had fluffy pink boas with smiling "real women" gracing the pages. What I mean by "real women" is "not models" or "celebrities" that I was accustomed to seeing for any type of selling toward women. I had imagined a group of gorgeous witches who could brew up magic potions and teach me the art of revenge. Wasn't there a powerful vindictive and manipulative magic that all women needed to awaken?

The art of vengeance, with grace of course, is what I wanted to learn how to do then. I had nothing to lose. Despite my disappointment with the website and what I imagined was a "womanly art," I called the number and signed up, again no questions asked. That's how desperate I was.

I cannot describe what went on in that classroom full of all types of women in all levels of, of what? Anger? Desire? Pleasure? Awakening? Self-realization? I cannot describe any of it. There was laughter, dancing, crying, a lot of truth telling, crazy shit that blew my mind, and of course the swamp.

We were asked to put a Hefty plastic garbage bag on over our clothes and scream and shake our bodies to aggressive music in our seats. The women in the room went wild. There was so much repressed rage in that room full of over three hundred estrogen based bodies, that I was horrified and gratified at the same time. I hated the garbage bag, and I didn't want to mess up my hair.

I stared at everyone, so I could copy them. I pretended to know what I was doing. I tried a stomp with my right foot and felt like a little girl having a fake temper tantrum to get attention. I let out a pathetic "harrumph" and then quickly looked around to see if anyone else heard or saw me. Luckily, the two women beside me were also out of their element and kept their eyes averted from me and everyone else. We were in the back row, and it is easy to hide and fake it from there.

Because of my failed attempt at letting out my anger, I concluded that I was just not that angry with the world, and reasoned that there were plenty of people like me who were not angry at the world, the Dalai Lama was one of them. These "happy people" have learned how to direct their pain and disappointment into something very productive. I convinced myself that I was one of those people, except that I wasn't doing anything productive to serve the planet then.

It took me a long while before I realized that I was in such a state of apathy and numbness, that I would not give myself the permission to go where I have never gone before … inside.

As I laid naked on the floor, my phone made that distinctive Face Time ring. It was my husband. I wished he would have called when I had my black leather dress on, and my bond girl makeup wasn't running down my face. I answered anyway.

"Oh wow." He said when my face emerged on his screen.

"I know." From the little corner screen, I could see my resemblance to Bellatrix L'estrange. "I can explain." But I didn't want to.

"Uh, should I be worried?"

That made me laugh. Before he would have remained silent waiting for some clue of what to say or do if I looked distraught in any way. "No, I just had a really good swamp," I answered.

"Oh. Good. How was it?" We've come a long way for that answer, which I was so grateful for.

I'm not sure if he really wanted to know how it went, I mean, how can he even begin to understand the value of trying to murder Bob with real wrath? And, I wasn't completely convinced he was really "OK" with this idea of swamping in the first place. We've had many conversations with him saying that I should be healed already, and that he was raised to brush things off and move on, but he's going with it for now.

I still had to ring out oceans of patriarchy and oppression, but I also knew that at some point I needed to get into an easy flow of gratitude and love for everything that was beginning to happen *for* me. I fully understood that my swamp was my swamp, and I couldn't suck my husband in with me.

I changed the conversation and asked about his meetings, his travel, his day, anything light, as I delicately tried to smooth my hair and wipe the black streaks off my cheeks.

I had no urge to explain myself, pick a fight like I used to do, make him responsible, or blame him for anything. I also didn't feel like there was anything wrong with me, which was huge. I didn't even feel guilty that beating up Bob was my big accomplishment for the day.

There was huge release in my body, and I settled into an ease that stimulated me. I decided to give my hubby a sneak peek of my nakedness before I hung up. It was my way of teasing him, and assuring him that I would not take his head off when I saw him that evening.

LESSON: You have permission to purge any anger you might still have in your body, and should.

SAFE SEX AND ARMORED BODIES

My initiation into the dark and chaos of the underworld began with untying that pretty little white ribbon to look deeper inside that pretty Tiffany blue box. Like Pandora's, there are dark and scary things in there, so I subconsciously avoided being curious about what kind of darkness lurked inside me. But I knew that is where I had to go in order for me to heal my soul and enter into the light of love and experience the vibrancy of living, for also in the bottom of Pandora's box was hope.

The myth of Pandora is ultimately about creation and new beginnings. It is the same in many cultures, this cyclical rhythm of death and destruction before rebirth and awakening.

"Thank you, Kali," I said to myself in the mirror as I finish wiping off the streaks of mascara from my cheeks. "Bitch."

Although my body was beat, my mind still wanted to make sense of it all, and my ego wanted me to go back to my old habits of hypervigilance: Where's the enemy? Where's the exit? Where's the safest space? Where's my invisibility cloak? My body was too exhausted to clench into her usual tightness.

Kali was another goddess that found me during one of my soul searching expeditions. She is responsible for the events that hit you in the face like a jagged edged rock. The impact of her entrance can be a rupture so great that your whole world is thrown upside down, and inside out. She, like the Femme Fatale, forces you to look in the mirror and decide your own fate. The Vedic philosophers and Tantra gurus tell me this is a good thing.

"So, Miss Death and Destruction," I stared at my myself head high and poised, my femme fatale almost revived. "When is my new life and rebirth going to happen already? Bring it on, sister."

Kali represents the feminine continuous flow between chaos and creativity, destruction and rebirth. She's supposed to teach me that something has to die in order for something new to begin. I figured that "something" was my old habit of freezing, staying invisible, not feeling, making up excuses, dimming my light, and fear. It was not about focusing on any of my ruptures themselves, but how I chose to use them as a powerful learning tool. I wasn't at that stage yet, and I knew that before I could transform into any form of greatness, or at least have a happy marriage, I had to squeeze out every ounce of old rage and shame in me.

The transition from my raving madness, dance party to settling back into to my "normal" self wasn't so easy. I was having a conversation with myself in the mirror, because I didn't have friends that would understand or welcome my need to swamp so much. "Remember, you are a badass," I said to myself, but it fell flat. I was really too tired for any more of this "tough assassin, I will kill you now" persona, so I decided to take quick a nap.

All the madness had then settled into my gut, making me want to curl up and grieve. So that's what I did. But this time I wasn't angry, I was just so sad for everyone. I cried for my dad who must have suffered so much more than we did, otherwise there was no way he could do such a thing to his family. I forgave him. I cried for my mother who must have been so afraid and yet so resilient to endure the daily violence. I forgave her too. I cried for my siblings and the wounds we shared that they may or may never look at. I cried for my husband who probably has a few things of his own to heal. I forgave him too. I cried for every person who has ever had to experience abandonment, fear, abuse, shame, or betrayal. Then I finally cried for myself, and forgave myself for all the things that I am not.

"When will it be over Kali?" I half whispered, half cried. I fell asleep.

I started dreaming that I lay naked on top of a marble funeral table in the center of a rotunda circled by a group of very handsome and masculine men with incredible physique. They were all so strong. The room was cold and light. I could see the men through my slightly opened eyelids. They are wearing armor and waiting for me to awaken. I dared not let them know that I was conscious. I lay as still as a corpse. They were whispering to each other that time was running out.

I wasn't at all afraid, but I was aroused by the idea that I was naked amongst all these beautiful men who looked familiar to me. My skin was perfectly smooth, almost glass like. My hair was longer than it is, and it elegantly draped across the table. My boobs and nipples were perfectly perky. Jewels adorned the trimmed small triangle of my pubic hair. I had a knowing these men were not there to hurt me, but instead to be of service to me. I wondered if my naked body aroused them too.

Five of the men circled around me and lifted the marble slab I was on over their heads. I noticed that all but one resembled past boyfriends, including my husband, who was not my husband in this dream. They were all way better looking in the dream, like mini gods. They took me into another room and placed me on a pillar near a burning furnace. I started to get really warm. For a second, I thought I was going to be cremated alive, which I thought might end all the suffering. But then it donned on me that they were just trying to melt the layer of ice that made my skin look so smooth.

My body became moist with sweat as I lay beside the furnace. The wetness felt good between my legs. I could hear a drumbeat echoing from a separate hallway. One of the men (the one that looked like my husband) took a torch and lit it from the furnace fire. He held it in front of him as he walked toward me. I opened my eyes and we stared at each other. I thought to myself, are you really going to burn me again? I had an eerie feeling that in our pasts lives we had a history of betrayal. His stare was all knowing, like we've been at this very junction before. He looked at me as if to say, "you should know the lesson by now." I could not move. Then he touched the fire to my skin, and my entire body ignited in colossal flames.

Instead of a searing pain, it felt like melted wax that does not burn. It made me giddy with delight because the feeling was just on the verge of pain, it was so pleasurable. Then clear smoke entered my nostrils and took me away with a wave of blissful hallucinations, like a trip on Ecstasy. Before I knew it, I was standing erotically on the table, dancing wildly in the flames.

In the golden light of my fire, the men watched with admiration. The last of the ice melted away and became steam. I was beginning to get more physically aroused, and thought that I should pause the dream and wake myself up to get my vibrator.

I saw myself shutting my bedroom door, and going into the bathroom drawer to find Tiny (the name I had given my little compact vibrator). I brought it back to bed so I could finish my dream with a little stimulation between my legs. I turned it on and placed it delicately at the tip of my clitoris, but didn't press too intensely. I just wanted to feel a little something.

I drifted back into my dream. I was now sitting on the table in prayer, alone. All the men, including the one that looked like my husband disappeared, except the one I did not recognize. He had dark hair and dark eyes that had a childlike glow. I saw him smiling at me. Though his face was unfamiliar, he seemed so familiar to me, like I was looking at the male version of myself. I felt the pulse in my pelvic floor grow in stronger rhythms. The familiar stranger sat on the table in cross legged position. He pulled me onto his lap so that I sat on top facing him, our bodies equally upright and our eyes locked on to each other's in divine union. I felt his sex enter mine as we breathed as one.

The pulsation spread into my belly and inside my vaginal walls. I felt a rush of warm moisture seep out. Warm waves rippled up to my nipples which started to throb, which caused a more intense sensation between my legs. Then my whole body erupted with an intense and ecstatic, quivering orgasm. I repeat. My whole body. Intense. Ecstatic. Pulsating. Orgasm. Whole body!

I woke up partly guilty. Was I just making love to another man that I knew but didn't know, that was me but wasn't me? I looked at my bedroom door, which was still opened. I searched for the vibrator but couldn't find it anywhere near me. I noticed that I was in the same exact curled up position that I first fell asleep in.

Whoa.

I felt so clear, so removed from my previous irritations and swamp, that I actually felt sensation in my *entire* body. I normally have a hard time reaching an intense orgasm during sex, and it's usually focused in the tiny little area around the clitoris. Now here I was, alone, not at all touching myself (in fact, my hands were in prayer position under my left ear), simply resting after a serious maniacal swamp session, and I had a full body orgasm.

I started laughing. "Is this the other side?"

I got it. My body, our bodies need to be free of the pain to feel, to flow, to love. I was having safe sex with an armored body, which meant I only felt safe with my armor on. This type of love making was thoroughly unfulfilling. My dream was clearly telling me that I desperately needed to take off my protection, feel my heat, allow the ice at my core to melt into a river of soulful rhythmic pleasure. I got up and redid my make-up. I needed a do-over.

LESSON: Pleasure does come after pain.

8. Hello Kitty

THE ANIMAL OF MY BODY

Releasing the tension, resistance, and shame of my traumatic past felt really, really good. It allowed me to truly get into the animal of my body: my primordial impulses, my innate magnetism, and the primal movement of my erotic creature. We all embody the natural laws of movement, hunger, sleep, release and pleasure, as all animals do. Unfortunately, humans insist that these basic instincts be shut down and shamed, shamed, shamed … especially me.

During the second day of my project, I remembered thinking about when I first met my husband. I deliberately skipped this part of the story up until now, because it makes more sense to learn how to embody our divine, sensual beings only after we've understood the energetic and/or physical offenses that must be released before our bodies can feel how deliciously our souls can move through the body.

He and I were both working out at Gold's Gym on 2nd Street, next to the architecture firm where I was working as a marketing assistant, it was my first "real" job. He asked the gym staff about me, and they told him not to bother because I was the Ice Queen who talked to no one. As you probably know, an Ice Queen doesn't have any warm blood in her body, and probably walks like an ice pick, which is not so warm and fuzzy. My husband was a morning person, I wasn't, so I kept to myself while I worked out, hypnotically (literally) going through the motions at the god-awful time of five-thirty in the morning.

A year prior, I had gone to a hypnotist with my college boyfriend's mom. She had lost a lot of weight through hypnosis, and I guess she saw me roll my eyes because the next thing I knew, she paid for me to attend the next session with her. I didn't need to lose any weight, but I did need to stop the frozen Sara Lee cheesecake fix I had since I was a child, I also wanted to drink more water, and stay on a decent workout routine so I could be more grounded in my body. I hated working out though, I didn't like being inside.

When I got to the hypnotherapy group session, the therapist had us put earphones on while we reclined in leather chairs in a blacked out room. "All right get into a comfortable position," he started, softly speaking into all of our heads. "Relax your body. I'm going to count backward as you get deeper, and deeper into relaxation." Soothing background music and the sounds of waves subliminally lulled us into a waking sleep. "Ten, you are relaxed now … nine your eyes are getting heavier and heavier … eight deeper and deeper into relaxation."

By the time he got to one, our critical minds were asleep and our subconscious was on alert. He asked us to imagine our favorite dessert, Sara Lee frozen cheesecake easily popped up in my mind, and I noted how easily our comfort food is there when we need it. Then he had us see our favorite desserts really big, big enough to cover the screen in our heads. After a minute or two of staring at our favorite dessert, he encouraged us to make the vision really small, and put this tiny dessert into the corner of our mind's eye. Then he asked us to fill the space with all kinds of vegetables. He added drinking more water and had us turn up the volume on our metabolism.

For two weeks straight, I was ravishingly thirsty, I started eating tons of vegetables, and I had no desire to eat cheesecake of any kind. I was impressed. Later, I asked the hypnotist if I could make a personalized tape so that I would keep drinking water, have better body image, eat better, start working out more, and begin to move more gracefully and confidently. I also asked him to record that my day start out with a workout, just in case I convinced myself it wasn't worth the time, that's how much I hated the gym.

I listened to that tape constantly. Miraculously, I started to see myself strong and slender, kept up with the water and eating healthy, my body movement became more fluid, and I rolled out of bed at five-fifteen a.m. every weekday to get to the gym by five-thirty a.m. I was so organized (a new thing) that I brought my make-up and work clothes to change into afterward. I should have asked the hypnotist to include truly *enjoying* the gym, but at least I was getting there.

So there I was, at five-thirty in the morning as the grumpy morning Ice Queen, trying to enjoy my sit ups. My husband told me that I once hissed at him when he tried to say hello as I was doing crunches in the corner. I don't remember that, all I remember is a constant wish that no one would talk to me because I was never sure if I had brushed my teeth. That hiss was more likely a stifled cry of pain. At that point, my abdominal core was nonexistent.

To make a really long story short, we both changed gyms and didn't see each other for a few months. We bumped into each other at a nightclub, another cliché meeting ground, and then at a park where he finally asked me out on a date in front of all my colleagues at my new advertising job. I stopped working out in the morning at the gym, but I continued exercising my body in different ways. My Ice Queen was melting.

On our first date, my future husband invited me to meet him at his apartment in the Mission before we headed to dinner. He had a funky one-bedroom apartment, just off Valencia street, decorated with real furniture and a real dining room table. Meanwhile, I was living with three roommates in an apartment off Union Street, in preppy Cow Hollow. We had a hodgepodge of furniture, and a revolving door of guests. This guy seemed so adult to me. He wasn't wearing a suit that night, just jeans and a t-shirt. When we left, he put on a leather jacket, grabbed two motorcycle helmets, and asked if I felt comfortable going to dinner on his motorcycle. Corporate grunge, now *that* was interesting.

I hopped on the back of his motorcycle and we drove up to Twin Peaks to see the city skyline and the Bay Bridge before driving down to the restaurant. I had my arms around his waist, and I could feel the steel, six pack muscles beneath his cotton t-shirt. Two thoughts went through my mind at that moment, one was that I should start liking the gym and workout my abs more, the second was wondering what would happen if I slipped my hands under his shirt to rub all over his belly and just feel his skin. I was beginning to feel that primal stir in my body that happens when you know you are going to mate with someone.

We had a great dinner that night, and I ended up sleeping over (and, yes, having sex). I don't remember leaving. Four months later I officially moved in, we got two cats (now sadly gone), seven months later we got engaged, and a year later we got married under a full moon on Kauai.

My husband was still asleep as I was thinking about how we first met. Our new cats, Oreo and Cookie, jumped off the bed and gave a luxurious stretch, which encouraged me to stretch, too. It felt so good to feel animal-like in my body. As I stretched with my cats, I was inspired to create my next icon and knew that I had to get back into the animal of my body to do so.

LESSON: Hypnotize yourself back into your innate primal body with visualizations.

HOUSE OF DREAMS

After the first icon, the Sports Bud, I woke happily exhausted by our fucking the night before, even though I waited patiently for lightning to strike me down. We never just fucked. I blamed my residual Catholic "good girl" conditioning, and the puritanical rules that I inherited by marrying into an emotionally conservative family for feeling like "just fucking" was such a bad thing. Lightning never did strike me down, so I guessed I was free to continue with this project.

As I mentioned, I grew up in a strict, religious household. We were supposed to act like proper Catholic children. Sex was something you offered when the time came, not enjoyed. Sadly, it was during my early twenties when I had my first orgasm, and only after my very first exposure to porn.

I lived in an apartment that my roommates and I called Daisy's Place. Our landlord was a Chinese woman named Daisy, who refinished the apartment with cold granite counters and modern glass book shelves. It was the perfect residence for new college graduates. My roommates and I lived in a platonic arrangement of two women and two men in a four-bedroom apartment.

During one of our rare evenings when we all happened to be home at the same time, Lane casually asked us if we had ever seen the movie *House of Dreams*.

"It's good," he added with a devious smile.

I had never even heard of it, but I loved a good movie, so I perched myself on the cozy swivel chair with the fuzzy yellow pillow, ready to share my analysis of what the movie was trying to convey. That's what I liked to do, pretend that I was too smart for my own good, believing that everything should be analyzed for their hidden messages. I claimed the best seat, up close and personal. Rikka made popcorn, and Rob got a pillow from his bedroom, they claimed the couch. Lane took the fake leather lazy-boy in the corner of the room. The lazy-boy was an unwanted gift left by the tenant before him.

I was expecting an artistic psychodrama with a love story embedded between weird but interesting scenes, layered stories that would unfold slowly for us, Quentin Tarantino or Stanley Kubrick style. I prided myself on understanding and predicting where stories would go before we got to the end. Rikka had a very innocent imagination, and waited for fairytales, castles, and romance. Rob and Lane were poker-faced, save for the smirk that they both had on their faces. Rikka and I were in for a big surprise.

The movie started off with various scenes that played, teased and taunted us. There was no shortage of romantic interludes and visually artistic moments. Each of the chapters started and ended with beautiful women, naked bodies, sex on the beach, on rooftops, women on women. There was a mediocre soundtrack beneath each scene, but it didn't matter. We were taken inside the mind of one woman's erotic fantasies, her house of dreams. It was my very first lesson in self-pleasure and witnessing the enjoyment of sex without shame. I should have guessed that Lane would put in a porn movie.

As I remember, *House of Dreams* wasn't like the aggressive porn with obviously fake enactments of sex that is so prevalent today. It wasn't the hard core, five-minute wham, bam, thank-you-ma'am scenes that sexually desensitize us. This movie must have been created for women instead of men, because there was no corny dialogue or many words at all for that matter. And, quite frankly, I learned a lot.

We sat in silence for the entire eighty minutes. I'm positive the guys had hard-ons, and I know that Rikka and I were squirming in our seats. We said not a word; not even a breath was lost between us. When the credits finally floated up the screen, each of us soundlessly went to bedrooms ... separately. Or maybe not. I'm guessing, but Rob probably snuck into Rikka's room, because she had a big crush on him, and Rob was a bit of a Casanova, women loved him. Lane probably pleasured himself to sleep.

I had never watched porn before, or seen anything like that kind of movie. I pretended that it was no big deal for me. I don't know who I was pretending to, since I was alone in my room. Maybe I didn't want to admit how inexperienced I was in the art of sex. *House of Dreams* must have awakened some dormant energy deep inside me, because while I curled up in bed and let sleep take me, my body surprised me. Without even touching myself, my body relaxed into my very first, most incredible orgasm, similar to the orgasm I had when I finally released all the rage from my Femme Fatale fit.

It turns out that these energetic orgasms are a rare and coveted experience. It is the goal of Taoists and Tantra practitioners, considered to be sex magic that awakens one to a new level of spiritual consciousness. It took a betrayal and my inner Femme Fatale to figure out how to release the resistance in my body and surrender enough for it to happen again.

That memory was what came to mind after I felt the warm semen escaping from between my legs from the night before, and watching my cats slink around. I had to conjure 29 more personas to fulfill this challenge, and I didn't want to do this if I wasn't going to enjoy it at every moment. I needed to embody bliss, even though it was so hard for me to feel sexy to begin with. It helped me to think about that evening when I silently snuck off into my bedroom and quietly had a most delicious orgasm, all by my innocent self. That memory encouraged an even bigger, more pleasurable full body stretch, and I felt very feline doing it.

My husband's routine was to leave early in the morning, by four forty-five a.m., so he thought I was still asleep when he bent over to give me a kiss goodbye. I dug my claws into him and bit his lip as a hint. Then I turned over, ignoring him, fell asleep again, and dreamt about pussycats.

LESSON: Sexual fantasy is not a bad thing, when used wisely it opens the door to pleasure.

HELLO KITTY

In my dream (no doubt inspired by the memory of my first erotic movie and first real orgasm), a mysterious pussycat snuck into a luxurious party full of beautiful people. They were wealthy, well-traveled, and well dressed. They stood with an air of chic exclusivity and privilege. The party was located in the Penthouse of an old and ornately decorated hotel. Maroon velvet curtains dressed the walls, mink couches were placed luxuriously around the room, and leather pillows gave it a hint of kink. Real candles twinkled in the crystal chandeliers that hung from the high ceilings. Both men and women were impeccably dressed in Tom Ford, Alaïa, and Alexander McQueen. Lipstick-stained laughter, whispered secrets, and gossip about luxury vacation homes, art, and trips across the globe filled the room. Exotic cocktails filled glasses held in manicured hands. The men oozed of money and power, while the women were dripping with sex.

The pussycat sauntered from one end of the room to another like a predator seeking out her prey. She wore a skimpy black, delicately beaded mini dress. The front draped in folds almost to her belly button, the fabric barely covered her nipples. It was obvious she wasn't wearing panties, because the back was so low, practically revealing the cleavage of her backside. The only thing holding up the scant piece of fabric was a skinny spaghetti strap, zigzagging down her bare back. Her sexual energy was magnified from the base of her groin all the way up through her body.

One elongated leg crossed over the other with five inch Christian Louboutin heels that made her hips sway from side to side as she continued to meander through the room, aloof to all, until she glimpsed someone interesting to her. Her body suddenly perked up in attention and stalked toward a dark-haired man at the end of the bar, and she purred. He became the object of her attention. She did not take her eyes of him as she slowly moved toward him. His body was strong and lean, his face rugged and sharp. The Tom Ford suit he wore was tailored to emphasize his masculine physique. He looked like Superman in Clark Kent's suit. The hair on his skin stood when she came nearer.

Pussycat walked up behind Superman, suddenly hungry for him, and only him. He turned to face her, accidentally brushing his leg up against hers. They stared at each other for a long time, the animal magnetism thick with tension. It wasn't clear if they were going to pounce on each other in a fight to the death for dominance of who was predator and who was prey. He broke out into a big smile first, prey she thought. Pussy could see a hint of what might have been dimples, and her heart melted. She grabbed his hand and led him to the elegant staircase and started to climb it. Superman could see glimpses of her nakedness as each leg stretched up for the next step. They got to the top of the stairs and entered a small reading room. It was dark, filled with wall-to-wall books of every genre. Perfect for a pussycat who loved to read. Standing against the bookshelf, they fucked and ravished each other wildly.

I woke up from my yummy dream state and stretched luxuriously again for a really long time. "Could I pull this off today?" I thought as I grabbed my phone and texted my husband, "Meow."

When I got out of bed, I went into the bathroom and felt the cold marble floors beneath my feet. I took a white washcloth from beneath the sink and ran it under hot water with a bit of lavender soap. I sat naked on the tub and watched myself in the mirror as I gave myself a sponge bath like only a good pussy would do. I was practically licking myself clean. "Hello Kitty," I whispered to myself.

As a newly embodied feline sex kitten, I had to figure out what to wear for the day. I had a transparent plastic container that I kept on the top shelf of my closet, which had a thin layer of dust on it when I took it down. The box that now plays the role of storage for my collection of headpieces was found behind a pile of books that my bookshelf had no room for.

After unloading tulle skirts, saris, seventies glitter, colorful robes, a variety of wigs, I realized how much I've collected over the years. I had a costume store right there in my closet. But nothing felt like "kitty" in that box. I did find a gold cat-ear headpiece that I purchased at Bergdorf Goodman's when I was visiting New York one weekend for yet another workshop.

I can be a cleaver stylist, I brag. I channeled Bastet, the cat goddess, and found a pair of fishnet stockings to wear under my leather pants, and a tight black top to pair with it. I wore the Gucci leather boots I was obsessed with for months that my husband had recently surprised me with. He started getting me random gifts after I got pissed off at him for giving expensive gifts to the "other woman." I added a black sexy bra and panty set from Agent Provocateur, as you know by now, was my new go to.

I straightened my hair with a flattening iron and put on dark liner above my eyelids to mimic Eartha Kitt when she played the role of the first Catwoman. I also called on the energy of my late cat, Snowflake. She was a mini black hole, so dark and cute, she could pull you right in. She had a rare thyroid disease which made Snowflake's bright yellow eyes overly big and round, and it also kept her body small – the eternal kitten. When Snowflake purred, her tongue would fall out of her mouth and stay there. She was a sweet, fragile, black ball of perfection – the perfect amount of sweetness to keep the feral out of my cat.

Ding. At that point, I got a text response.

"Okay. No fair, you have to send me a picture. Bursting with love for you. I adore that you love being playful," was my husband's response to "Meow." I smiled at that.

Black lace lingerie set and fishnets. Check.

Black sleek leather pants and clingy black top. Check.

Cat eyes. Check.

Cat ears. Check.

I even had a pair of black leather gloves to wear. Check.

When I walked into the kitchen, I told my boys, "You are getting cereal this morning." I said it as kittenish as I could while dramatically pouring milk over their Cinnamon Toast Crunch. I didn't give myself time to make a warm breakfast for my two middle schoolers (which turned into a trend during this project!). I've been accused by my boys of being an overprotective mother, which may or may not be true, but a nourishing breakfast was important to me. I grew up eating Pop Tarts and drinking Sunny Delight (which is on a Top Ten Foods Not to Eat list) for breakfast, they would survive this. Of course they were in heaven, because all they know (by me) is that cereal was not *real* food, but just a treat marketed as food for lazy people. They sarcastically asked if I was getting lazy.

My boys scarfed down their breakfast and didn't bat an eye to my cat ears. When the other two kids in our morning carpool got in the car, neither took notice of my kitty ears either. I dropped them off at school and that was that. I would be fine taking this look to the streets.

As my morning routine dictated, I drove the four boys to school, got myself a chai latte, and either worked out or headed straight to my studio. I decided to head to the La Boulangerie coffee shop near their school instead of my typical Starbucks fix, just to be curious as a cat. One of the Marina Moms, the typical north side of town blond parent who wore ballet flats, cropped pants, and a designer brand parka like jacket, looked me up and down and asked if I was going to a birthday party. I know she was thinking that I was probably working as the entertainment at the birthday party, so I just smiled. Then I saw my girlfriend Andrea in her car, she mouthed, "What are you up to this time?"

"Call me," I gestured with my hands as she drove off.

I decided I needed to slow way down today, just like a cat would.

When I got to the coffee shop, I decided to have my drink there instead of "to go." I was glad to see that they offered their coffee and tea drinks in large bowls, perfect for my kitty persona that morning. I picked up the bowl and lapped up the chai latte with my tongue. I didn't care if anyone thought I was weird or not. I took a selfie with my tongue in the bowl and sent it off to my husband. I didn't realize how exhausting it was to lick up an entire bowl of milk, poor kitties. I then headed to my studio to do some photo editing, enjoying my leisurely pace.

After a few hours, I went home to take a catnap that I didn't really need. I took off my leather pants and lay on the bed with my fishnet stockings. I just wanted to take a selfie in catnap position. I sent the picture of my naked bum and legs in the fishnets curled up with my high heeled boots still on and sent it off to my husband with the caption, "time for a catnap." He was so excited by that vision and sent back another picture of a small black gift box. It was like the special rodent gizzard offerings that the wild cat in my sister's neighborhood left on her doorstep every day in appreciation for her feeding it. That wild cat offering, I was told, was a very special gesture.

I had to leave another two hours later to pick up a few fourth graders and get them to baseball practice. I grabbed some chocolate milk and goldfish and when the four boys got into my car, I handed them the snacks and said, "Here you go, kittens, have some treats." Not one of them noticed my cat ears, or got the reference of milk and goldfish. Maybe they were just ignoring me. I sat in my car for the next hour waiting for practice to be over. I just couldn't bring myself to stand on the sidelines with the other parents in my black leather pants and stiletto boots, I didn't feel like explaining what I was doing. Besides, sex and relationships were not topics that these parents talked about.

When we finally got home, I was glad that stew was still cooking in the crockpot and all I had to do was roast some vegetables. It was nearly six, so I shooed our cats away from the large window sill facing the street and perched myself on it while I waited for my husband to return home from work. I tried to stare at him with great intention, but he didn't notice me from the street. When he came in, I gave a little purr and pounced off the window sill and cuddled up to him with a smile, then immediately walked away. This is a push-and-pull technique that I learned from watching our cats daily. My husband started to play along and dangled the black gift box at me. I tried to swat it with my right hand and growled at him when he lifted it too far above my head. When he finally gave it to me, I opened the box to find the most amazing black diamond scorpion ring I had seen at a gift shop in Los Angeles when I last visited. Not that material things could make up for a broken heart, but I was being spoiled. I nuzzled around his body and then plopped into his lap and licked his cheek.

LESSON: Erotic fantasies awaken your soul to her amazing past life love making memories.

SEDUCTION OF THE SENSES

That evening, I really turned up the heat in a different way than the night before. I was intentionally going to feel pleasure for *me*, like the woman in *House of Dreams*, like all cats do. I was going to teach my husband the art of seduction of the senses. I would be the receiver.

I brought in some chocolate, put on soft music, and lit vanilla scented candles that I placed all around the room. It created beautiful light and it smelled delicious. I asked my husband to be present, and not approach me until I approached him. I told him I wasn't going to speak; I was only going to use body language to communicate with him. I crawled over him, hovering my hair over his skin. That was my invitation that we could play together. I nuzzled my head into his chest until he started to stroke my skin, I gave a purr-like moan to let him know he was on the right track. I used my nose to push the coconut oil over to him so he knew that a massage was required next. As I mentioned before, sensual touch produces oxytocin, the "love" hormone that creates the sense of bonding between couples, and I wanted a little more bonding. I had learned from the many courses I took, that sensual touch and massage before sex enhanced relaxation for deeper orgasms, built trust, and was a powerful form of healing in relationships. Touch is what helps premature babies survive.

When I had my feel of bonding, I broke the silence and turned over and spread my legs open. I told him that this pussycat needed stroking. He first used delicate strokes on the upper left quadrant of my clitoris, a technique we learned from Steve Bodansky who wrote *Extended Massive Orgasm* (more on that story later), and then he used broader strokes as he brilliantly stroked me to orgasm. For the first time, I didn't worry about my husband not having a release; cats don't care about anyone else but their own pleasure.

Afterward, feeling completely satisfied, I rolled over and picked up a piece of the chocolate with my mouth and offered it to his lips. We shared a bite of the dark chocolate. The night was a successful seduction of the senses.

Later, my husband told me how turned on he was by my turn on, and that it was sexy that I knew exactly what I wanted, and how to show him what I wanted.

LESSON: Seek embodied pleasure for yourself. Your turn on, turns on everyone else.

ANIMAL MAGNETISM

Before you go off and call your local hypnotist or put on a cat suit, you might want to know a few things about where we energetically source our erotic pleasure, or life force energy. It's also helpful to know how to create a magnetic field of energy that pulls in and manifests desires, and the electric field of energy that ignites and activates intentions. In the animal kingdom this is called animal magnetism.

The magnetic field is also called feminine energy in some circles, while the electric field called masculine energy, having nothing to do with biology. It is the yin to the yang, the receptive to the penetrating, prey to the predator, and the moon to the sun. In other words, the electric and magnetic field of energy, or chi, is the polarity that keeps the fire in relationships burning with passion. It is also the energy that keeps individuals radiating with beauty and sex appeal. When I was in my kitty persona, I channeled the feminine energy of fluid movement. Later, I learned how to channel a more ferocious lioness like energy that could stalk her prey. Mastering both is not such a bad idea. The first step for both men and women to create polarity, is to keep all their energy focused in their first and second chakras, or power centers.

Let me back track a bit to briefly explain the chakra system. According to one of my teachers, Deepak Chopra, chakra is a Sanskrit word that translates into a "wheel of spinning energy." Most ancient teachings of the science of life, like Ayurveda, focus on the seven major chakras within the body, and sometimes two more just above and below the body making nine.

Deepak Chopra explains that these spinning energy vortexes are ruled by spiritual laws of consciousness, and when they are working properly in continuous motion they increase our life force energy, create harmony and wellbeing, and can manifest love and happiness in our lives. When we are fully actualized, we can then be of better service to humanity and the planet. That's a win-win to me.

The first center is the root chakra, which is located at the base of your spine. The root chakra is the energy center that governs how grounded we feel, our security, our worthiness, and how much fear we hold. If we are not balanced in this energy center, we might feel insecure and express fear in our relationships. It is the place where jealousy or scarcity mentality comes from, the fear of not having enough goodness in the world to go around for everyone. I found my Femme Fatal persona deep in my root chakra. She helped me go from Victim to Warrioress. Her grounded sense of security helped me to annihilate the fears of my ego. Of course I had to keep practicing, but that revelation came to me when I embodied her rooted power.

If we don't have a sense of our fierce inner Femme Fatale, fear and unsafety can create the shadow side of our sexy kitty personas too. We might turn into feral alley cats who can only experience love and life in the fight, flight, or freeze survival mode – me for most of my life, which didn't feel good or safe or sexy. It is best to first feel secure and grounded before moving on to the second center, or sacral chakra.

The sacral chakra is the magnetic and expansive energy also known as our creative and sexual energy centers. This governs pleasure, sexuality, procreation, and manifesting desires, creativity, and how we approach love and intimacy. This chakra also has to do with self-acceptance and abundance. When blocked, it can produce sexual shame. It is located about two inches below our belly buttons.

Whether you want to call on a feline kitty, a ferocious lioness, or a sensual snake, these two chakra centers are where we can access our inner primal creature to create the polarity necessary in a juicy relationship. Most women don't feel fully grounded or safe, and this leads to keeping their sacral chakras closed, while aggressively penetrating with their heart centers. Meanwhile, most men haven't learned to open their hearts, so women don't feel received by them, and the men feel smothered by the insistent love energy directed at them.

Men seem to be more naturally rooted in safety and have active and open sacral chakras. If a woman is not grounded and unaware of how to open her sacral chakra safely, then a man's sexual energy may feel oppressive or aggressive to her even if he isn't intending to be forward. So like opposing magnets, we are actually pushing away from each other, putting out the fire of passion and shutting the door to intimacy.

To stay rooted is a meditative process of focusing all my attention on the base of my spine and lower pelvic area. I imagine a ball of light energy in my root chakra that turns into a cord of light and shoots down through the earth past all the earth's crust, the plastic layer, the molted liquid layer to the center of the earth's metal core where I wrap my energy cord and tie a pretty bow around it. From the center of the earth, I imagine collecting earth's magnetic energy and pull it back up the cord into my lower pelvic area and then swirl it up into my womb space, the sacral chakra. Attention and intention is key.

I know this opening of the sacral chakra business works because my friend Juicy J, a plump (her own words!), menopausal fifty-year-old divorcée, who stands just under five feet tall, is a sex magnet. She is more bunny rabbit than sex kitten, but she has this magnetic thing down.

Juicy J rarely wore make up, and I'm not sure if she styles her hair often. She used to consult me on how to be flirtatious and how to approach the opposite sex. We were sitting on the beach in Miami the November before I started this project, talking about sex, desires and how to attract men. It was the first time I wore my gold kitty ear headband. Princess Nou, who (I was convinced) was a beautiful Persian Princess in hiding, sat topless, exercising her body confidence. Madness, the fourth in our group who I gave this nickname to, was a gorgeous artist from New York, she was another madly confident sex lover who spoke frankly as her wavy black long hair spilled over her skinny Kate Moss like body. We were a pod of support that promised to hold each other accountable for personal growth. None of these women knew how hard it actually was for me to sit on the beach with kitty ears on pretending my confidence. I didn't tell any of them about the affair until way later, I was still in research mode. They simply thought I was a prude, recovering Catholic, not a wounded betrayed woman. That's how pained I was.

Juicy J was never out to look for sexual experiences, she was just a joyful flirt who loved sex and men. Men of all ages flocked to her like bees to honey. Cab drivers, executives, pool boys. "Look at me. I'm fat. I'm fifty," she said on the beach as she grabbed her belly. "I must have heroine in my pussy because men are addicted. They can't get enough of me."

Juicy J was a shorter, hotter-mess version of the actress Amy Schumer; she used the word "pussy" in every other sentence. As far as I could tell, Juicy J did have sex with many different men, with a lover in practically every city. Juicy J danced on tables and would fall dramatically on the floor in a fake faint when a good friend entered the room, making them feel like they were the only thing she cared about. Juicy J would break out in song, belting into her own fist as if she was the headliner at a karaoke rock concert. It didn't matter if she was out of tune. She was always center of attention; everyone loved her.

What I came to understand was that Juicy J put all of her attention on her pussy, as she likes to say, and sacral center. She may not have been the slow, sultry cat that I was going for, but she proved that simply being open to her sexual center was magnetic enough. And that is good enough proof for me to know where I needed to focus to get into my primal cat body to create the animal magnetism I was looking for.

LESSON: keep your energy in your root and sacral chakra to create that intimate magnetic pull.

NINE LIVES

From where I stand now, my shut-down and injured heart days seem like they were many lives ago. My first life was one of child-like wonder, even if it lasted a short time. My second life included trauma, offenses, and conditioned rules dictated by others. My third life was unconsciously following these rules, as I stayed frozen in my body, asleep to my natural rhythms. My fourth life was a rupture that shook me awake and broke me open. My fifth life was taking the first step on the journey to know and understand myself better, this happens to be the longest and hardest where we enter the cave and dive into the dark side, it is the context of this story. My sixth life was to accept what is and turn all the shadows into light. My seventh life is to share how I came to this very point of healing, and serve in a bigger way. My eighth life is to awaken to a higher consciousness, which is happening right now. I can feel it. And my ninth life is still in the making.

Like the cat, we too have nine lives. Cats are mysterious creatures said to have mystic and psychic qualities to them. Maybe their nine lives have something to do with the nine dimensions.

I was starting to get my magic back, and I believe it was because I learned to deeply tap into the specific energies of each persona I embodied. Some of the more significant archetypes had to be accessed through the different power centers. Attending to my chakras helped me open up my subtle fields of perception that "woo-woo" people call the clair- senses: clairvoyance, clairaudience, clairsentience.

We all have a little magic in us, we just need to remember how to get access and use it for the highest good. Adulting, society, religion, and the fear of being labeled a nut case closed me off from my inner knowing. It is interesting to note that the story of Jesus walking on water and the story of Moses talking to a burning bush are considered divine, while women who use their intuition, plants, and rituals to heal are crazy. It is important for me to keep reminding others that we used to get burnt at the stake for this.

In my twenties, I had an opportunity to open up to my magic, but I chose to shut it down because of fear. One of my dearest friends called me up before dawn one August Sunday morning with ecstatic joy. I was living with my then-boyfriend, now-husband, at the time. My friend on the other line started jabbering on about how he had just died and left his body, saw his body from above, but was lucky enough for his soul to land back into his body at the exact same time in space. He told me how he was beginning to leave his body during work, and his colleagues were starting to notice. He was speaking so fast and with such enthusiasm, I couldn't help to encourage more details.

I loved my friend Buzz. He was handsome, funny, and smart. He went to Stanford, then to Harvard, and had a great job which we *never* talked about. The two of us only conversed about synchronicities: our favorite songs, the world between the worlds, the soul, ice cream flavors, and magic. We predicted the future, talked about past lives, and we debated about how many alien colonies were really out there. That morning's conversation wasn't so weird, considering. The only thing off about it was the time, five-thirty a.m.

My then-boyfriend groggily told me to call Buzz back later so we could sleep in more. They were once roommates, so he knew how much Buzz could chatter. But when I relayed the conversation back, we both decided that it was a bit troubling, so I tried calling him back to invite him over for breakfast. No answer.

There was no answer all morning. We found out the rest of what happened later that day. A few friends were headed over to the Sausalito fair and were stuck in traffic on the Golden Gate Bridge. Buzz had decided to go for a morning ride then too. As our friends heading to the fair slowed down to a stop, Buzz slowly snaked his way through the traffic on his motorcycle. I would have thought he was headed for the ice cream shop in Sausalito, where he would take me sometimes, just because he liked riding across the bridge. Our friends turned and saw him idling right beside them.

"Hey Buzz!" one of the guys said. "Whatcha doing?"

"Just going for a ride." Buzz smiled and continued through the traffic jam.

About thirty seconds later, they saw a crowd of people peering over the side of the bridge, and Buzz's motorcycle had been deserted on the side of the road. One of the guys ran out of the car to the edge of the railing and watched as Buzz's helmet sank into the Bay. There was a giant seal right next to him staring straight up at all the onlookers. When Buzz's body sank all the way in, the seal retreated into the water.

When I found out, guilt oozed all over my body. I shouldn't have gotten off the phone with him. I should have known something was wrong. Could I have stopped him? Buzz's body was never found.

In the middle of that night, I was woken up by something. Actually, something pulled me up from lying down to an upright sitting position. The room got really cold. I didn't know what was happening, I was still partly asleep, but my bones started to chill. Then I saw right in front of me a foggy figure of a man. There were no details, just an outline. I tried to strain my eyes to see clearer, but I could only see the foggy shape. Then I felt a finger touch me on the tip of my nose. It was wet and cold. I freaked out.

"I'm not ready for this, I'm not ready for this, I'm not ready for this." I stared frozen at the apparition across from me.

All of a sudden, I felt hands on my shoulders as my body was pushed back into a lying position. The foggy image drifted away and the room suddenly felt warm.

"That was weird."

"You saw it too?" I was so grateful.

"Just saw you sit up and fall back down."

I replayed my experience.

For months after, I would pick up the phone to hear only static on the other end. Whenever I stayed on the line longer than I should, I would here the song "Imagine," by John Lennon, Buzz's last theme song before he jumped over the bridge. We had a habit of creating theme songs for people. If I was mountain biking in the Marin Headlines, I would get a soft push up the mountain. Sometimes I would get a whiff of jasmine scent out of the blue. Buzz used to talk about rainbows all the time, and when my husband and I got married a couple of years later on Kauai, there was a double rainbow across the bay.

All these phenomena have been said to come from spirits who are trying to communicate with you on the other side. I went to a psychic who told me that I should not be afraid of my powers, but that made me more afraid of my powers. So I shut them down.

This devastating story might seem like a non sequitur, but stay with me. I know now, that awakening to your unique super powers is key to awakening to your sensual body, which is key to feeling really sexy in your body, which is the key to seduction, which is the key to manifesting a juicy love affair with your partner. Your *whole* being is important, and that includes your magic.

My point in sharing this story is that this experience was an opportunity for me to open to some of the inherent gifts that women have naturally, but I didn't. The Universe wants us to wake up to our super powers, and our sexuality is one of the most important. It is a portal that connects to the pineal gland and helps us to reach for higher dimensions of consciousness.

If we don't open up to our inner magic when they first expose themselves, then the Universe is going to make you work harder for it. For me, betrayal was so much harder to get through. Had I simply said "hello" to Buzz's spirit, I might have come to this awakened place sooner, who knows. Most people are afraid of death and don't want to deal with death, but to me, a betrayal is just as painful a death because the couple we were died.

Sometimes I get downloads from Buzz telling me that he died so he could live, and that he was trying to teach us that something has to die before another thing can be rebirthed. That makes sense to me; my marriage died the day I found out about the affair. My old self died then, too. I was handed Pandora's Box by the council of nine, and like Pandora and the cat, curiosity got the best of me and I opened it up to all the misfortunes of my past self. But I don't think that was a bad idea at all. My magic is back, and it helps me to tap into the energetics of each persona in myself and others more clearly.

Cats being nocturnal can represent our dark and mysterious sides too. Since they have nine lives, they can also symbolize death and rebirth, a natural law of the Universe. Cats are also associated with unpredictability and healing. Nine also happens to be the numerology of wisdom, initiation, and global consciousness. Whether or not you believe in such symbology, it doesn't hurt to curiously slink into the mysteries hidden in our most sacred space in our sexual bodies. When I was working with a pelvic floor specialist, she told me that I hid all my emotional scars in the back of my vaginal wall just behind my cervix. When I started attending to that chakra center, my body and those energetic scars started to heal.

I recommend experimenting with a feline persona, either kitty, lioness, Catwoman, Bastet, or even Sekhmet. You can do it fully dressed up and embodied, which is so much fun. Or, you can try it out first energetically. Tapping into your sexual centers, finding pleasure in everything you do including how you move, and curiously examining what you find is key to awakening to the next level of your sexy, unbetrayable, powerfully provocative self.

LESSON: Remember you are a magical erotic creature with nine lives and the power for rebirth.

9. The Executive

PARKING LOT PLEASURES

When I got up in the morning for my next persona, I dressed in a pencil thin, fitted black dress that landed just below my knees. It had a square neckline that showed off my cleavage. It was very sexy chic, with a profession flair. I put on a pearl necklace that my mom lent me for an engagement party, I had never returned it. Knowing my mom, it was probably fake, but it was a good fake pearl necklace, so it would do. Being a bit of a shoe whore, I already had the perfect Ralph Lauren black and white, wingtip stilettos that matched. I chose not to wear any lingerie underneath.

With a straight posture and a very professional demeanor, I created a list of personas I wanted to try out and schedule. I changed my mind constantly. The mermaid tail and phoenix wings I wanted were too expensive, and took too long to make. Plus, I wondered how to be productive without legs, and I didn't really trust myself with fire. I quickly realized, I was better at spontaneously creating each persona the night before, or the day of.

I was a quarter into the thirty personas when I decided to create a contract that told my husband how I wanted this project to go, and what I wanted from him sexually. This would be a good exercise since I never thought about what I really wanted. When you don't know what you don't know, you just don't know where to start. So I copied the language of a legal document I found on the internet, and just changed some words. I titled it the "General Goddess Worship Agreement." Not exactly the template for a sexual exchange contract, but it did look and sound very professional. I didn't think to create a contract a la *50 Shades of Grey*. I was still so naïve then.

It was time to actively include my husband in this project of mine, by active I mean offer him a stake in it. Where the previous icons could be done without partnership, the upcoming personas worked better practicing with a partner. The contract would help me understand better why I was doing this project, what I really wanted to get out of it, and how I wanted my partner to serve in it. This project, after all, was about how I could be and feel sexy in my marriage, in spite of being betrayed. My husband didn't really have a choice in the matter, he still felt guilty by what he did. He knew that I wasn't really over it *yet*, even though I did my best to pretend otherwise. This contract would be a nice gesture. And if I was out to create the craziest love affair with my husband, I had to break free from my inner critic, be grown up about it, and keep it fun.

When I was pleased with my contract, I called up his assistant and asked her to put me in his calendar for the late afternoon, as a "personal meeting." My husband had a busy schedule; he didn't look at his calendar until minutes before his next meeting, unless of course he had to travel to it. I knew he would be surprised when I showed up in the office.

I put the contract and a few adult toys in a portfolio box with handles that I usually use for photographs, and drove myself downtown to his office near the Embarcadero. I thought it would be fun to open the box as Inspectress Gadget, and have to pull out the contract from beneath a bullet vibrator, a set of stainless steel Ben Wa balls, and some leather cuffs.

For someone who was supposedly "shut down," I had a few unused adult toys in my top drawer. Maybe my subconscious mind took me to Good Vibrations years before, predicting that someday these sexy gadgets would come in handy, or maybe I always had a little bit of kink in me and just shoved it way down.

I was lucky there was room in the garage right under my husband's office building, parking is virtually impossible downtown. I was even luckier that I got a spot right next to his car – if that isn't a sign from the Cosmos, I don't know what is. I thought about writing a cute note and putting it under his windshield wiper from a "secret admirer," but that didn't seem so professional to me. Instead, I decided to use the vibrator as I sat in my car in the parking lot. I know that was not so professional either, but I was in the process of giving "the business" a whole new meaning.

As I lifted up my skirt, I was nervous that someone would see me, but it also excited me at the same time. I was using a very powerful vibrator it seemed, because within minutes, I was convulsing with orgasmic pleasure. I put my index finger up between my legs to collect a little juice and I smeared it on my husband's car windshield for good luck. I had learned from The School of Womanly Arts that putting "pussy juice" behind your ears, or spreading it around was a blessing for good fortune in more ways than one. I wanted to test it.

I also made myself a mental note to try having parking lot sex with my husband soon, just because we had never done that together. It would be a novelty, it would be risky, and it might even be more fun to just plan it. Who knew that I would get off on parking lot pleasures. The thought alone got me excited to use the vibrator again, but I stopped myself, put on my blazer, and headed up the elevator all flushed and invigorated.

LESSON: Do "The Business" in a variety of places for novelty and good memories.

BUSINESS UP FRONT, PARTY IN THE BACK

When I got to my husband's office on the 34th floor of the building, I was escorted to the lounge area. I don't know if I was imagining it, but everyone looked at me suspiciously. I rarely went into the office; I had visited a maximum of five times in over ten years. Every time I did visit, I would playfully spread rumors that I was the second wife, then later down the line, I would announce to his assistant to spread the rumor that I was his third wife. I couldn't remain twenty-eight years old otherwise. No one got my humor.

While I was sitting on the couch in the lounge, he walked out of the bathroom and saw me. He looked confused. "We have a meeting," I told him matter-of-factly, as I stood up and grabbed my portfolio box. I think he was nervous for a second, wondering what I was planning to do in his place of work. All the walls in the office were glass, there was no hiding anything in there. He gave me a quick kiss on the cheek and walked me over to his office, which also had glass walls. We sat at his conference table. I took off my jacket and I watched him take me in.

"Why the pleasant surprise?" he said, then lowered his voice. "Do you have a bra on?"

"Oh." I paused and looked him in the eyes, smiling. "I didn't know it would be that obvious." I sat next to him and crossed my legs *Basic Instinct* style and added, "I didn't wear undies either."

"You look sexy," he said as he looked over his shoulder, hoping that no one could read our lips. "I'm getting a hard-on."

"That is not very professional is it, your hard-on?" I responded casually, as if we were talking about the weather. "But thank you." I gave him a wink.

"You aren't playing fair."

"Well, that is exactly why I'm here." I opened up my portfolio box. "To play fair." His eyes widened at the toys in the box, and he looked back over his shoulder. "Don't worry," I said. "No one can see what's in the box." I pulled out the contract beneath the leather handcuffs and the vibrator, the Ben Wa balls rolled around the other toys like balls in a pinball machine. "Oh by the way …" I pointed to the vibrator. "I used that while I was sitting in my car just before I came up. It's a really good stress release technique that all powerful business women should use. I might have to start a trend." I smiled at him a little longer than was needed. "Now we have some negotiating to do," I paused dramatically, "so you feel like this experiment of mine is 'fair.'" I used my quote fingers to emphasize the word "fair." "Let's read this contract together, go down it line by line, and if you are in agreement, you can add your initials. We can negotiate the ones you would like to change." I should have been a lawyer; I was so convincing.

Although I treated this document as if it was legally binding, it was pretty much a business up front, party in the back contract, with a dash of Rated-R.

LESSON: We can be business-like and sexy at the same time … It's "and not or".

CONTRACTS AND AGREEMENTS

Why do lawyers deliberately write up complicated contracts that make no sense? I guessed because it would make it easier for them to get out of, or confuse their clients so much that they would give up on reading the fine print. The one I borrowed off the internet was no exception, but since I created it that morning, I made sure to convey that this was a working copy.

I placed a blank copy of "The Contract" in front of my husband and we went through each section and filled in the blanks together.

GENERAL GODDESS WORSHIP AGREEMENT

This agreement ("AGREEMENT") establishes the partnership ("PARTNERSHIP") between goddess ("GODDESS") and hero ("HERO"), and the agreed upon worship ("WORSHIP") AGREEMENT between the following parties:

_____   _____

and is undersigned and set forth this _____ day of _____ in the year of _____.

The undersigned parties hereby agree to the following provisions as conditions of the GODDESS WORSHIP AGREEMENT.

SECTION 1 – Goddess Outline

1.1 The PARTNERSHIP will be named GODDESS WORSHIP for the purpose of worshipping the GODDESS (name)_____, by the HERO (name)

_____, and all "business" will be will conducted at (address) _____ and/or other luxurious travel destinations per choice of PARTNERSHIP.

1.2 The PARTNERSHIP will commence on the date listed above, and will end at the "end of time," or when the Universe collapses. At that time, renewal opportunities can be discussed in person, while bathing, or lounging, or in a relaxed state. No communication to be started minutes before bedtime.

1.3 GODDESS WORSHIP AGREEMENT is a working document subject to change by GODDESS and in agreement with HERO.

SECTION 2 – Initial Worship Agreement

2.1 HERO will contribute to the initial WORSHIP investment according to the following rules: honorable, truthful, and respectful communications, plus a word bath full of sexy and enticing phrases, stories, or fantasies to the GODDESS each day.

2.2 Small gifts of any price and size, such as lingerie, shoes, jewelry, or handpicked flowers from the anyone's garden should be offered to the GODDESS throughout the week by HERO.

2.3 PARTNERSHIP agrees to experiment with each other's body parts for pure pleasure research, the use of toys, tongues, genitals, fingers, etc., may be used where deemed appropriate.

2.4 HERO agrees to accept the many roles and faces of the GODDESS and respond accordingly. If at any time the PARTNERSHIP becomes uncomfortable with one of the many faces of the GODDESS, PARTNERSHIP agrees to communicate clearly (see Section 4.1).

SECTION 3 – Interest on Investment

3.1 HERO may collect gifts, compliments, gratitude, acknowledgments, and adoration from the GODDESS as appropriate to his level of worship to her. GODDESS agrees to provide ample feedback to HERO on his duties to serve GODDESS.

SECTION 4 – Disputes/Arbitration

4.1 Any misguided conversation that leads to an argument will be halted immediately. The HERO and the GODDESS must strip down to their naked bodies and rub oil all over each other, specifically on the penis and vulva before continuing on with the conversation.

4.2 If the conversation continues to deteriorate, the HERO must remove himself from the presence of the GODDESS and self-pleasure until in a relaxed state (or vice versa). The GODDESS will be allowed to vent, rage or cry in the privacy of her own space and self-pleasure as necessary (or vice versa). HERO agrees not to offer judgment or try to fix anything for GODDESS (and vice versa).

4.3 If all else fails, the PARTNERSHIP must agree to reincarnate, at that very moment, into higher beings, apologize to each other, and start the conversation over. PARTNERSHIP agrees to enter the bed chamber with issues resolved.

SECTION 5 – Management

5.1 GODDESS WORSHIP will be considered successful by how much the GODDESS deems the HERO'S presence and attention each day. Communication via text, phone, email at least 1 (one) time per day is sufficient. Honesty, reliability and devotion will determine success of WORSHIP.

5.2 Pleasuring of the clitoris and the sacred spot of the GODDESS is of the upmost importance in determining if HERO has managed his role properly.

5.3 GODDESS agrees to stimulate the pleasure centers of HEROs body.

5.4 HERO is expected to devote himself mind, body, heart and soul to the GODDESS.

5.5 PARTNERSHIP meetings will be conducted each evening. Exciting and stimulating experiences both clothed and unclothed will be expected from both parties and to each other. New experiences are greatly encouraged.

5.6 If either party feels stagnant or bored, the issue must be addressed immediately and an emergency meeting will be called. An emergency playdate will be conjured and put into practice the following day or evening.

5.7 PARTNERSHIP agrees to be flexible and have fun.

SECTION 6 –Non-Compete/Dissolution

6.1 Should either partner choose to leave the PARTNERSHIP, willingly or unwillingly, he/she shall do so with grace and integrity, and only after both PARTNERS have exhausted all means of healthy communication, forgiveness, sexual healing, etc.

6.2 While in PARTNERSHIP, partners agree to not take any position, nor engage in any activity, with any company, persons, etc. that are deemed crazy, dishonest, have bad karma, or are evil competitors to the PARTNERSHIP, for a period of eternity.

6.3 PARTNERSHIP may agree to experience expert activities, companies, persons etc. that sexually and emotionally enhance the Partnership, and will be discussed when needed.

SECTION 7 – Jurisdiction

7.1 This AGREEMENT is subject to the laws and regulations of the Universe, as well as any applicable energetic laws of Karma.

7.2 This AGREEMENT is subject to changes at any time and with consent of PARTNERSHIP.

We, the undersigned, agree to all the provisions listed above, and sign this document of our own free will. So be it.

Signed on this day of _____ in the month of _____ in the year of _____.

(GODDESS)_____

(HERO)_____

We sat in his glass walled office pretending to go over these official papers and laughing at some of the requirements, my husband made a few changes that made the worshipping more of a two-way street, and we signed on the dotted line.

I think we should all create some sort of contract at the beginning of all partnerships that includes exactly what they mean to each of us, in detail. I never verbally said that betrayal was out of the question. I just assumed that everyone thought the same thing. The contract should include that we will seek guidance before negative feelings and resentments get out of hand. No one told us that child rearing was going to take the life out of me. No one taught me how to navigate the needs of kids, my husband, or myself. No one told my husband that being a provider was going to be so stressful, or that the stress could turn even the nicest of guys into a brutal asshole. No one taught us how to ask for what we wanted or needed either. I've never seen a prenuptial agreement, but I do know that they are contracts mainly concerning material assets should the marriage dissolve. Why are there no negotiations being made emotionally, psychological, sexually, or spiritually? These are the real conflicts that plague marriages in the first place.

Contracts are great, and they can open up difficult memories, even if they are playful, like the one I created. When I included the non-compete/dissolution section, I had to ask myself what I would do if this happened again. For a long time, I was convinced he would do it again. I hated that I wanted to look at every one of his texts, and wondered if his haircut appointments were really haircuts. Poor guy chose to work only with men for the longest time.

Even though I didn't think he *could or would* have an affair again, given how much pain he saw in me. I didn't know if he *wanted* to do it again. It was easy for him to compartmentalize his affair to a thing that he did *before*. He was good at wrapping it up in a garbage bag and throwing it away, like it never happened in the first place. I was just the opposite. The toll it took went through every cell in my body, and I couldn't help to remind him of that.

One day he was so frustrated that I was still not "over it," he suggested that I should have an affair to know what it was like, but just not to tell him about it. I was livid. Did that mean that he liked having an affair? Of course he did, that's why he did it and kept doing it until I found out. But how dare he think *I* would do such a thing. At the time I thought it so insensitive to encourage me to go out and have an affair when the wound was still raw. I didn't feel date-worthy. What guy would agree to sleep with me just because? I didn't know how long it would take me to even look at another man in the eyes.

This suggestion was either a way for him to stop feeling so guilty, or he wanted something to blame me for in the future. And then he said he didn't want to know about it. I was the one to feel the pain, but he would be spared. Even though I was furious at the suggestion, a part of me did wonder what it would be like to experience another person. I wondered if anyone else would ever find me attractive. I wanted to be wanted. I did want to know if I was desirable to others. So when he said it to me a second and a third time, I told him that I just might take him up on it.

I didn't have the courage to put in a clause that said: GODDESS is allowed to have an affair, and promises not to share with HERO, and this affair is not grounds for the dissolution of the PARTNERSHIP. I knew that I was healing much faster now, because I realized that in his own way, he was trying to make me feel whole. It was powerful and liberating to know that I was free to do what I needed and wanted, even if I didn't plan on it.

I put the signed papers back into my portfolio, put on my jacket, shook his hand and left the office. When my husband got home, he continued with the roll playing and said, "Wow, you must have had a really hard day at work today. Can I offer you a foot rub?"

He got many points for that. I took off my heels, and we sat on the couch. I put my legs over his, giving him a peek of my nakedness as he rubbed my feet and I grabbed for my toy box.

LESSON: Contracts allow you to think about what more you want out of your relationship.

THE INTERVIEW

When I dream, I dream vividly. I'm never sure if my recurring dreams are messages about the future, or about the past experiences I still needed to process. Some of my dreams are weird, some foreboding, and some erotic. Sometimes the scenes are from my childhood, sometimes the scenes have giant spiders, strange rooms that I have to go through, or I'm flying. I'm always surprised by my erotic dreams because I always feel like I have lived them before. As I said, this project was activating my dream state.

After my roleplay as the business executive, I dreamt about "The Interview," an erotic dream I have had over and over again for the past few years. Jungian analysts say that dreams are the psyche's attempt to express important things to us, to find out what our egos don't know or understand.

In my dream, I was the founder of a company who interviewed and trained the alpha male: strong, goal oriented, a natural leader, the honest warrior type. The alpha male was composed, unassuming, intelligent and attractive because of his intense and pure energy. There was a shortage of this type of man because of the shadow side of this type of man showed up as arrogance, domination, and oppression. Unfortunately, very much like the powerful men today.

In my dream, that type of man was dying out and a new breed of man was emerging and needed to be "trained" by women. My job was to train these men to be of sexual service to the growing number of high-achieving business women. It wasn't an illegal operation, because women, in my dream, ruled the world. The women, in my dream, did not diminish or abuse men. My business offering was a cross between a dating site, organizing an arranged marriage, free will, and teaching sex magic. The bonds always worked out because my company was so thorough in investigating the deeper parts of how people connected on an emotional and cosmic level. We even had an on-staff astrologer and psychic to measure compatibility.

My exclusive clientele were the most powerful women in the world, because in this lifetime, we were not afraid to use our sexual powers and shame did not exist. We knew that sexual energy was an important source for power, and when used with heart and compassion, we could save the world. The more powerful that women became, the more that we were serving humanity by creating new technologies that were sustaining and nourishing. There was a balance of power for both men and women in my dream, because women were more collaborative than the previous rule of patriarchy. Women needed and wanted powerful men to support them.

The men who passed the interview process were given a new wardrobe, lessons in manners and grace, we pushed their bodies with extreme peak performance workouts and nurtured them afterward, we taught them how to be amazing and present lovers. These alpha men led the industries that supported the women who created them, so that the women could create even more. Not one man felt emasculated, just the opposite, they were able to exercise their strength, use their minds, express their sexuality, and have an open heart. It was Utopia in the making.

The man who came into my office was tall and muscular. He had dark blond hair, blue eyes, and a boyish grin. He was wearing street clothes: jeans and a t-shirt. We wanted them to come in "as they were." He took a seat on the couch opposite my desk. My uniform was a one button blazer with nothing underneath and a slim short skirt, all in black. We wanted to arouse the men visually, so we could measure the energy of his heart in comparison to the test he took before the interview. The goal was to make sure that men learned how to open their hearts, drop into their sexuality, and be able to come back into their heart centers easily. This was a full rewiring of the male nervous system that was so used to being head and dick centered. We believed it was the heart, without letting go of their sex, that would uplift these men into the alpha male.

After the interview with me, he was taken into a private room to watch erotica. He wasn't allowed to self-pleasure. A woman was left in the room with him to make sure he did not self-pleasure himself. We knew this was torture for him, and it was torture for the female assistant who volunteered to watch it with him. In reality, she was one of the executive women who tested to be the most compatible for him on paper. She brought him to all the rest of the stations to measure their connection.

He was then taken into another private room styled in a minimalist way. In the center of the room was a massage table. Electric devices were put on his body to start measuring his impulses again. She began to stroke his cock to orgasm as they continuously looked into each other's eyes.

My dreams are never complete stories, but they can probably be pieced together to create the whole. In this dream, I was the owner and the assistant. It was the middle of the night when I found myself stroking my husband. I slowly crawled on top of him, imagining him to be an alpha male of my creation, I told him about my dream while I took myself to orgasm.

Einstein again is quoted as saying, "Imagination is everything. It is the preview of life's coming attractions." If that's the case, I hope that my dream about sexually empowered women who rule the world, will come true someday. Maybe my subconscious is telling me that there is something we women need to teach men, if they would only let us. Or maybe, it's simply that "sexy" is infiltrating even the deepest recesses of my being. Either way, I'm learning to use my dreams as a tool to manifest my future.

LESSON: Start writing down your dreams, they are trying to tell you something.

10. The Madonna and the Whore

JESUS FOLLOWED ME EVERYWHERE

I was raised in a very Catholic household. My mother prayed with rosary beads every single day, and made us go to church with her every single Sunday. My dad made it to church too, which was embarrassing for us, not to mention hypocritical. We would sit in the back of the nave so most of the congregation wouldn't notice us. My dad always fell asleep at church, and always started snoring. We ignored him. I pretended I didn't know him, and refused to look away from the priest at the altar. But everyone knew he belonged to us. Martin, a boy at my grade school always caught my eye when we got to church. I don't think he was mocking me, I think he was sending me telepathic messages of empathy. I wondered if his parents were dysfunctional, too. At the end of church when the chorus began to sing, my dad would wake up and start singing loudly with them.

There were religious relics on every wall and in every corner of our home. Little porcelain angels and cherubs were placed on window sills and shelves. A large statue of Mother Mary stood near the doorway. Plenty of smaller images of Mother Mary were placed in various areas throughout our home. Plastic rosary beads could be found in glass bowls on the side tables, and there might have been crucifixes, big and small, in every other room. My mom even had a few small plastic vessels in the form of Mother Mary that held holy water. The dining room was where a large photograph of *The Last Supper* hung on the wall.

But it was the large framed photograph of Jesus that affected me the most. It was the classic image of a bearded Jesus with a vibrant halo that surrounded his long, brown hair. He wore a white smock that was the backdrop for a floating heart encased in thorns, with a crucifix above it. If you took away the halo from Jesus's head and added a surfboard, he might have made the perfect surfer dude. If you replaced the surfboard with a rubber mat and the heart with some mala beads, Jesus might have made the perfect yoga teacher, or Haight Street hippy.

I used to be scared of this picture of Jesus because his big, sad eyes were always looking at me. I would run to one corner of the room, and noticed that he was still watching me. I would run to the opposite side of the room, and he would *still* be watching me. I ran under the dining room table where I could still see him, and there he was *still* looking at me. I once made my younger sister and brother stand shoulder to shoulder with me in front of Jesus. When I counted to three, I ordered them to run in opposite directions. When we finally ended up in different parts of the room, I yelled to my brother, "Is he looking at you?" My brother nodded, not taking his eyes off Jesus. I yelled to my sister, "Is he looking at you too?" My sister stared at Jesus Christ and nodded as well. I yelled, "He's looking at me too!" We screamed and ran upstairs. There was a Jesus Christ image up there too. No matter where I was, Jesus followed me everywhere.

My father taught C.C.D. on Saturday mornings in our basement, or at least he was supposed to. C.C.D. stands for Confraternity of Christian

Doctrine (I just learned), which is a Catholic education program geared for kids on the path to Confirmation. Although my father was *supposed* to teach C.C.D., he asked me to teach in his place when I turned fourteen. He was too busy playing poker all night long. He either didn't come home, or was still asleep when the C.C.D. kids came over. I'm not exactly sure what I taught these poor children, except that I was positive Jesus Christ followed us everywhere. When I was twenty, my friend Jeanette and I went to the A.C.T. theater on Geary Street to see a show. The young man at the door collecting tickets looked at me and said, "Excuse me, but I think you were my C.C.D. teacher, did you ever teach C.C.D.?" I laughed and asked if he had turned into an atheist. He looked at me, puzzled. I apologized and confessed that I had no idea what I was doing then, and hoped I didn't taint his religious path. He said that I was his favorite teacher.

One story in the Bible I was obsessed with was that of Adam and Eve. Even if it was only a paragraph long, I imagined it to be something very dramatic and profound. The image of two innocently naked people in a garden all to themselves was so erotic to me. And then top it off with breaking a rule because of a slithering snake, my imagination went wild.

If I were in Eve's place, I would have eaten the fruit from the Tree of Knowledge, too. I might have eaten all the fruit off the tree. Who wouldn't want to know everything? Eve was my idol. I didn't hear much about feisty Lilith growing up, but I ended up liking her, too. She was Adam's first wife, who refused to be submissive to him so was banished from Eden. The whole story doesn't make sense, if Adam and Eve were the first people how could there be a Lilith. I knew someone was making this whole thing up to benefit them – the patriarchy again.

Everything from the dismissal of equality, to shame, to the fall of man is blamed on women. Religion brainwashed me into believing that I was a born sinner, and I made myself "wrong" for just being me. I shied away from any attention, tried to dim my light if it showed too much, and mastered the good girl archetype. When I got my ancestral matriarchal curse, breasts, I started to hunch over, and wore sports bras that made me look like I had a "uni-boob," as one boyfriend called them. He was trying to say in his Neanderthal ways that I had nice boobs and shouldn't hide them. I should rewrite the biblical story.

The story is really a metaphor for sexual awakening and its power to experience life fully, at least to me. My Eve and Adam are on a lush, deserted island where the Tree of Life and the Tree of Knowledge stood miraculously in the center. God would have said to Eve, "Go find the Tree of Knowledge and eat of its fruit, for you are now ready to lead Adam into the magic and wonder of the body. There will be a serpent lying dormant at the base of the tree who will remind you to eat it, lest you forget."

So Eve wanders off into the dense forest in search of the Tree of Knowledge. When she gets there, she and the serpent discuss the meaning of Kundalini rising and sexual awakening. Eve will be the first to awaken sexually, as girls are the first to mature. Eve is prepared to teach Adam the way. Eve takes a bite first, and feels the sleeping serpent in the base of her spine begin to awaken. She feels it uncoil up through her spine to stir the other chakras centers in her body. She knows that Adam must eat the fruit to also awaken, so she tells him to take a bite. Eve's feminine energy, Adam's masculine energy, and their naked bodies merge in sexual union, just like the cosmic energies of the Universe. My story of Eve would be the awakening of humanity, not the fall of man.

Changing the biblical story inspired me to start changing the victim stories of my past to be the empowering stories that they really are. As we rewrite our stories, our many personas transform into their most superior versions.

LESSON: Find your own religion, and create your own stories.

THE SACRED WHORE

It was a Saturday morning, and my husband rolled over to try and get an intimate nibble of my nipples. I stopped him and said, "That is going to cost you." He didn't understand my hint and I think he went back into pattern and felt a little rejected. I continued with my tease and said, "You know that I'm extremely talented with my tricks, so even just a little piece of me is going to be *really* expensive." I stroked his morning hard-on slightly. "That alone is worth $150."

He was catching on and asked, "How much for a full session?"

I had to think about that for a second. What would I charge if I were a high-end call girl? That was an on-going problem for me, trying to figure out how to price things for the couture outfits I used to make, for my photography sessions, for the workshops I taught now and then. I never knew how much to charge. I always put in way more creativity, hours, dedication and work for my projects than I invoiced my clients for. If I couldn't figure out how much my services with clients were worth, how was I going to figure out how much to charge for the services of my body? "I charge over $10,000 for the evening, more if I spend the night," I said. "But because you're pretty hot, I'll give you a discount."

"How much?" he asked.

"$5,000 in cash," I answered, then added, "in brand new, one hundred dollar bills, please."

My husband was enjoying the conversation and tried to get a freebie nibble in. I scolded him: "No. I need to see the cash first." We negotiated that he could give me the cash in full later, and I would give him a nibble now, for free.

We had to tag team for the three baseball games between two boys that day. I was playing mom/kid-sitter/driver by day, but I considered my *real* job to be a high end prostitute by night – at least for these next twenty-four hours. I slipped on black see-through, mesh lingerie and thigh-high silk stockings under my jeans and t-shirt. My husband had purchased this matching set for me long ago, and it was the perfect first time to wear it.

At the baseball field, I climbed up the bleachers and sat with two other mothers from my sons' school. We did the usual small talk, which I was never good at. There was a complaint about the large baseball team, the changes at their school, and if the boys were going to sign up for next fall's Midweekly. The Midweekly was a San Francisco exclusive dance program, where high society manners and old-school dance steps were taught. The boys were required to wear ties, and the girls were required to wear white gloves. I heard that some of the boys were in it for the snacks, and most did not remember their ballroom dancing moves when it was all over.

Sandy asked what I was doing these days, and I gave her a toned-down version of my project, how I was experimenting with how couples in long-term relationships could reignite the spark. By then, I had read every book on relationships and could sound smart by regurgitating theories, but to actually embody a practice made my own theories on the subject come out as a higher truth.

They were intrigued. I wasn't surprised. Almost everyone I knew had something going on with their relationships. And the ones that didn't just seemed bored and compliant. It was so rare for me to recognize the bliss and the joy and the true intimacy that I thought would radiate out if a couple were truly fulfilled and happy with each other. I could tell just by Sandy's questions and body language that she was having problems with her husband. They both looked like they were in shut-down mode.

There are definitive signs when a couple has lost their spark. Both bodies are rigid, they don't look each other in the eyes, they stand far apart from each other, they don't smile at each other, they are no longer demonstrative, there is tension in the jaw and throat, and you can feel the energetic resistance or dead space. There is usually no "aliveness." There's a certain edge to their voices when they speak to each other or about each other. One or both might have nervous energy, looking around to find the other and anticipating a complaint or giving one, just to name the obvious few.

Out of the blue, my husband ran up to me and grabbed me from behind. I was surprised; he was supposed to be at the other field. He told the other ladies that he just wanted to stop by and give me a hug, but he whispered to me that he wanted to get a peek at what I was wearing underneath. I whispered in his ear that I couldn't wait for our "arrangement" that evening.

"You are like no other man I've had before," I told him, "and I have so many new tricks I'd like to try on you."

The other dads lingered nearby. My husband literally came and left within five minutes. He was starting to be known as a really attentive husband. I could see Sandy watching us; I could feel her yearning for something more, because when her husband came up beside her, she stiffened, looked away, and sighed.

When I got home, I immediately went to our bedroom to freshen up into my high-end whore clothing. I was planning on an afternoon delight. On the bathroom counter, I found five brand new $100 dollar bills. I smiled at first, then got mad pretty quickly. I had said $5,000 not $500. Many things went through my head. Was I not worth $5,000? He got the hairdresser a dog that cost $2,000, and what about the jewelry, and what about the things I didn't know about? I should have asked for twice that much! I started to think that I wasn't going to be able to pull off a sexy prostitute anyway. I equated the hairdresser with being a high-end prostitute who was just looking for a Sugar Daddy. Was my husband going to compare our sex moment to her? I began to get really insecure again.

Then I said to myself, "Fuck it. If he thinks I'm worth $500, then he's going to get a mediocre $500 unimpressive hand job." I might even start yawning while I'm doing it. I decided that $500 wasn't worth the beautiful lingerie that I had planned to put on. I was going to change into cotton grandma briefs, if I could find any.

I went into my closet and opened my lingerie drawer searching for a pair of ugly underwear that might have been saved from the massive elimination of all my rejects. I noticed that on the top of the dresser, there was another $500 in crisp, new bills for me. I laughed and realized that my husband was now toying with me.

I decided to put on the hot pink lace lingerie set as planned, plus a pink angora button down sweater, white hot pants, and high Jimmy Choo pink shoes. I stained my lips bubble gum pink. I stayed in the bathroom until I heard my husband come into the bedroom and get on the bed. I walked into the bedroom like a sexy streetwalker.

"Thank you for the deposit," I said, "but I don't take anything off until I have all my money and count it. And I don't ever kiss on the job."

He handed me an envelope with more cash in it. I took the envelop and opened it, then sat on the edge of the bed and counted out a total of $5,000 in cash, all brand new $100 dollar bills. I fell in love with him all over again. He was playing *with* me, not just responding to me.

I fanned the crisp new bills over my chest and let them fall between the mounds of my breasts. I had him take a picture before we started, telling him I did this with all my clients, just to keep track of them. Plus, I was still posting my mischief on the private chat room for my sister goddesses and wanted to prove that my husband was playing along so brilliantly. From the small goodie bag I held, I took out a bottle of edible massage oil that heated up when it was rubbed onto skin, and a black silk eye mask for him. I asked him to lay back on the bed, and I began to undress him slowly. I pulled off his shirt first, then ran my fingernails over his bare skin. I unzipped his pants, and used the bottom of the massage oil bottle to probe for a hard on. He wasn't hard enough yet. I pulled off his pants, and tossed them onto the floor. I looked over his body as if he were a rare and beautiful specimen.

I slowly unbuttoned my angora sweater. The demi cup lace bra I wore, lifted up my breasts to look round and perky. I pulled down the hot pants I was wearing and let them fall to the floor, which showed off the tiny little matching lace G-string. I allowed him to look at me as I started to stroke his sex, and then I used the mask to cover his eyes.

I described everything that I was doing to him as I did them. "I like spreading oil all over your beautiful body," I said, as I rubbed the oil over him. "Your nipples taste like vanilla," and I gave his right nipple a little bite. "I'm unclasping my bra now. I like the feel of my breasts over your skin," I continued as I rubbed my body up and down his. I continued to touch and talk sensuously. "I consider my work Sacred," I told him as I took his hand and guided his fingers to feel the heat and wetness between my legs. "I am your Sacred Whore."

I lovingly touched every part of his body with mine, as if I was healing all his wounds and asking for forgiveness for shutting down, for not trusting him from the beginning, for not giving him the benefit of the doubt. I used my body to heal my own wounds and I asked myself for forgiveness, and that made all the difference in the world. Taking full ownership, regardless of what it looked like, and forgiving myself was another key to letting go of the blame, and transmuting it into something else.

"I want to be your only client," he whispered as I began to stroke his hardness faster.

"That is such a tempting offer," I replied.

"How much for you to spend the night?" he asked.

"Tonight, I'll stay for free," I whispered back, and kissed him gently on the lips.

LESSON: Forgive yourself and claim your worth.

THE ALCHEMY OF THE LOVER

Being a whore for a day was an edge for me. I was paid money for sex, and it made me feel shame the morning after, even if it was pretend and with my husband. I wasn't positive if I felt shame for the money, or because I actually *enjoyed* the uninhibited sex and I willingly allowed my body to be of service. I was so trained to believe that pleasure, especially sexual pleasure, was a bad thing, and I could see how much my worth was directly tied to how uncomfortable I was with my sexuality.

As our sexuality is governed by our sacral chakra, so is money, so is shame. There is so much disdain around money and sex separately, that when we put them together, the shame is that much more intensified. Most people don't realize that they use sex as an exchange, whether money is involved or not.

The sacral chakra is also where our inner prostitute lives. We've all lied to ourselves, gave too much of ourselves away, held too much back, or ignored our truths for something fleeting, shiny, new, or safe. As my friend Maddy once said, "We're all prostitutes in one way or another."

This can show up as the lonely, desperate, single woman who disguises herself as a sex-loving hairdresser, who will give her body and her sex away to the poor married guy who thinks his wife is shut down – without even a second thought about the wife (me in this case) on the other side. What this type of woman is really doing with her body and her sex is trying to secure her certainty, her significance, her connection.

It can also show up in the lonely guy, disguised as an unhappily married man, who picks fights with his wife to validate his decision to have sex with another woman and who gives expensive gifts to the woman he's fucking so he feels good about using her for sex. What he's really doing is satisfying his need for variety, and also his need for significance, his need for connection, and his need for control.

It would be unfair of me to ignore the other part of this whole equation, the clueless wife who feels so disconnected with herself and with her partner, that she turns her back on her partner in anger, resentment, and insecurity. She withholds sex because it fulfills her need for control, while the self-pity fulfills her needs for significance. According to Tony Robbins, if I remember correctly, you only need two out of the four basic needs to be met (through positive or negative actions) for actions to become a powerful addiction.

I remembered having a cup of tea with one of my girlfriends, Carrie, who lives in Marin. Her teenaged daughter, Ellie shared with Carrie that her "friends" gave away blow jobs because they believed there was power in that act. She claimed that her "friends" were sexually "in charge."

"Do you believe that?" I asked Carrie.

"These girls have a different idea of sex; they seem to think they have the power," she replied. She added that she was just glad her daughter was sharing, and wanted to listen without judgment. I asked Carrie if she knew if her daughter masturbated, or knew if her daughter was aware of what *she* liked sexually. I completely ignored this "friend" charade.

Carrie shrieked, saying that her daughter was still a virgin, also ignoring the friend charade. I suggested to Carrie that a technical conversation about her lady parts was obviously way overdue. Carrie disagreed with me, saying that there was something romantic about two kids fumbling through their first time together, and that she didn't think the dry, technical talk was so necessary.

If you haven't figured it out by now, I can be a bit of a provocateur, so I questioned her even more. "So you think it's okay that the boy Ellie decides to sleep with someday is going to play with her, probe her, penetrate her even though she's never explored her own body?" I looked at Carrie and added, "And it's okay that she's never touched herself, or has a clue about what pleasure means to her, but it's cool if he gets to ejaculate inside her anyway? That's so romantic."

Carrie didn't answer me. We didn't talk for a year after that, so I guess I crossed the line. But this is how we end up with a strong inner prostitute, by not knowing and taking ownership of our bodies, or knowing what pleases us. I would know, I was in Ellie's shoes once too. Carrie was fulfilling her need for control and connection, her daughter was fulfilling her need for significance and connection. Where have you given away a part of yourself to fulfill these basic needs?

These thoughts were going through my mind the next day, because my husband decided to get up and go surfing early that morning. It was that very excuse (or taking his Ferrari for a spin,) that he used to leave early and visit the hairdresser during our weekend time. Did I have an eerie feeling about it back then? Yes, I did. I just ignored my intuition then, and it only enhanced the worthless feeling of my inner prostitute.

I wasn't triggered or wildly insecure, I just had a residual pang while I contemplated how my world kept twisting and turning into this interesting story that was my life. I was learning to flow along with it, instead of resist it. I was getting so much better at seeing my story in a detached way, which helped me learn more about what my karmic lessons were with my husband.

Karma in a relationship, by the way, is about the lessons we are trying to learn and overcome on the 3D level (this earth plane). From a higher standpoint, the challenges in our relationships encourage us to look deeper into our souls, to know ourselves better, and to awaken us to a higher truth. Some couples will be inspired to renew a commitment, to forgive a betrayal, or to leave if it no longer serves the relationship in the best way. I know with my entire soul that fear, betrayal, shame, self-worth, guilt, control, jealousy, patience, and trust are just a few of the lessons for me in this lifetime (darn it). If we know what we are supposed to learn, we can turn those lesson into gold.

I could never have an affair with a married man because I witnessed the excruciating pain my mother had to go through. I promised myself that I would never hurt another woman. I'd like to change Eleanor Roosevelt's quote from "There's a special place in hell for women who do not help other women," to "There's a special place in hell for women who betray other women." It suited my situation better. I know betrayal is one of my biggest karmic lessons to overcome in this lifetime. I'm supposed to turn it into gold, or bliss. That's how karma works, or we just have to keep repeating the lessons over and over again (no, thanks).

Our pains fuel love. Our pains are the source of power to get to the next level of overcoming. They are our karmic tests, to see if we are capable of loving anyway. When you transform that pain and use is toward love, you begin to see your life as a reflection of who you are on the inside. Your relationships become mirrors of you, projections of you. The key is to send love to everyone, knowing that they are just projecting the thing you need to work on. This is unconditional love. When you do that, you begin to clear the karmic lines, and you get to experience the gift on the other side.

I realized quickly that the personas that were coming through me were personas that represented the shadows that I needed to work on. I needed to take my shame and unworthiness and turn it into self-acceptance and worth. The path of the prostitute I found, is the alchemy of the lover.

LESSON: The prostitute becomes the lover; betrayal becomes bliss.

LIKE A VIRGIN

"Forgive me father for I have sinned" I sent a text. I was still feeling a little guilty and figured that I would embody just the opposite of the whore. I was going to redeem myself and become a virgin. The great thing about Catholic school is that they taught you how to pretend to be a good girl or a virgin, even if you weren't. I decided that I needed to confess my sins.

"Last night I acted like a prostitute, asked for and accepted money for sex. Forgive me father, for I liked it." I sent another text.

"Please tell me how I can be reborn in your eyes. I desire to confess live, on my knees to you ..." I sent a final text.

I pulled out a pair of white loose gauze pants that I reserve for the summer time, and a white flowy top. I had a plastic gold cross that I wore when I was the "Papa Don't Preach" version of Madonna for some dress up party with the other Madonna's. I called up my mom to borrow some rosary beads. When my mom brought over the rosary beads, I put a white tulle skirt on my head (yes, I owned a white tulle skirt), fell down to my knees with my hands in prayer position at my heart center, and asked her to take a picture. She said it reminded her of what I looked like when I had my first communion, when I walked up the aisle with my childhood friend Mark Gilkey.

Since my mother lived next door, I'd told her what I was doing when she first saw me in the cat ears. When I told her that this time I was confessing to being a prostitute yesterday, she said, "Ay! It's Lent, can't you pretend something else?"

"Too late, Mom. I've already started." I looked at her beneath the tulle skirt veil. "Maybe you should pray for me at church."

I took the boys and my mom to get bagels for breakfast, and while we were waiting I heard the ding of a text. It read, "My child, that is the gravest sin I have ever heard confessed.... You may be beyond saving ... Unless you are willing, to commit another sin to atone for the first." I burst out laughing.

My husband was putting his surfboard into the garage as we were pulling into my usual street parking space. He looked over at me and said, "You're supposed to be a Catholic virgin, but I can see your bra through that shirt."

"Shoot," I said, "do I have to add that to my list of sins?"

Being a good Catholic girl is not at all hard for me. I had no shame or guilt about the virgin. This was my comfort zone, and I knew it was why I was sexually blocked. This Madonna/Whore thing was unveiling great truths about me.

I took my husband into the bedroom, got on the floor and sat down on my knees, while he sat on the bed. I kept my head down in remorse and embarrassment. "Forgive me father for I have sinned," I started.

"Go on, my child," he played along.

"I was walking the streets last night and I found a man who would have sex with me," I confessed. "I ravished him and he gave me $5,000. I massaged him, and licked him, and gave him a hand job, and so much more I am too embarrassed to admit."

He whispered to me, "What do Catholic priests do after a confession?"

"Punishment," I whispered back. No one was in the room, but we both thought that whispering was better than breaking the spell of our game. "It's usually in the form of a thousand Lord's Prayers and another thousand Hail Mary's." I remember thinking that if the priest didn't give me a lot of prayers for my sins, then I didn't make up a good enough one.

THE MADONNA AND THE WHORE

That's what I resorted to doing when I was young, make up sins because I was supposed to be a sinner. "But you can just spank me?" I continued in a whisper.

"I cannot spank a virgin like you," he said, a little embarrassed. We were getting into different territory it seemed. "But I will think of a very good sin for you to commit to atone for your naughty sins. A sin for a sin, that is how it works in my church. Now, why don't you take off your clothes and say ten Hail Mary's."

I took off my clothes and said ten Hail Mary's as he watched me. I was impressed that I remembered the prayer. I suddenly felt a little bit guilty, too. Even though I had denounced the Catholic church, I still had reverence for prayer and something higher than myself.

"I want you to think about all the sins you want to commit and write them down for me," he added after I was done. "This way I will know before you sin again."

I loved that suggestion. It got me thinking about all my hidden fetishes and fantasies. We agreed that I would maintain my virginity with no touching at all that day or the next, not even a caress on the arm or the holding of hands.

All day I would walk really close to him. He would "tsk tsk" me. When I habitually reached for his arm, I'd catch myself and pull away just in time. He almost forgot and tried to give me a kiss, but stopped so close to my lips. The longer we didn't touch, the more I felt the energy between our skin. And the more we couldn't touch and almost touched, the more I wanted to touch him. It was interesting. This is a trick I would recommend to everyone.

LESSON: No touching is an erotic game that ignites passion.

THE RESURRECTION OF THE DIVINE MAN

The Madonna/Whore complex is a real thing for many men. It is the compartmentalization of women to perfection. The Madonna is the good girl next door who is the marrying type. She's the nurturing, compassionate, asexual, mother of his children. The Whore is the tainted, sexy, hot mess that all men want to fuck. She's the fantasy, not the marrying type. Obviously in my marriage, I was the Madonna, and the hairdresser the Whore.

According to Sigmund Freud, men with this complex have a hard time maintaining their sexual arousal in their committed, loving relationships because their wives are the women they see as pure and motherly. They often desire women who have been degraded, probably to feel like saviors, to satisfy a hidden raw part of their own sexuality, or to validate a sexual hierarchy (I am using my own theories here). "Where such men love they have no desire, and where they desire they cannot love," Sigmund Freud wrote. I think many men have a bit of the Madonna/Whore complex in them.

My husband was raised with high-society and country club rules. His mother did not like me at first. I was probably more Whore than Madonna to her, mostly because I did not have blonde hair, and I was from the other side of the tracks. When we got engaged she said to him, "What is this going to do to your career?" There was always a right way to do things and a wrong way to do things. Marrying me was the wrong way to do things.

Many mothers of high-achieving, white men either smother them to death or don't give them any affection at all, yet expect them to fulfill their dream of raising the best provider, father, husband. Sex isn't in their equation either. Many of our mothers hide their sexuality, so I get why sex and love are separated into two categories. The thing is, women are both sexual and loving. That is our truest nature.

When I started to really look into myself, I realized that underneath my virginal good girl persona, I did have a wild, sexy side. In college, I wasn't so Madonna like. I wasn't Whore like either, but I was sexual. It was the combination of kids, and perhaps my husband's subconscious thoughts that mothers can't be sexual that I started to close up more than I thought I could. I brought this idea up to him way after the project, and he agreed it might be true. In fact, I started to ask our male friends what they thought about this idea, and most had to admit that they couldn't see their wives as wanton sexual "whores."

The Virgin Mother Mary is the epitome of the nurturing, compassionate, and unconditionally loving woman. She, as we all know, is the mother of Jesus Christ, while Mary Magdalene was demoted to prostitute by the patriarchy. I happen to believe in the ancient Egyptian stories of Mother Mary, Magdalene, and Jesus being descendants of the Isis mystery schools, where they taught sex magic as a way toward enlightenment. That is why Jesus had such an incredible aura around him, because Magdalene and he practiced this magic together as lovers. I mean, come on, before Jesus Christ was Christ, he was a human. Together, it was both the loving aspects of Mother Mary and Mary Magdalene that helped Jesus Christ spread love, and resurrect from the dead.

I was once told during an Akashic Records reading that in this lifetime I had both Mother Mary and Mary Magdalene incarnate energy. I interpreted that reading to mean that I could be both a nurturing loving woman and a sexually loving woman, and I would be able to figure out how to share that. I also interpreted that reading to mean that I would someday help to resurrect the divine man. This inspired me to write a love letter to the sacred masculine:

Dear Sacred Masculine,

I want you. I really do.

I want to know and worship every ounce of your body, mind, and soul. Not all at once, but slowly, so I can savor every single morsel of you.

I don't want to claim your freedom, but I do want to unleash you toward a higher consciousness that pulls in desire and amplifies a cosmic kind of love.

If I must tempt you even further – yes, this type of love does include mind-blowing sex.

I long to know your power. The power that lies beyond aggression, competition and the diminishing of others; especially women.

It is the kind of power reserved for superheroes and gods; solid, enduring, capable, and otherworldly. This is a power of pure potential. It ignites and contains a chaotic and ever expanding Universe – a whole woman. When you use your power in this way, I will shower you with the appreciation and attention you deserve.

A feminist man is really sexy.

I want to hold and be held by the safety of your flesh, so that I may free my wild side from societal cages, surrender in tenderness, gyrate with creative life force, and show you what my erotic creature is greedy for.

I am a huntress of desire who equally wants to be hunted, a warrioress for truth who will show you the way, a seductress of sacred sexual connection who wants to love, make love, and fuck. I am a tornado, a soft breeze, a blazing fire, candlelight, *the depth of the ocean and a peaceful river. I am a shapeshifter that feels and emotes with the full 88 keys of a piano –* can you handle me? *I need you to be the sacred container that can, and then I'll blow your mind.*

The heat in my heart and in my groins only ignite in safety – you have no idea the power of the Divine Feminine allowed to reveal her true nature.

I wish to hear your fears and your deepest desires. I am both a nurturing Mother Mary who bleeds with unconditional love, and the shameless Mary Magdalene whose calling is to resurrect the Divine Masculine from the ashes of a dominating patriarchy through erotic love.

Surrender to me, so I can show you the proper way to dominate in love and love making.

I crave to be penetrated by your focused gaze. First through my eyes, then into my heart and soul. I want you to worship my entire body as she is, especially at the center of my sex, where the magic of all creation begins. Linger on me, tease me, tempt me, taste me, and now penetrate me with your body.

I want to love you in your naked truth – a grown man who journeyed within himself to heal the boy and find his heart, who has compassion for others, and continues to be devoted to his highest self.

No one can emasculate the Sacred Man.

It is the merging of the Divine Masculine with the Divine Feminine that will awaken this world to a new way of relating, and magnify the love that this earth so desperately needs right now. Will you melt into me with sacred love and ecstatic bliss to get there? I want you to.

With love, adoration, and so much desire for you,
The Sacred Feminine

I hope that my words resonate and you too have the need to be and feel everything. I really believe that the journey is to first understand and accept our many selves, including the Madonna and the Whore. We then need to excavate our shadow sides and learn to transmute the lower vibration emotions associated with them and turn the darkness into gold. Then we need to fall madly in love with every self in us. And that's when we can find our core, the place of infinite possibilities, the sacred, the divine. This whole process can lead us to know our soul's purpose, it can call in a lover, it can heal a marriage, and it may even help to resurrect the divine in all of us.

LESSON: We are divinely both Madonna and Whore with the power to resurrect the divine man.

11. Geishas and Mail Order Brides

ONLY ON CONDITION

What do you really, really, *really* want? How far will you go to know love?

Not many people think outside the box. We stay small, we stay safe, we stay within the walls of conditional love. Conditional love is what most of us practice, because that is all we know. We don't have the courage or the ability to let go of our subconscious fears of being alone, getting it right, or accepting that we have conditions in the first place. The journey to unconditional love is a long distance run, a spelunking expedition, a climb up Mt. Everest, and triathlon all rolled into one adventure, where we travel the nooks and crannies of our hearts and souls. It is through the testing, tasting, tempting, and exploring the truths of who we *really* are, and what we *really* want way deep down inside, that will finally get us to love, another and ourselves, unconditionally. So, will you get naked and personal to reveal the conditions you put on your relationships?

A lot of our married friends migrated out of the city and into the suburbs when they had children. They wanted the big lawns and the better schools, even if they would end up sending their kids to private schools anyway. I told my husband that I could never live in the suburbs again, thank goodness he felt the same. That was one condition we agreed upon.

Our married friends ended up moving to places like Palo Alto, Woodside, Menlo Park, and Atherton like many high-achieving, family-oriented couples do. The women quit their jobs and raised the kids, while the men became impressive investors, entrepreneurs, and consultants for the many successful Silicon Valley industries that were popping up everywhere. Life was good, and is still good for all of them. I just couldn't do it. I didn't feel like I belonged in that crowd, I felt like an outsider. There was no diversity, no African-Americans, few other minorities, no gay or lesbian couples, no one with purple hair or tattoos, no one with a flamboyant, artistic flair. And from what I gathered, everyone had similar childhoods. I was the anomaly, so like I said before, I shared none of my past.

Even my good friend Kirsten, who I met in college, didn't know *everything* about me. But, she intuitively warned me about moving down to the Peninsula anyway. She grew up in Atherton, and admitted it wasn't a normal place to grow up in. The first time she introduced me to her high school friends, it was at a party in someone's second mansion, just a town away from their primary mansion. It wasn't clear if the parents were divorced, or if it was just a second home for the heck of it. We were still in college then, so I was impressed by this huge, modern extra home on the hill. The host, a college kid himself, offered his guests matching terry cloth robes to use after hot tubbing. There was plenty to go around. Then we visited another one of her friend's home, which was a huge white house with white Venusian columns, white rugs, a white marble staircase, and pristine white furniture. I could image Filipino maids in uniforms in the other room. The best part of this scenario were the two West Highland white terrier puppies that ran throughout the house with diapers on. It was a wealth bubble of epic proportions.

When Silicon Valley started to really boom, that entire area started to morph into its own category of people, the Atherton-Americans. They were über wealthy, über educated, über innovative, über scheduled, and über traditional in many ways. This new breed of Atherton-Americans were our friends, and subconsciously I didn't think I could keep up.

I grew up on the other side of the tracks, in a development of homes where every fifth house was internally laid out, and externally painted, in the same exact way. The walls were thin; the carpets were cheap. My parents had custom-made plastic covers for the couches, and used plastic runners on the floors, even though we had to follow strict rules that did not allow us to be messy. My dad gambled, slept on the couch with lit cigarettes in his mouth, and had another family on the side, while my mother worked two jobs. Living in the suburbs for me was like ground hog day; the same type of houses, the same routine, the same dysfunction, the same trapped feelings. I wanted out. My future would not include arrogance, violence, a smoker, a gambler, a cheater, or someone who did not want to be accomplished.

My husband grew up in Monterey, off the famous twenty-eight-mile drive. Although his family wasn't rich either, the community he lived in seemed more civilized than mine. Most of his family's friends were traditional couples. The men were the bread winners with respectable professions such as doctors, scientists, or owners of lumber companies. The women, were homemakers. They played tennis at the country club, walked their dogs along the pristine beaches, and went to the Episcopalian Church on Sundays. His mother praised success and high society. There was plenty of sameness in that community too, the same pleasantly formal people, the same social interests, the same polite conversations. And like many white, educated men, my husband was privileged with the same opportunities; the best schools, lucrative jobs, and women who took care of themselves. I'm sure he wanted to maintain that level of civility or reach higher. To me, his future would not include someone who couldn't fit in, who wasn't educated, who wasn't attractive, who wasn't interesting, nor would his future include someone who would rock the boat too much.

Wealth, a healthy family, and world travel is a dream come true for many. Believe me, I am so grateful to have been plucked out of the "trailer park" into the world of opportunities … *and* I still believed there was more to love and life than the material world that riches had to offer. I am so grateful that my husband was bold enough to look over my dysfunctional past and take a risk with me anyway. And I'm so grateful that my insecurities and rigid boundaries did not fully sabotage my choice to step into a world I never knew existed.

As spoiled as this sounds, I still had that empty feeling that there must be more to life than houses, family vacations, good wine, and shallow conversation. I knew that I wasn't going to be happy with only material success, but I certainly never wanted to go back to the tacky façade of my upbringing. My desire to merge the material and the spiritual was a champagne problem, and one many soul seekers in search for purpose beyond her family or job have, no matter where we are on the ladder of "success."

Before I could figure out what I really, really, *really* wanted on a soul level. I needed to reconcile the shallow part of me that feared scarcity and needed material safety, with the compassionate part of me who loved the underdog, rooted for them, and wanted them to know that their circumstances did not matter, only their hearts and souls did. I needed to accept that I was still living and acting in a world where we did have requirements. Have you ever said "only on condition" to anyone?

If the answer is yes, then congratulations; you've done the first step to really knowing unconditional love, which is admitting to that human part of you. Thinking about "conditions" is how I came up with the next icon.

LESSON: Admit to the conditions that keep you from
unconditionally loving.

LOVE BY MAIL

My husband and I weren't going to see much of each other until late in the evening, but I could still role play as different women without actually seeing him. I was thinking about the most obvious "conditional" love there could be, and mail order bride popped into my head. That is what I would do, have him choose a mail order bride. This might give me more insight into what his conditions were, and my own.

I googled "Mail Order Bride" and found out that it was a real thing, not an urban myth. It depressed me. The sites are full of seriously beautiful international women from Russia, the Ukraine, Asia and Latin countries. I noted how many beautiful people there are in the world, and noted how desperate the situations must be in their countries to be bold enough to jump into a marriage with a stranger in this way. I wasn't convinced that these sites weren't controlled by gross men who were really sex traffickers exploiting innocent women, and taking advantage of lonely men. One site even warned customers that it was not their fault if other members tried to harm them in some way. It sounded suspiciously like Russian mobster to me.

"Dear Sir, I received your Mail Order Bride Application, but need more details on your preferred dream bride so we can be sure to find you a perfect match." I pressed send on my text to my husband. By now, he was playing along, and that required him to put the puzzle pieces together himself.

"A Petite Brunette please," he didn't skip a beat. I thought it was cute that he would describe me as the perfect mail order bride. I hoped he wasn't focusing on not trying to trigger me into jealousy. He had gotten overly sensitive in that department. I was never a jealous person, but after his affair, I scrutinized all the ways he looked at or flirted with other women. Even though I was fine, he kept up his vigilance.

"We only have blondes, sir."

"Do you have any brunettes that wear blonde wigs?"

"We will see what we can find you."

In between clients and mom duty, I created two profiles: Sybil and Fantasia. I used broken English to describe my husband's dream bride choices and they were filled with many inside jokes. I sent him a description of Sybil along with a photograph of me in a long, curly blond wig, and a description of Fantasia in a short, blond wig with bangs. I was kissing a chess piece.

Sybil, 5'4" – 32DD – 104lbs:

Hello, my name is Sybil. Although my name may suggest I have multiple personality disorder, I assure you that is not true. I am a brunette who likes to be blond sometimes. I speak seven languages, but none very well. I can give you relief when you are stressed out. I have many, many talents. I was a former ballerina and would like to be U.N. Ambassador. I am very clever. I would never, ever come to your country only to desert you later.

Fantasia 5'4" – 32DD – 104lbs:

Greetings man from states. I am Fantasia. I do not come from states. I speak seven languages of love. I am looking blond, but I am brown haired. I am excellent chess player. I am excellent crossword puzzle maker. I love to cook only the French food. I have written many songs for the artist formally known as Prince. We do not speak any longer. I never lie. I come to you because you are famous in my country, and I know I make you happy.

After he received his choices, we had a couple of phone calls so he could "interview" these candidates. On the call I sounded like I had a mixture of a Russian/Spanglish/Pigeon accent.

"What kind of relief I give after stressful day?" I asked as Sybil. "I am good at rubbing on the body ... you know what I mean, sir?"

"No. Please tell me more," he fired back.

"Voulez-vous coucher avec moi," I mimicked the only French I knew, lyrics from the song Lady Marmalade that was featured in the movie *Moulin Rouge*. "You like my French?"

Then I said in my regular voice, "Sorry sir, your time is up." And I hung up on him. I called him right back though, introducing Fantasia.

"Hello man from states, you are so famous in my country. I know I will make you very happy ending ... you understand what I mean?"

He laughed and repeated, "No. Please tell me more."

"It is very top secret, only Prince knows what I am talking about, but we're no longer on speaking terms. I never lie, you can trust that you will be very, very happy."

"Sorry to interrupt," I said again in my regular voice, "but your time is up and you will have to choose among the two candidates. Please look over their profiles and text me your choice when you are ready."

He chose Fantasia.

I wasn't planning on dressing up as his potential bride, because Fantasia technically would still be in Russia, or the Ukraine. I figured since we weren't going to see each other until later that night, this day's persona was just going to be about the profiles. When I got home after dinner with some friends, he was already in bed. I whispered in his ears, "Your dream bride will come to you soon, and you will be the happiest man on the planet."

When I got up the next morning, I saw written in pink lipstick, "Fantasia, lunch?" on my bathroom mirror. He added his number just to let me know he was serious. Fantasia became the next icon.

We agreed to meet downtown for lunch at Ozumo's, an upscale Japanese restaurant frequented by the financial crowd. I don't know if my husband thought I would actually go downtown looking like a mail order bride, but I did alert him through a text that, "I might be late because I am arriving from out of the country. I will not be in fancy clothes. Maybe you have time to buy me something fancy?"

I put on the short, blonde wig with bangs. I was instantly transformed. I wore tight jeans, high heels and a tight purple wrap-around sweater, something I used for the S-Factor dance classes I was now obsessed with. In fact, my girlfriends in my class got to witness me as a blond, because that's where I was just before I went to lunch. I also carried a big hand bag and wore big sunglasses. I looked like a call girl. When I got to the restaurant, the receptionist looked me up and down suspiciously.

"Table for two," I said when I realized that I got there before my husband. I was quickly directed to a table in the back. I could feel everybody's eyes on me as I followed the receptionist, my heels clicking loudly on the wood floors, to my seat.

"I do not understand a place that does not cook the fish." I texted my husband as I waited for him. I imagined that a woman who would choose to be a mail order bride would have never had the opportunity to eat expensive sushi.

When he finally arrived at the table, I held out my hand to shake his and said, "Hello, I am Fantasia." To the crowd, it must have looked like we were members of one of those dating websites for Sugar Daddies and Sugar Babies (rich men and hot gold diggers) on our first date.

We talked about his busy day, and I reminded him that I was very clever and great at giving relief. In between "real" conversation, we discussed meeting at home after work so I, as Fantasia, would know for sure if I wanted to marry him. "I must inspect you thoroughly," I told him.

Later, I waited at home in my Fantasia wig. The kids were out having hamburgers with our neighborhood friends and their kids. We had a quick dinner together before he pulled out his computer to finish up some work. I went into our bedroom to tidy up, when I noticed the rejected wig I left on the bathroom counter. I decided to change hair styles.

I went out the garage door in the long, blonde wavy wig that turned me into Sybil. It was cool outside, so I quickly made my way to the front door and rang the bell. My husband answered the door with a confused look on his face. He seemed a little freaked out to see me in the long curly wig instead. "Where is my twin sister Fantasia?" I demanded.

LESSON: We choose who to love and how to love, and should choose love every day.

DOUBLE TROUBLE

We lost touch with the Millers, a couple we met before we got married, after they moved out of the city to have kids. Spring wasn't exactly a Mail Order Bride, but was from a Mormon family who married outside the religion, which was a really big deal. It's hard to say if they were truly in love or not. Jason was a handsome, successful man who was shorter than the average guy, while Spring was a tall, young, pretty blonde, who was trained to get married. Jason bought Spring all the right things, sent her to cooking classes, and had her get a bachelor's degree. She worked out three hours a day, and did not apologize for herself. I really liked her.

Spring once told me a story about Jason and one of his colleagues. They were all at a conference together in someplace like Colorado. Jason's colleague offered to drive Spring and Jason back to where they were staying. I guess the two men were always competitive with each other, and the colleague would tease Jason about finding someone "over his pay grade." Jason and Spring took the back seat of the car. Spring told me that Jason asked her to pull up her skirt and sit on his lap so they could have sex while his colleague was driving, and as they talked to his friend through the rear view mirror. It was Jason's way of winning that moment's competition. Spring had no problem with it; she was on wife duty and was happy to help her husband "one up" his competitor. I called on the spirit of Spring to help me embody an unabashedly sex-devoted Sybil.

My husband looked at me with my long waving hair and said, "Sybil?" Then under his breath he whispered, "Uh oh." He obviously didn't like this look, I wondered if it reminded him of the crazy lady who cooks the family bunny rabbit in *Fatal Attraction*.

I said in my really bad attempt at an Eastern European accent, "I love my sister I must be here with her ... and maybe you, too." I barged in the house looking for Fantasia and walked back down the stairs to our bedroom. He went back to his work while I decided to put on Fantasia's wig again. So when I walked into the kitchen in Fantasia's wig, he looked up and was relieved. I told him that Sybil was downstairs resting. Then I gave him a sexy plead, "Could she please stay with us? We can make you very, very happy." This would be my first pseudo-threesome.

Throughout the night, I would switch wigs when my husband was not watching, just for fun. When the kids got home, I asked them to tell me which wig they liked best. The benefit of being known for loving Halloween is no one thinks it is strange to try on wigs for no reason.

I remembered a time when my former roommate Rob had just moved to New York, and my husband and I were there for a wedding that I was invited to attend at the last minute. The bride and groom insisted that only engaged couples were allowed to participate because their guest list was well into the three hundreds. At the last minute, the bride invited me because she heard that we got two cats together. "That's almost like being engaged," she told me on the phone when she formally invited me to go. We met Rob at a bar somewhere in the East Village. I loved going to New York, I didn't drink that much, I didn't need to. I was fully entertained by watching people, and I was doing just that when this middle-aged couple came up to me and started a conversation. They looked like they could have been from Walnut Creek, California, a conservative suburb about twenty-five miles east of San Francisco.

"Are you here with anyone?" A tall Asian woman with sleek short black hair asked me. She was wearing all black; a simple black sweater and black slacks. Her husband or boyfriend, I wasn't sure which, was standing right next to her in all black too; a black mock turtleneck and black jeans. He was in his late forties it seemed, because I could see grey hairs trying to dominate his blond. I was taken aback by how nice these New Yorkers were to me, I expected the aloofness that I was used to.

"Yes, I'm here with those two guys over there." I didn't bother to tell them which was my boyfriend, it was way too loud for that.

"We live just around the corner, in a really nice apartment" she told me, "Where are you from?"

"San Francisco," I answered. They both smiled at me.

"You look like someone who is into it," they said.

"Into what?" I replied smiling. They spoke in a code that I couldn't quite figure out.

"You know," the man paused, "into *it.*" He emphasized "it."

"Sure," I said, "I'm into just about everything." And I was into everything at that moment. Life was exciting for me, a new boyfriend, a new job, me visiting my friend in New York, and me suddenly getting an invitation to a beautiful wedding in The Golden Triangle of Greenwich, Connecticut.

"We can go back to our apartment if you want?" The woman offered. I was getting the impression that she thought my two guy friends might be more comfortable in their apartment. How nice of her, they knew I was from San Francisco, and those two guys were my friends. For all they knew, they were a gay couple, and this bar felt really "straight."

Rob came up and sat next to me at that point. I asked him if we should go back to their apartment. "Why?" Rob asked in a whisper.

"I don't know why, they just asked us. And apparently they have a great apartment."

Rob was my adventurous friend. I met him through my last college boyfriend. Rob was doing the walk of shame one early morning, and was wearing sweat pants and a blazer. We told him to get into the car and we'd take him home, but we needed to stop for breakfast first. The morning turned into apartment hunting, as Rob and I were both looking for an apartment to live in. That's when we found Daisy's Place. We didn't have the extra two roommates we needed, and we had no furniture but one king sized bed that we ended up sharing platonically for two weeks. We were so poor right after we rented that apartment, that on Saturdays, we would go to the local coffee shop with sixty-seven cents between us, and could only order a side of cheese. That's how we became friends.

"They aren't asking us to go," Rob explained to me, "they are asking *you* to go."

"What do you mean?" I said. "They seem so nice, they wouldn't be so rude and only invite me."

"Yes they would," Rob said. Rob whispered into my future husband's ears and I saw him perk up and get a little protective. They were overacting I thought.

He turned to all of us, including the couple, and said out loud, "I think it's time to get going. Let's go back now."

I turned to the nice couple and told them it was nice to meet them, and maybe next time the stars would align. They each gave me a little too long hug goodbye.

In the cab home, Rob explained that the couple were swingers and they wanted me to have a threesome with them. That image did not compute. I was so naïve; the couple looked so conservative to me. "Do I look like a swinger?" I said to myself. Apparently I do. That was the closest I had ever got to having a threesome, and here I was potentially fulfilling that premonition with Sybil and Fantasia and my husband.

At bedtime, I asked him to close his eyes as I whispered in his right ear how much I loved him. Then I whispered in his left ear how I loved being his bride's sister. I would let him open his eyes only when

I changed wigs and sides. We ended up getting confused which blond I was and couldn't stop laughing with each other.

The mail order bride to Fantasia to the threesome was the most fun we had in a very long time. I believe this silliness made us set down all our weapons to experience more joy and bliss together. The laughter made me feel safer in my body so that I could open up more too.

LESSON: Silly brings us closer, and can be sexy too.

TEA CEREMONY

During my thirty-day challenge, my icons were inspired by emotions, cliché sex symbols, and issues I wanted to overcome. They also came from memories of when my husband and I first met. Shortly after we started dating, and before I officially moved in, I wanted to do something special, but inexpensive for his birthday. It would be our first celebration together. I was telling my cubical neighbor at the advertising agency I worked at, that I had plans to get Japanese food and dress up like a geisha and do a tea ceremony for him. I was inspired by a scene in the original *Karate Kid*. Caitlin told me that she lived in Japan for a year and learned how to do the tea ceremony from a real tea master. She offered to teach it to me over lunch. As I reflect back, it seems like there was always an invisible hand helping me to prepare for this love project of mine.

The Japanese tea ceremony, or Chanoyu, is considered a revered artistic and spiritual discipline. The ceremony is a sensual display of grace and aesthetics. It is beautiful to watch, and feels good to express gratitude in this way. Every posture and movement, from preparation to cleaning the utensils to serving the tea, is a gesture from the heart in honor of the guest. It is an act of unconditional service. I didn't have all the traditional instruments, nor did I remember exactly what to do, but I did keep in mind that I wanted to give, without any expectations in return.

That night, I asked my new boyfriend to have a fire going by the time I got to his apartment. He didn't know what I had planned, just that I was taking care of dinner. I put white powder on my face, styled my hair into a bun on the top of my head, and wore a silk robe that I covered up in a parka so I could pick up sushi from a nearby restaurant without offending anyone.

When I got to his apartment, I asked him not to enter the living room where I was preparing for the ceremony. He didn't question my pale face, or the wardrobe fail. I lit some candles and put down a soft blanket near the fireplace. I placed the tea utensils and sushi in a beautiful arrangement on the blanket. When I was done, I asked him to come and sit in silence on a pillow, while I went into the kitchen to make a kettle of matcha tea, remove my parka, and take off my shoes.

I entered the living room in silent slow motion, carefully attending to the tea kettle of hot matcha. I moved soundlessly and gracefully over to my side of the blanket, and set the tea kettle over to my left. I knelt down on my pillow and gave him a low devotional bow. He asked a question that I ignored, quietly telling him that words were unnecessary.

In meditative silence, I grabbed a red cloth napkin from the right side of the display, and began to purify his tea cup with three exquisite caresses around the rim of the bowl. Then I dipped the napkin inside the bowl sweeping its center three additional times, before setting it down in front of him. I did the same for my cup.

With focused attention and slow movements, I picked up the silver spoon lying beside the tea kettle and gracefully stroked it three times from its end to its tip, and put it back down again. I then picked up the tea kettle and used the red napkin to christen its spout three times as well.

I set the napkin down for the final time and gently poured tea into his cup and then used the silver spoon to stir the contents of his tea three leisurely times to the right. He went to pick it up, but I stopped all movement and looked at him without breathing. In the stillness, he understood that he was not yet to enjoy his tea. I poured the matcha into my bowl as well and stirred.

When the ritual preparation was complete, I picked up his bowl of tea and turned it three times in my palm then handed it to him. I picked up my tea cup and turned it three times in my palm, raised it to my brow before lowering it to my lips. I looked him in the eyes, and in unison, we both took a sip of tea. We sat in quiet peace for a long time, drinking our tea, enjoying the crackling sounds and beautiful glow from the fireplace.

After I was done with my tea, I set it down and bowed toward him again. When I pulled myself up to sitting position, I was blushing. We had only been dating three months, and all of a sudden I worried if I had done too much too soon. But he loved it. We ate our sushi and made love by the warmth of the fire afterward. This memory came in handy for my next icon.

LESSON: Serving with ritual, beauty, and reverence is an act of unconditional love.

VIBRATING IN THE VORTEX

For the record, I'm not into polyamory, and I think a threesome can fall into the polyamory category. Polyamory is the state of being in a romantic relationship with more than one person. It is different than an affair because everyone involved in a polyamorous relationship are transparent about how many partners they have, and how many they are sleeping with. All participants consent to the arrangement, however it's laid out.

The first time I even heard about the term polyamory was at The School of Womanly Arts. Many of the women in the program had freed their sexuality to a point where they wanted to share themselves openly with others. I felt so old school and prude when I met all these women who were so open in their relationships. There was a point when I thought polyamory was the way we were all supposed to intimately relate to each other. It was the reason why people cheat, I told myself. I was so obsessed with the polyamory concept, and wondered why it didn't work for me, that I initially called my project *The Polyamor-me Project*. I thought I was so clever to have created such an exciting love affair that had a polyamorous feel, yet took place in a monogamous reality. But Polyamor-me is a tongue twister, and people started to think I was doing a polyamory project, so I was in search of a new name.

Among the many poly women, I met Lauren, who had a primary boyfriend and lovers on the side. Lovers sounded like such a better word than husband, so that's when I started calling my husband my lover. It made me feel more free of the conditions of marriage. I highly recommend you start calling your husbands or long term partners, lovers right this very second. Send them a text right now saying, "Hi, lover." (Sorry for the digression.)

Lauren was a voluptuous and sexy woman, with long curly blond hair. She is an incredible sexual healer, helping men and women heal from sexual wounds. She was the nicest thing on the planet. If she was polyamorous, I thought, lots of lovers couldn't be a bad thing. Many of the poly people I've met assured me that it is a good thing. But, no matter how much I tried to open up, I just couldn't wrap my head or my heart or my sex around polyamory for *me*. Maybe it's too complicated for me, or I'm too lazy, or I have too many conditions, or I like going way deep with just one. Who knows, but what I *do* know is there are pros and cons to both ways of loving. Even Lauren told me she still feels jealousy, regardless of her choice to participate in a polyamorous lifestyle.

What I have also come to know, is that there is no such thing as unconditional love in a conditional world, that is why it is important to recognize the naked truth of our conditions. We are all looking for the perfect situation, the perfect relationship, the perfect person, the perfect love story. By default, this mean we all have conditions that we want met from our "perfect" anything. The great news is we don't need to feel guilty for having conditions, because our conditions are simply reflections of how we, according to Abraham Hick's and the *Law of Attraction*, are vibrating in our own vortexes.

If you don't already know about the *Law of Attraction* and Abraham Hicks, let me give you a brief introduction. Abraham is "infinite intelligence" from the energetic realm, who teaches the simple cosmic *Law of Attraction*, which uses positive thoughts to manifest anything we desire. Abraham has been channeled for about thirty years now by a woman named Esther Hicks. The key to the *Law of Attraction*, is getting into vibrational match with what we desire.

The problem is, we don't really know how to match our vibrations with our intentions. If it was so easy, we'd all have amazing bodies, the loves of our lives, abundance, and world peace by now. Getting into the vibration of love to call in the love we want means we've got to be in love with love. The only way to be *in love,* is to *be* love. The way to becoming love is, you've guessed it by now, to love all aspects of yourself: your victim, your prostitute, your innocence, your rage, your primal sexual body, your beauty, your power, and your conditions. Stepping into these sexy personas, and making them work for you, helps in getting to the blissful feelings that are vibrating in the vortex ... just saying.

When we start to vibrate at a higher level, we no longer have conditions, we simply become deserving of our desires and start acting as if we are sexy, or enough, or unbetrayable. We don't expect anything from our loved ones and they are free to match your vibration, or you call in those that do match your vibration. Your world begins to lose all conditions, and you are free to love unconditionally. The more you feel love, the more you become love, and the more love you have to give away, you end up experiencing this blissed-out, ecstatic flow of love energy that keeps gaining more and more momentum. We all have that love vibration memory seed embedded in our cells someplace, all you have to do is call on it and let it land in your heart.

LESSON: Step into your love personas, and you step into the vortex of your desires.

MEMOIRS OF A GEISHA

My husband was a trooper, I really had to admire him for playing full out with me, and I really wanted to appreciate him for his willingness to keep it going. I don't know if I've emphasized this enough, but he comes from an unemotional, traditional, draw-inside-the-lines breed of characters, and he worked in a conservative industry with friends who wouldn't get it. During this crazy thirty-day project, we were getting along better than ever, and we were rekindling a deeper intimacy than we had ever known.

The very first time I ever dressed up and played a different persona, was when I gave him the tea ceremony for his birthday. It was a fond memory that brought love and joy into my heart. I thought I'd recreate that moment, as time and family would allow, and honor him as I did so many years ago, but this time as a sexier Geisha.

I took my time getting ready that morning, and remembered what my Japanese design teachers, Ms. K (short for Kubukawa) and Shizuko, taught me; the process of creation was just as beautiful and important to the end result in the Japanese culture. I incorporated precision and beauty in everything I did that day, and I slowed way down.

I put on a purple silk Kimono, the one I had used for a client's photoshoot, and put my hair up into a bun on the top of my head. I took a few flower buds from the orchid plants we had around the house and decorated my hair with them. I once again patted my face with white baby powder. I practiced being the demure, yet slyly coy Geisha who knows of art, music and culture. I remembered the scene in *Memoirs of a Geisha* where Sayuri Nitta, the grey-eyed premier geisha was learning how to stop a man in his tracks with a single look. I tried the look in the mirror.

When my husband got home, I greeted him at the door like the most highly respected geisha would. I became the illusion of the unattainable, perfect woman who holds the key to a mysterious world of delights. I made him feel like he was the most honored of men. I walked through the house like a moving piece of artwork. He was mesmerized, so were my kids, and so was my mom who came over unexpectedly. We sat down to take-out sushi together, my husband in a button downed work shirt and slacks, my kids in their dirty school clothes, and my mom in casual jeans and her leopard print slippers. Then there was me, in full geisha regalia.

I only completed a mini version of the tea ceremony because we kept getting interrupted by the kids knocking on our bedroom door. My mom was still there, and should have been able to entertain them. But they probably wondered if my Japanese outfit meant the Samurai swords that were once on display, were going to resurface again. I had decided to hide them because of my kids' barbaric attacks on Bob. They weren't allowed to play with them in that way, but I didn't trust that they wouldn't accidentally behead each other if they were tempted to annihilate Bob tsujigiri-style, even if the blades were effectively dull. I made my kids go to bed and went back to tend to my husband and our tea ceremony.

After the tea ceremony, I drew him a bubble bath with essential oils that would relax his natural fiery nature, a concoction I learned from the Chopra Center, and sponged him clean. After the bath, I offered him a shiatsu-ish massage and then fed him delicacies of chocolate and strawberries. I made up an elaborate story of how I was cast out of one geisha house because of a jealous rivalry, and was never deflowered by a patron. I told him that although there were many gentlemen who wanted to deflower me, I was saving myself for him.

I allowed my Kimono to slip from my shoulders to reveal my color-coordinated bra. I feigned more shyness, and refused to let him touch me. I let my kimono fall open even further, every time I made a refusal. We ended the evening like we did those many years ago, with soft sweet lovemaking. I didn't say it to him at that moment, as I thought it would change the tone of the evening, but every touch and gesture was filled with gratitude for him sticking in there with me, and forgiveness for all the things I had blamed him for in the past. I mentally took the memory of being betrayed and replaced it with the memory our first tea ceremony, our first motorcycle ride, the birth of our children, our wedding day. So many other insignificant but fond memories poured into my mind then too. I told myself that the betrayal wasn't the end of the story, my story was still being written. A little tear filled up my eyes.

"Is there anything wrong?" he asked.

"No," I said gently and squeezed him a little harder, "I'm just so grateful."

LESSON: Our stories always have good endings; we just need to catch up with them.

12. The Dominatrix

MOTHER OF DRAGONS

There is a reason we all love Khaleesi, the Mother of Dragons. Hers is a story that is being acted out in the collective today. A demure woman at first, Daenerys in the *Game of Thrones*, is treated as a second-class citizen by her brother, both remnants of the exiled House Targaryen. She barely speaks, and attends to her brother's every whim, including being betrothed to a warlord in exchange for an army.

Slowly, she begins to transform. No one sees her innate power, and she is too often dismissed by men who rule. Daenerys becomes Khaleesi, the Mother of Dragons, the queen of powerful armies, the Unburnt, Breaker of Chains, and the one who walks away naked and unscathed from a blaze of her own creation that slaughters alive the very men who threatened her life with hideous violence. She becomes the icon of female dominance.

We are in the Age of Aquarius my dear sisters, the age of the feminine. It is time for us to know what we are made of, so let's tap into our female power.

During my thirty-day project, a friend of mine who led the communications department at Google, invited me to see the HBO Premier of *Game of Thrones*, a full red-carpet affair with all the actors and the author, George R. R. Martin, present. My friend's partner couldn't make it, so I was replacement date. HBO chose San Francisco for the premier to simultaneously promote their new internet channel, HBO Now, that would feature the season's first *Game of Thrones* broadcast. It was a big deal in San Francisco.

I ran around the city searching for the signature blond, long hair with braids wig that copied Khaleesi's hairstyle that season. It was hard to find, I supposed the Mother of Dragons might have been the most popular costume that past Halloween. I finally decided to buy a regular long, blond wig and braid the temples myself. My Sybil wig was not blond enough, had too many layers, and made me look more like the seventies actress Farrah Faucet. I wanted to authentically honor the badass character that was my new idol.

I wore an off-the-shoulder, full-length dress and carried around two dragon figurines by Safari Ltd., that I borrowed from my sons' toy box. This was one of the times I was glad not to toss all their, now unused, little animal toys. My kids were obsessed with dragons, dinosaurs, and animals of all kinds. It was embarrassing how many of these figurines I bought them. When my boys were small, they would line up magical creatures alongside domestic beasts in a puzzling arrangement all over the house. If our dog, Boomer, stole one to chew on, all hell would break loose. I took the two largest ones that didn't have our dog's teeth marks on them. I tried to sew one of the dragons onto my shoulder, but it wasn't working, so I kept it in my palm, and the other I stashed away in my purse to pull out whenever there was a flat surface for it to stand on.

My friend didn't have time to dress up as he was coming straight from work. We planned to meet on the corner of Van Ness and Grove so we could walk over to the War Memorial House together. I was lucky we found each other; the streets were packed. We stood in line and waited for the red carpet guests to arrive, and I noticed (like always) that I was the only one dressed up in costume.

In line for the premiere, I felt the same lonely "I'm the only dress up nut" sensation in my gut. There was a reporter a few yards away who caught sight of me and started taking pictures. Then die-hard fans started thanking me for playing full out, telling their friends to come see. One woman said she wanted to be me. I'm guessing she wanted some of my boldness, not my wig. I was hoping the higher ups would notice and escort us to the front of the line and up the red carpet. My kids even appreciated this icon, who wouldn't?

Inside the theater, we got to watch all our favorite actors and the author take seats in the orchestra area, and then my eye caught another Daenerys. This very tall, beautiful specimen came over to say hello. He did not look good as a woman, but it was clear he had practiced dressing as a woman many times before. He said he was jealous that I had a dragon. I teased him about the importance of owning a dragon, even if he was just the *other* Mother of Dragons. He nodded sadly. That's when I pulled out the second dragon from my purse and handed it to him. "Here, take care of this," I instructed him, "he's yours to train now." My twin Khaleesi jumped back in excitement, and gave me a hug before he found his seat a couple of rows back.

I sent my husband a text, "Moon of my life, my sun and stars..."

"I love ALL of you," he texted back, which was in response to all my personas that he was privileged to get to know.

When Tyrion Lannister walked in, everyone cheered for him. He looked over and gave me a wink, I brag. The transformation of Daenerys was like my transformation from being a self-conscious, wounded, betrayed woman to someone who had to fight her own demons, burn the old stories, and learn to ride the dragons of my own psyche. I was a ruler in the making. I found redemption, and the power to shape my failing relationship with my husband into a mighty kingdom worth fighting for.

LESSON: Never underestimate the power of dressing the part.

POWER DYNAMICS

The distinct imbalances of influence, authority, leadership, clout, privilege and money are directly associated with the shadow side of power. Dominance, oppression, and manipulation are the bells and whistles that distract us from the curtain of false power that hides the tiny, little nervous person behind it. That tiny little person is a wizard at self-sabotage, simply disguising fear and insecurity. You can let fear have you, or you can have it.

Real power is never *over* someone; it can never be taken away, and is always sourced from within. Real power is knowing your strengths and weaknesses. Real power is truth, authenticity, humility, and grace. Real power is never giving up and choosing to finish that marathon, even if you have to stumble and crawl across the finish line. Real power is feeling the pain, moving through it to the other side, and finding the pleasure in it.

The reason we have a hard time stepping into our power, is the idea that power comes from the dark side, ruled by the Darth Vader, Lord Voldemort, and Lucifer types. The truth is, power does come from the shadow side, and can only transform into gold if you know how to master it and ride it like a dragon. If you allow fear to have power over you, that is when it allows the devil inside to rise. Shadow simply means the repressed and hidden feelings, thoughts, and urges that are living breathing realities within us. It is the repression, refusal or resistance that creates the shadow over the repressed thought, fantasy, need, or desire. Darth Vader feared the loss of those closest to him, Lord Voldemort feared death, Lucifer feared his own God-like qualities. To ignore our shadow is self-punishment, and that is what creates the demons, or projections, of our deepest fears.

Sex, as you know by now, is one of humanity's greatest shadows. Although every species engages in some sort of sex to reproduce, there is still so much guilt in it. "Sex is natural, sex is fun, sex is best when it's one on one," sings the late George Michael, so why do we still make such a big deal out of it, get hurt by it, write books about it? Why do we unconsciously wear chastity belts of right and wrong, and prefer our virgins over our whores, our angels over our devils? Adding pleasure to the mix creates an even bigger shadow. We've been trained to suffer, not to feel orgasmic. That's why the things that smell, taste, look, hear, and feel good to us are called "guilty" pleasures. If everyone just admitted that their bodies were meant for pleasure, sex would be welcomed as a tool for connecting, healing, and spiritual awakening, which might lead to the end of militant organized religions. When we add power to this sex and pleasure equation, uh oh, we enter taboo territory. Here come the nooses, the torches, and the stones.

In ancient matriarchal cultures, a woman's sexuality was her power *and* her pleasure. Anne O. Nomis, an art historian, authoress, and revered Dominatrix living in Australia, teaches that sex rituals resembling the tools and practices in today's B.D.S.M. communities, date back thousands of years to the Goddess Inanna. In fact, all the literature on ancient Goddess Religions explore and validate the power and reverence for female sexuality. The Goddess' sex magic rituals helped heal and awaken mankind. Over the ages, these rituals became taboo and pushed down into the recesses of our psyche, only to rise in horrendous acts of oppression, torture, slavery, and rape. I believe that the practices in the kink dungeons tap into those taboos in an effort to heal these epigenetic wounds and transmute the shame associated with it.

Understanding that our sexuality is a source of power and owning that power, is the only way we can never be overpowered or disempowered again. It is sourced from the sacral chakra (where most of our shadows live) and channeled out through the solar plexus, or third chakra. To know our power is to understand that it is a dynamic energetic exchange requiring opposite poles; the masculine and feminine, predator and prey, dominant and submissive *energies* that our primal bodies know innately. Mastering both our masculine and feminine powers is the secret code to harmony within, and it allows for the beautiful flow back and forth into an electric or magnetic conduit for passionate intimacy. It is worth mentioning again that most women penetrate with their heart energy, while men keep their hearts closed to it. Most men penetrate with their sexual energy, while women keep their sexuality closed to it.

What we've ended up doing in our relationships is create protective veneers that distort the intensity of our connections. Men who are trying to be more sensitive can get castrated or humiliated by their female counterpart, and are often seen as weak. Women who gain power through an unhealthy use of their masculinity usually cut themselves off at the waist. They are seen as non-sexual beings often rejected by men. A couple who only exchanges in passive energy with each other have no juice between them, a couple who engages with only penetrating energy between them might feel a controlling or competitive tension that turns into a vicious fight.

Learning to embody a healthy balance of penetrating and receiving energy is confusing. We have no role models for the elevated man or woman, The Rock and Wonder Woman might be an exception. What we need to do is cultivate and experience a balance of power within us, before we can exchange power with a partner. Balance is essential to self-mastery, and polarity is essential to mastery with another. But first, let's master our dominance, our erotic power, and to do that we must call in our inner Dominatrix.

LESSON: Turning pain into pleasure is your superpower.

SPEAKING ABOUT SPANKING

While my dad's fury had no boundaries, my mother's helplessness was infuriating. I learned very quickly to extend my energetic body outward to create an intense bubble of protection. I had to be ready for anything. My hypervigilant inner warrioress was on fire, lest the Incredible Hulk might once again erupt out of my father and humiliate us in public.

I also learned how to quickly shapeshift into an obedient servant, as I witnessed my mother's ability to dutifully submit with the vulnerability of blind devotion. I didn't realize that I was raised with impeccable templates for the Dominant and Submissive roles played in the dungeons of the kink world.

Though my only exposure to this mysterious and underground world at that time was the book *50 Shades of Grey*, which I read with a fake cover on it one summer, and before that, *The Claiming of Sleeping Beauty* by Anne Rice, I believed the Dominatrix would be an easy persona to embody as part of my experiment.

We didn't have anything close to a Red Room, or any of the equipment, but I did have leather pants, a black bustier, black boots and a lace collar that I turned into a mask. I couldn't find the leather cuffs, and I didn't have the guts to ask our housekeeper if she knew where they were. I'd have to use what I had, and come up with inventive ways to become a fierce, but loving Dominatrix.

That evening, I ordered my husband to lay on the bed. I used a pair of socks to tie his hands over his head. I said to him, as I channeled the *Game of Thrones* scene where Daenerys demands sex from her advisor Daario, "Take off your clothes." I kept my legs apart, with my hands on my hips, and stared at him a little arrogantly and sinisterly. Then I froze.

He sat there waiting, but I got performance anxiety. I started to feel ashamed by what might come out of me. I knew that I had a really dark side that I was afraid of unleashing, I had seen it go rogue in my father, and I wanted no part of that. I didn't want to share the images that passed before my eyes of how much power can destroy. I didn't want my husband to see my visceral disdain. I pulled myself together, put an eye mask on him, and decided to give him a sensation massage full of surprises instead. I dug my nails into his skin, I used ice cubes, I tickled him with a feather, I whispered in his ears how I might torture him, that I might give him a spanking. It missed its mark; I was trying too hard, or not enough. I know my husband wanted me to fully take charge so he could finally surrender, really surrender. But I couldn't. I didn't realize how much effort I was using all these years to disassociate myself from any kind of power. All power meant to me was violence. No wonder I kept myself so small.

After our "session," my husband lay snoozing on the bed, while I immediately went into my office to do a Google search for Dominatrix training. I was disappointed in myself. I could embody, dress, and energetically template all the other personas, but this one gave me an unreasonable charge, I wanted to figure out why. As the shapeshifter that I was becoming, I wanted to master all the archetypes that were expressing through me. And as a self-help addict, I knew I would have no problem diving right in, even if I had to go to the seedy dungeons for enlightenment.

An entire new world opened up to me. I don't know why I was so surprised about how significant the Bondage and Discipline, Domination and Submission, Sadism, and Masochism (B.D.S.M. for short) subculture was in San Francisco. Every year leather bound explorers of this kinky world flocked to the Folsom Street fair where they walked around in masks, latex cat suits, collars, or nothing but strappy leather harnesses. There was a lot of music, celebration, and spanking stations. I've seen the pictures. San Francisco was also home of the Armory, where Kink. com filmed B.D.S.M.-based pornography. This small city of technology wizards, old money, an artsy crowd, and extreme foodies was also a hub for the booming world of kink. How did this escape my knowledge until then?

I went back into the bedroom and interrupted my husband's snoring by shaking him awake. "Don't judge," I told him.

"Have I been judgey?" He asked me, a little worried. He was working on his tendency to be critical.

"No. But speaking of spanking …" I paused.

"I don't want to have a spanking," he said, "that's not my thing."

"How do you know it's not your thing?" I questioned. "I've never spanked you."

"Is it your thing?" he asked.

I had to think about that. It might be, it might not. I wasn't sure.

He then said in a voice that was reticent, "Do you want me to spank you?"

"I don't think that's a good idea." I laughed. "I want to get this whole Dominatrix thing down first."

"What do you mean?" He gave a big yawn. It was a hint that he was too tired for me to redo the Dominatrix.

"Well." I paused. "I just sent in a message to a real Dominatrix, asking her to train me. What do you think about that?"

He didn't skip a beat. "You'll probably be really good at it." That was all he said before he rolled over and went to bed.

LESSON: Know what you don't know.

JUST CALL ME VANILLA

Over the next couple of years, I met and trained with Dominatrices in San Francisco and in New York, two more in Paris, and did a one-week intensive in Italy with the Australian Dominatrix, just to name a few. All teachers were very different from each other. Clearly, when I set out to learn something, I make sure I learn from the very best. And my husband was right, I ended up being really good at the arts of the Dominatrix, my version at least.

Although I could write an entire book on my experiences with this mysterious and occult world of dungeons, punishment, and fetishes alone, I'm including it in *this* story as an example of what I call future envisioning. Future envisioning is a really effective magic trick that helps you get into the same vibration as your manifestation vortex. All you have to do is talk about or act out your desires in front of friends as if they have already happened. The more you can envision your future and feel the joy of your desires, the easier it is for them to become a reality. When you share it with friends, the Universe is that much more inspired to make it happen. It is creating the future outcome, and then without any tension, allowing yourself to catch up to your dreams. Remember, dreams do come true. There are still some dreams that I'm waiting to be realized. So, you have just become an accidental participant in a part of my future envisioning. Thank you for that.

When I got back from my first workshop in the arts for female dominance led by Midori, an internationally renowned sex educator who is also an artist, performer, and writer, I told my husband that if I ever needed to, I could make a shit load of money as a Dominatrix. Midori is an excellent negotiator who really wants to keep participants in this playground safe. She is both playful and professional at the same time. Midori prefers the term sex educator over dominatrix.

Another dominatrix I met was the infamous Cleo Dubois and her teaching partner Minax. Cleo is a shamanic type of dominatrix who creates intense rituals, inflicts pain with great precision and love. Although I was intimidated by her, I think she is magic. Her husband was a famous photographer who practiced being suspended in the air by hooks in his skin to create what they called "out of body experiences." My experience with Cleo was intense, and at the same time nurturing.

In New York, I took classes from (and photographed) the impressive Kasia Urbaniak, who was once the highest paid Dominatrix in New York City and now teaches women how to dominate in conversation using verbal defense, among other skills. In Paris, I met the most famous dominatrix of all, Catherine Robb-Grillet, a very demure looking woman in her late eighties, known for her elaborate rituals, who could still command any room.

I stayed in an Italian villa for one week with Anne O. Nomis (I love her clever use of a pseudo-name), who traveled from Australia to teach the technical aspects of the Dominatrix, and offer us wisdom from her book, *The History and Arts of the Dominatrix*. I lived in a villa filled with professional and want-to-be-professional Dominatrices, as well as the lifestyle players. These were all normal-looking people with regular jobs. We all went to the museum in Florence together and had meals out. One would never guess what kinds of things went down among these seemingly traditional-looking tourists, and that was part of their allure, too.

And then there is the elegant Betony Vernon, who has impeccable taste and a gracious quality to her. She welcomes guest to her beautifully decorated lair she's named Eden, always in a gorgeous gown. Betony also creates exquisite custom-made toys and B.D.S.M.-inspired jewelry. I fell in love with her aesthetics immediately. Betony calls herself a sex anthropologist; I call her a sorceress of erotic intelligence.

At my first few experiences, I expected scary looking biker chicks in leather, but my classes were filled with average looking women who ranged from sex workers to B.D.S.M. lifestyle enthusiasts. I felt like I was the only one in the room who did not have any knowledge of the B.D.S.M. world. When we introduced ourselves and shared why we were there, I told them to just call me Vanilla. I felt so out of my league. I continued to consider myself "vanilla" with every other experience, because compared to everyone else, I was vanilla.

This world was about "playing" with dangerous equipment that could potentially cause some real harm, emotionally and physically. Negotiations regarding safety, boundaries and aftercare was of upmost importance. This was a specialized art of negotiation that I could have used early in my marriage. It was clear and precise, there was no room for projecting or guessing what the other person needed, and no room for not knowing your own boundaries. If you were going to create a scene with a stranger that included flogging, then you better know what you can handle and what you can't. I could see now why some of the teachers of this lifestyle were upset at the portrayal of B.D.S.M. in *50 Shades of Grey*, and it is why my first experience with my husband fizzled. It is important to be transparent, to know your boundaries, how much time you have, and what you need for aftercare and for how long. Everything was laid out, no stone unturned. I didn't know what my husband wanted before, in the middle, or at the end, even though we were married and had kids together. And what about this aftercare business? He often fell asleep after sex, or I'd turn over unsatisfied. Aftercare (a little cuddle for ten minutes, or breathing together, or holding hands) sounded nice.

We really went into the details of negotiation, emphasizing that it was just like playing as kids, the bossy ones would make up a game, tell the rules and the rest would agree or negotiate the game. That is exactly what I did as child. I remember playing with some friends and setting a scene that required a horse and a shop keeper. I dictated who the shop keeper was, who the horse was, and I even commanded everyone to help me collect rocks so I had a lot of money to spend on my horse. I rode the horse to the shop keeper, led my horse to water, and patted my horse on the back. I was a little dominatrix in the making. B.D.S.M., according to Midori, was simply adult play. I could relate to that.

Toward the end of most workshops, we had an opportunity to bring in a submissive or they were brought in for us. My husband has not a submissive bone in his body, and he wanted me to explore this on my own to see if it might become a "thing" for me before I dragged him along. We created our own boundaries around my exploration, and I was good to "do what I needed to do" in the name of research.

Most dominatrix teachers have a black book of subs they could call on for those of us who did not have our own personal subs. I wanted a masculine man for me, because I knew that I liked big, intense energy. I was used to it as a child. I didn't want to be abused or overpowered by the masculine energy; I was just used to and like the enormous swell of potency that masculine men often reek of. Anything less was too easy for me.

When the men entered the room, I would search for a masculine Thor, but I never ended up seeing a Thor type. Most of the volunteer men were natural submissives, which made sense. We practiced creating scenes, announcing our presence, negotiating the details and stating our boundaries. It was harder than I thought, but I finally got used to it. I easily found out what they wanted and could suddenly drop into a role of a snobby Upper East Side of Manhattan heiress walking her puppy, a Goddess training an initiate, or whatever role was needed.

When I first met Cleo, it was in her private dungeon. She was annoyed by me at first, because I didn't know what I wanted or what I wanted to accomplish. At that point, I just wasn't happy with the outcome of my fabricated Dominatrix. She pulled out a flogger and taught me how to use it on the wall, then she had me use it on her. I flinched every time the flogger hit her body, even when I did it lightly. She scolded me that I was not to flinch, that a Dominatrix does not flinch when wielding a flogger, but I couldn't help it. At my last attempt, she grabbed my flogger and gave me a whip on my leg. Ouch.

When I attended a workshop a few weeks later, I practiced with flogging again. I was paired with a woman sub who told me that she really enjoyed being flogged and to just trust that she would let me know if it was too much. I flogged her lightly, and she wiggled her body, telling me it was okay to give her more. We continued like that until I was using great force and with great precision. The lead dominatrix walked by me at that point and said, "I knew you had flogger in you." It felt good to let out energy in this way, and it was tiring. I thought, if only my mother and father had found this world, maybe their relationship wouldn't have been so destructive.

Cleo Dubois, in my opinion, is a master of constructing scenes and ritualizing them. She was what I imagined the Goddesses in the ancient art of erotic play to be, or she was the Marque de Sad incarnate. I mean that in the best possible way. Cleo's shaman-like healing energy made me feel safe in this taboo experience by the sacred space she created. She had us practice our scenes that we would then negotiate with her volunteer subs. I found out that I was really good at imagining elaborate scenes. I knew exactly where to channel my energy, again in the sacral chakra, where I would tap into the other person's desires and merge them with mine. My interviews with the subs were detailed stories of demons and angels, temple initiates, the hunter and the hunted. I just needed a bigger room, or a private field.

This seemed much easier than polyamory, because you could just leave your play partner, who might be a stranger, and didn't have to worry about emotions or real life. For a brief moment suspended in time, you could work out some issue in a sexual way, creating a new constellation to clear the block for the next phase of awakening. I didn't have any interest in making B.D.S.M. a lifestyle to the extent my new friends did, but I could incorporate its *essence* in a way that suited us and our vanilla relationship.

I started practicing verbal scenes with my husband, which was the perfect amount of kink for him. When we were making love, I would whisper into his ears an erotic story about a woman who found him unconscious in a field after battle, naked and torn. The beautiful woman in nothing but a sheer silk dress couldn't wake him, so she started fondling his entire body to get him to stir. Oral sex, public nudity, an unknown erotic savior all in the safety of our bedroom and in a whisper. He got to travel with me into my fantastical erotic imagination, and I could tap into what his secret desires might be, without forcing him to reveal what he wasn't yet ready to reveal. I was able to incorporate even more erotic play and language with the various personas I had within me.

The heavy judgments of this lifestyle are usually by those who don't know much about it. B.D.S.M. is definitely not for everyone, but there were nuggets of wisdom I found invaluable. I have taken the best from each of the Dominatrices I traveled to and incorporated the teachings in a way that works for my monogamous, long term marriage. I found that some lessons don't always translate properly for vanilla couples, simply because most professional dominatrices don't have conventional relationships. I also took the essence of these teachings and included them into my work and art. I wanted my clients to get a felt sense of their erotic souls, their beauty, and their power in many different ways. One of my dearest friends Natalie, on her own journey of awakening, decided she wanted to experience a persona ritual with me. She is a future Oracle with magical powers that run deep, I can't wait for her to unleash them. Natalie came to my studio where we started with grounding and energetic boundary work, then we tapped into one of her personas through a guided meditation, and then we came up with an image and naming of that persona, which was the submissive devotee. I asked Natalie if I could talk to her "devotee" and had her move in a different location. From there, I had a deep and honest conversation with her inner devotee using my inherent tapping-in skills. Usually at this point, I have a make-up and hair artist come in and I incorporate what I've learned to photograph my clients as their personas, giving them an opportunity to feel and witness another side of their being. Natalie wanted to go deeper. I had already anticipated what she needed from previous phone sessions, so I brought in a very masculine man I prepped to play the role of Hades, King of Death, the ruler of the underworld.

In a slinky dark silk gown, black thigh-high boots, and flogger in my hand, I verbally created a scene as I had done in my dungeon classes, except without direct punishment. I guided both Hades and the devotee through a labyrinth of sacrificial love, death, and rebirth, power and surrender. The field of energy we created was full of ancient wisdom we could source from. Nat was in tears, metaphorically giving up her children, her husband, all of her worldly possessions, and everything she had ever loved to this incredibly handsome Hades, who would spare her soul from eternal damnation and allow her to rise like the Phoenix into her own power. There was no touching, except maybe holding Nat's face; there was nothing sexual about it, but the energy was an erotic animating force that allowed Nat to go deep, to let go of the regular world, as she tapped into her own esoteric alchemy. Nat shed all the things she used as excuses to hide her power. Aftercare for Natalie was slow sensual, unchoreographed movement. The event was deep and transformative, she would go home to her husband with one more protective layer shed from her energetic body, and a sacred knowing in her physical body. I realized I was sourcing from the ancient teachings of deity yoga and constellation work. Ritual is powerful.

After my experiences in the dungeons, I fantasized about having a mansion deliciously designed, where every room was decorated in different styles for different rituals. It would be Christian Grey's Red Room on steroids (the typical dungeons in San Francisco and New York City are not exactly the most tasteful or clean places). I wanted a gigantic elegant playroom where I could take my lover (my husband) and dive into fantasy, only softly curated for monogamous, vanilla lovers like us. I could bring in clients to awaken and photograph a variety of personas with a plethora of scenery. Or, just have elaborate and tasteful events that were erotic displays of beauty and unconditional love. This is my future vision, check back with me in a few years.

LESSON: Use future envisioning and erotic ritual to manifest the life and love you deserve.

TRAMPLE ME

What I noticed during my sojourns into the dungeons was quite a bit of fake power, too. It was clear that some women would have rather surrendered, while others just wore the right clothes as a mask of dominance. Their commands would flop because they didn't really believe in what they were saying. Yes, a powerful stance is important. Yes, a commanding voice helps. Yes, a bull whip has the power to put someone in their place. But believable power is being true to your own nature which is sourced from deep within. No one has your code of power, your specific ray of light. Any type of cookie cutter process will not resonate. Looking like you are powerful, present and paying attention, is not the same as being in the presence of your unique power and paying full attention to your partner in that space.

There is great power in the role of the submissive too, maybe even more so. When I was "studying up" on how to be an incredible Dominatrix, I realized that the rules, regulations, boundaries and safe words of the submissive gave them incredible influence as well. They are the ones who got to say yes or no to a proposal. They are the ones who desire the feelings and sensations that punishment, humiliation, surrender, and letting go offer. In reality, the Dominatrix is in service to the Sub, especially so in a professional setting.

I was servant to a man who loved having me walk him around on a leash, desperate for me to give him a whack on the bum for any misbehavior. A few of my interviewees renegotiated scenes that suited them better. Another sub would stare at my stilettos, as if to stay "trample me," yearning for me to walk all over him.

I was in a bit of a dilemma. My husband is anything but submissive, and I've already shared that I was a pretty damn good little Dominatrix-in-the-making. Maybe my hypervigilance aggravated his rigidity and vice versa. Maybe we weren't experiencing authentic and truthful resonance, because we were both trying to one up each other, like two alphas. If only one of us could learn to yield at the perfect moment, that would allow for natural flow of polarity that draws couples together instead of pushing them apart. Since my goal was to master the various energies and use them as a tool to get along with my husband, and to take it out into the world of multidimensional beings with multifaceted personalities, I needed to master how to switch back and forth in these two polarities. I didn't want this to be a fake act; I wanted full embodiment of the personas as they naturally flowed through me. I felt like I was doing a great job at surrendering, until I met Bodhi, a Shibari Master.

A Shibari Master is skilled in the ancient Japanese art of rope bondage. Shibari was originally used in the martial art of restraining captives during imprisonment and torture. The Samurai were required to treat their prisoners with respect, so the style of tying was a presentation of the honor and status of the prisoner. Shibari later became an art of erotic spirituality.

I originally signed up for a workshop to learn how to create rope artwork on bodies so I could photograph the beauty of it. I didn't have a partner to practice with at the workshop, so I wasn't accepted. Lucky for me, the day before, the Shibari Master called me up and asked if I wanted to be the model because the original model backed out at the last minute. After we spoke on the phone though, he was wary about my ability to surrender. He said I sounded too bossy (he had no idea how bossy I could be). I told him I was a shapeshifter and that I could definitely surrender, although I wasn't sure if I really could to his standards.

After we got to the space, he put me in a Japanese silk robe. When the guests arrived, he and I were perfectly stationed so each of the participants in the semicircle of men and women could witness the demonstration clearly. He asked me to take off my robe when we were ready to start. I looked at him like I didn't want to be naked in front of people I didn't know. He looked at me as if to say, "Didn't you know what you signed up for?"

I didn't know what I signed up for. I never do.

Then he asked the class to take off as much clothing as they were comfortable with. Most of the participants got naked. Alright, I thought, I'll just keep my underwear on. The things I do for research.

Before he began his instructions, the master explained to the group that I might not be an easy one to surrender, which at the moment was true. Then he started to wrap the rope around my arms and torso, he brushed the rope along my skin in a most gentle way and pulled it tight, he did this with so much tenderness and care two more times around my body. I immediately turned into jelly. I had no idea how good it would feel to be bound up and tied. He could do anything to me. He flipped me this way and that, and my body just flipped and flopped. I had no choice but to surrender, if I fought the ropes, I would get a rope burn and they would only get tighter. It looked beautiful and I felt like I was back in the womb. This was true surrender, and it felt really good. I could see how one in complete control could make another feel safe and secure. I could see how surrender in safety could feel and look like devotion. It was erotic hypnosis that was just as effective for letting go as my previous experience with the hypnotist and my cheesecake addiction, only better. Vulnerability was what made the dominant want to take precious care of the sub. Vulnerability is power too.

I started to come up with ways to use psychological ceremony of power dynamics and curate it for the non-B.D.S.M. crowd, and for those who are tired of their monotonous, long-term vanilla love experiences. Hello, Kinky Vanilla.

There must be something about the need to experience a little suffering in life, so that we know what the opposite feels like. How would we know what pleasure was if there was no pain? It's the elegant duality equation of the cosmos; the profound and the profane, the light and the dark, and the highs and the lows that brings us to a sacred center. To master the flow between the opposites to find the pleasure in the pain is finding your gold, your fountain of youth, your tree of life.

The sacred texts say, "as within, so without," and "as above, so below." We are separate beings with separate souls, yet we all share this one great big spirit. In the big scheme of Universal things, nothing matters, yet everything we say and do matters.

I was beginning to see the truth that there is a unifying energetic force of love, individually expressed through all entities in this life. It's the Law of One in a diverse cosmic playground. When I finally got this concept, and it landed in my body as truth, a whole new world of possibilities opened up for me. And that became my true power.

LESSON: Finding the essence in the flow between the opposites is true power.

13. Dakini, Sexperts, & other Gurus

WRITTEN IN THE STARS

Your past and your destiny, is your karma and your dharma. It's the story you wrote before you decided to enter into this planet through your parents. That is why you were born on the day you were born, and in the constellation you were born into. To help you fulfill your life's purpose and ride the wave of its current. Understanding even a tiny bit of your soul's purpose, helps you to overcome some of these damn lessons of betrayal. I also learned this at the Chopra Center in San Diego, while on the path to being a certified Ayurvedic Educator.

I was introduced to a deeper type of astrology than the horoscopes you read in the tabloids. At the time, I was still very skeptical of psychics and woo-woo stuff, even though I was getting certified in Consciousness and natural healing. If you know anything about Deepak Chopra and his teachings, it is all about the quantum field, meditation and spirituality based on ancient Vedic philosophy. It is as woo-woo as you can get, except he is a medical doctor who uses science to back his claims. My struggle with all of this was deeply knowing that I was a starseed and had some sort of magic in me, but also needing to be practical and "normal" in the world.

I made an appointment with two of the Jyotish astrologers that Deepak Chopra recommended. I chose to do it twice specifically to catch flaws in the system. Both of my readings were similar, with a slightly different lens depending on the reader. In essence, my sun sign is in Aquarius, my moon is in Scorpio, my rising sign is in Leo, and my Venus is in the galactic center of the Universe. These are all fixed signs, they told me, apparently a difficult chart to have. As my past has proven, my charts were on target.

Dr. Suhas is a brilliant Ayurvedic doctor and Jyotish astrologer from India. I believe he's psychic too. When he read my charts, he said, "I feel for people like you who have a chart like this, your childhood was not easy." He nailed that one. Dr. Suhas also confirmed by either looking at my charts, or intuitively read, that I had two boys. But then he asked me, "What about the other one?" I gulped. How did he know?

I had never told anyone the story about the abortion I had when I was nineteen years old. I never even told my husband. My high school sweetheart (a really great Catholic boy himself and the epitome of Apple Pie) and I were still a strong couple our first two years of college. We used the pull-out method for birth control, because that's what Catholic kids did. We knew, without having to discuss it, what to do about the pregnancy. We drove in silence to Planned Parenthood. When he dropped me off, he gave me a big hug. I stoically walked into the building to have the procedure done.

When it was over, I lay on the operating table in a foggy daze. All I concentrated on was the electric sound of the procedure. It made me cringe. There was no question that I was going to get an abortion, we were both just kids in no position to have our own. When the procedure was done, I lay on the table and started to cry. The doctor was really gentle with me, he put his hand on my arm and let me know that it was okay to cry, and that he would leave me to myself for a little bit, if that is what I wanted. I did; the solitude was perfect. My boyfriend and I didn't speak about it again, nor did we share the experience with anyone else. I felt devastation and gratitude at the same time. So much guilt coursed through my body, and I sometimes wondered if it was a girl or boy. I imagined a girl. I also knew that I did not want to raise a child at that stage in my life or ever. My childhood was so painful and violent that I didn't trust my child would be lucky enough to bypass that type of experience. I couldn't imagine how I would ever be able to keep an innocent being safe in this world, even if I had a great boyfriend.

It was a shock for me to hear those words come out of Dr. Suhas's mouth. I told him the story of my abortion. He only nodded and looked down at my charts again. Then he said to me, "Why are you still with this man?" That shook me even further. What did he know about my relationship? Did he know that my husband had an affair just by the charts? I thought when he mentioned betrayals due to Scorpio in my 4th House of home and family, he meant as a child and I associated it with my father's betrayal. I was still pretending to the outside world that I was an unbetrayable woman, but somehow Dr. Suhas knew. I couldn't answer his question. I was upset at it actually. He asked what I would do if my husband left me. He was really pushing me to understand myself and my situation more. I could not answer him.

He changed gears and assured me that everything was going to be okay. He said that "it didn't matter." My Venus in the galactic center of the Universe, was apparently making her presence known and would soon position herself as a cosmic force to welcome in the new Age of Aquarius, also known as the Age of the Feminine. All this made zero sense to me, but Dr. Suhas pointed out that by 2020 my karmic lines would be cleared and life would be really good to me. Were there still more surprises to come, and did I have to wait that long?

The other Jyotish master I called was Brent Bevcar, he used slightly different language but gave me a similar reading. He pointed out to me that I had a lot of planets in Scorpio, and that my journey was about transformation, the occult, and sexuality – and then sharing it. At that time, I was so non-sexual, so it didn't resonate. And sharing it? No way. No one was going to know how neurotic I was.

Then of course, as a good self-help addict would, I started looking into other types of astrology, like Evolutionary, Esoteric, and Galactic. I consulted Shamans, Akashic Record keepers, Mediums and Psychics. Many of the practitioners saw the same theme; I was to know the heartbeat of the Universe, the difference between conditional love and unconditional love; I was an incarnate of multiple personalities and understood the individual aspects of the multifaceted self in relation to All That Is; I could channel many deities, I had many past lives in ancient Egypt and India, where the occult teachings of Tantra and sex magic for the purpose of spiritual awakening was one of my paths. Everyone emphasized that I was a master of the shadowy underworld. The spiraling in and out of death and rebirth, the transmutation of pain into pleasure that create the fabric of who we are, and turning our karma into dharma is something I do know about.

But at the time, it was thoroughly depressing. All I wanted to do was get away from evil. All I wanted was easy normal love. All I wanted was to experience a nurturing life that felt safe and cozy. I didn't really care if I was sexy or sexual; I had to do that because my husband was dissatisfied. I believed it all and didn't believe any of it. I went back and forth telling myself they were all frauds fabricating hogwash, and to having a deeper sense of knowing that maybe I really was a sexual being that had a multifaceted soul, could be a healer through my own healing, on the verge of awakening to a higher dimension. If there is even a slight bit of truth to the influences of the Cosmos, then we might as well work *with* them.

LESSON: Keep your mind open to the Cosmos, her wisdom is waiting to guide you.

EXTENDED MASSIVE ORGASM

As I mentioned, I became obsessed with my charts, and that I was supposed to be this extremely sexual and passionate person (with Mars in the Eighth House of Pisces, unaspected). It couldn't be true. My husband wouldn't have cheated on me if I was so sexual, and I would *feel* sexual if I was so sexual. I didn't feel it. I had to relearn this innate gift, so I went to many a sex guru to find out what was "wrong" with me. By the way, everyone is a sexual being, sexy can be unleashed in everyone, and polarity, intimacy, and attraction can be cultivated in everyone.

As you know, my journey included taking almost every class out there and meeting with almost every "expert" out there. The first person I went to see in the sexuality department was Steve Bodansky (who came highly recommended by many of my new friends), he and his partner Vera wrote the book *Extended Massive Orgasm*. I loved reading it, and I started recommending it to everyone. I still think everyone would enjoy reading it.

Many walls had crumbled and the ice around me had melted some. I was starting to feel more sensual, which meant I was using my five senses more to feel everything in my body. But sexual was not something I associated with. I thought sexual meant that I wanted to have sex all the time, that the wind would turn me on, that I could feel pleasure for everything, that my whole life would feel orgasmic. I also thought it meant that every sexual experience would be like that orgasm I had when I watched *House of Dreams*. That was my goal.

I knew mechanical and technical sex well, which didn't do much for me except give me an "achoo" like release, if I wasn't faking it. I was looking forward to having full body orgasms with a partner, not alone. I wanted a sacred "out of body" experience when I was having sex in partnership. I wanted to feel stirred walking up the grocery isle. I wanted every day to feel like bliss. That wasn't happening, so I decided it was time for me to get some hands-on treatment. And it was time for my husband to join me. I spared him the larger, coed lectures and workshops that I was going to. He wasn't interested in "healing" or self-improvement courses. He had no choice but to join me in this experience with the Bodanskys. I promised him it would be a private session, and that it was for my issues not his, I didn't want to give him the wrong impression that I was dissatisfied by anything he was doing. Plus, reading a book is just not the same as doing the practice. Each person will process the words differently, only remembering what resonates with them at any moment. Especially something that is so visceral. I believed in working with guides who wrote the book, or experienced, first hand, the very thing I wanted to experience. I warned my husband that if he didn't want to learn how to give me an Extended Massive Orgasm, somebody else would.

We drove east across the Bay Bridge on a Saturday morning. I noted how much warmer the east bay was than foggy San Francisco. I was nervous that morning. I wanted to seem professional to Steve Bodansky, I don't know why. I didn't want us to appear like a couple who had issues. I aspired to show Steve that we were a progressive couple just upping the ante a bit. I asked my husband to change into a white, button down shirt instead of the cotton Captain America t-shirt he was wearing. I decided to put on a cotton maxi dress and step into my high heeled sandals for this nine a.m. on a Saturday morning appointment, where I knew I was going to get naked from the waist down anyway. First impressions count, I said to myself.

The address took us to a cluster of apartments that reminded me of the timeshare presentation we got suckered into when we first visited Hawaii together. We took the tour of the property and sat through an intense sales pitch all because we wanted a free dinner at the fancy Princeville hotel. Tourists and realtors to the left and right of us were popping champagne bottles in celebration for their spontaneous purchases. Meanwhile, my husband and I sat horrified by our determined saleswoman who managed to hold us hostage for three hours, never giving in to our many excuses for why a timeshare wasn't the right thing for us. I can't remember exactly how we did it, but we pretended to go to the bathroom and ended up climbing down the back steps to ditch the relentless shark.

We walked through the nondescript apartment complex and found the Bodanskys' apartment on the second floor. The building could have been a larger version of the office developments reserved for dentists, therapists, and insurance brokers. I vaguely remember a shaggy welcome carpet out front. I knocked on the front door. I felt someone look out from behind a peep hole.

A kind middle-aged man with a Burt Reynolds mustache, and a dark ring of hair around his bald head, opened the door. He looked like he hadn't left the seventies. I don't know why, but I pictured a man who could write a book called *Extended Massive Orgasm* to look and feel like a sex machine, to me that was Jason Momoa or Chris Hemsworth. Shame on me, I knew that I was just projecting my view of sexy onto him, so I stifled any judgement.

Steve Bodansky was in sweats and a t-shirt, my husband looked over at me and raised an eyebrow, bummed that he wasn't in his. Steve invited us into the one-bedroom apartment he shared with his lovely wife Vera. Vera was many years older than Steve, maybe even twenty years older. You go girl, I thought to myself. I heard that Vera had recently experienced a stroke that took her voice away, and she was forced to move much more slowly than she was used to. So in silence, Vera stayed in the background.

I hoped we didn't come too early, there was still a little breakfast on their kitchen counter, and dishes in the sink. Their coffee table was filled with documents and what looked like bills being paid. There may have been the makings of another book that I saw too. I kept imaging that I saw a box of kitty litter on the floor, but I can't remember ever seeing a cat. I don't remember much of the décor, but I did notice the chaos and clutter of unpretentious, normal living.

In *Extended Massive Orgasm*, Steve writes about the importance of treating yourself or your lover like a "Visiting Dignitary" when it comes to creating a special place for love making. Remember, I grew up with plastic on our couches, which allows me to be comfortable anywhere and everywhere. But with my Venus in the galactic center of the Universe, beauty and harmony is very important to me, and it makes me overly picky. Although well intentioned, the Bodanskys' living room wasn't quite the space I imagined worthy enough for a "Visiting Dignitary." Was I being too snobby? Maybe, I thought, he would take us into a session room filled with plush, jewel colored pillows, the scent of jasmine, a candelabra, and fresh red roses.

Steve didn't give us an introductory spiel, so I started off the conversation by saying, "I've done just about everything, and I want my husband to learn how to properly stroke my clitoris so I can experience an Extended Massive Orgasm." I was picking up bits and pieces of the language from his book. I was telling a white lie, of course, I didn't do just about everything in the touch department. This was one of the first things I was doing to address my nonsexual and inaccessible nerve endings.

Steve sat down on the couch, and I took a seat on the chair opposite him. My husband remained standing. I could see the adorable Vera in the corner of my eyes shuffling around in her slippers. Steve didn't really say much, I guessed because he was better at hands-on training. But I talk when I'm nervous, so I asked Steve if there was an equivalent practice for men, I skipped over the men's section in the book. My husband just stood there listening like a champ.

He did not read *Extended Massive Orgasm*. Prior to this meeting, I only told him that he was going to learn how to rub my clitoris because there was a very special and very specific way to do it, according to the book. Steve leaned back in his chair and answered my penis question in his slow and deliberate way, "I'm really into leaking, right now."

"Leaking?" I questioned.

"Yes, it is when you rub the penis slowly and pre-cum comes out," he answered.

"Oh, yeah. Right." I tried to sound like I had heard that before. Maybe I was hearing everything wrong at the moment. I tried to glance over at my husband to see his expression, but I didn't want to burst out in laughter for our lack of knowledge. We made a little more small talk, and then I finally said, "So, I've brought my husband along with me to learn the first steps to, you know, your technique."

"How much do you know?" Steve asked him.

"Well, I think I know some things," my husband said, "but I don't know your technique."

"Okay. I'll set up the nest and I'll show you how to stroke the clitoris to get to orgasm." I noticed Steve left out "extended" and "massive." I didn't bring my very straight-laced husband into this unconventional experience to learn how to give just any old orgasm; I wanted the Extended Massive Orgasm that Steve's book promised. Steve then turned to me and said, "I don't use gloves, but I will wash my hands." He pointed to the bathroom. "Feel free to go into the bathroom and do what you need to do to feel comfortable. We will be in the next room." He got up, went into the bathroom to wash his hands, and then took my husband into the other room.

I didn't know if it was a normal thing in the orgasm world to not use gloves. I don't like it when massage therapists use gloves, so I decided it was probably normal. I went into the bathroom and felt like I was prying into their private grooming habits. I don't have a clear memory of everything in the bathroom, but there was generic shampoo, maybe Johnson's baby shampoo, in their bathtub shower combo. There might have been a plastic shower cap for Vera. I used a bar of soap to wash my hands. Toothbrushes, toothpaste, a hairbrush, and medication were on the counter. I took a pee and washed my hands.

The next room wasn't a dedicated room for sessions; it was their bedroom. There were no roses, jeweled pillows, the smell of jasmine, or candles of any sort. I soon concluded that "Visiting Dignitary" was reserved for lovers not clients. Bright daylight filtered through the veiled window; Steve had placed a single dark towel on top of their duvet cover. There was a pillow for my head and two pillows to support my knees that would help when I butterflied them opened. He had a clean washcloth also. In a professional tone, Steve asked me to get naked and hop on the bed. I did as I was told.

So there I lay, naked on the Bodanskys' bed with my feet together and my knees falling outward. Unwaxed, my lady parts were boldly exposed in the bright daylight. I was grateful for the pillows that supported my knees; I wasn't that flexible. I wanted to die ... of either laughter, or humiliation, or both.

Steve, the professional clitoris stroker and author of *Extended Massive Orgasm*, stationed himself to my left. My traditionally-raised, Ivy-League-educated, businessman of a husband stood at the edge of the bed. And then silent Vera, who jumped up onto the bed like a cat, sat on her knees and watched from the back corner. Little tiny murmur sounds escaped her lips; I wasn't sure if she was giving approval or just purring – maybe that's why I imagined kitty litter in the house. Vera reminded me of a cat.

First, Steve showed how to spread open the labia of my vulva and find my clitoris. He showed how to find the left side quadrant of this tiny little organ and stroke gently. It was all very practical. "See," he said, "it is erect." My husband nodded like a good student, his hands clasped behind him. During one of my previous workshops, I had witnessed a live demonstration using a similar technique, the woman who was being "stroked" made all these guttural sounds that lifted and fell depending on the wave of her orgasm. I was silent.

"How am I doing?" I asked Steve with a sincere look in my eyes, "Is there anything happening? Am I getting aroused?"

Steve looked at me for a moment, probably thinking, no you must not be getting aroused if you have to ask that question. This is how I know the power of the mind, or at least the power of my mind. I was so intent on getting it right that I never left my head. I never dropped into my body to feel anything that they were doing. I had two men stroking the most concentrated pleasure center in the human body, and I was worried if it was working or not.

"Yes," Steve assured me, "your pussy is flushed and moist." Phew, I thought. Steve then turned to my husband and said, "Would you like to give it a try?"

My husband looked nervous, like he might actually fail at something. He silently moved close to my body. Steve used his own finger to rub my husband's arm to give him an idea of how much pressure and how much speed to use on me, and then Steve gestured for him to start stroking. I still did not make any sounds like the woman I watched in the live demonstration. She moaned and groaned in a perfect rhythm of ups and downs; part of me wondered if it was all rehearsed. I had mastered the fake orgasm myself, so that thought floated around in my head for a while. It seemed fake for me to try and sing along with the strokes, while Steve and Vera were staring at me in broad daylight, my legs splayed open like a science project.

Steve showed us how to use the towel to clean up the lube that was used, and said it was supposed to ground me. I never reached an orgasm. If I couldn't get a mini orgasm with the master stroker of the Extended Massive kind, then there definitely was something wrong with me.

We drove home in silence for a while. Then my husband turned to me and said, "What the fuck was that?"

We fought the entire way home, not knowing that the technique would come in handy later.

LESSON: Experts can help only so much; you need to find your own way.

DAKINI LOVE

Before I met my husband, I found this book called *The Art of Conscious Loving* by Charles Muir and Carolyn Muir. It was a how-to book based on the authors' teachings on intimacy and touch, rooted in ancient Tantric tradition. I am not going to pretend that I can explain the richness and depth of the Tantra tradition, but in its most rudimentary form, Tantra can be explained as a philosophy of intimacy that explores polarity; the dance of Shiva Shakti, the masculine and feminine principle, the yin and yang, or the flow of electric and magnetic forces that are always in Cosmic creation. It is said that the sexual practices of Tantra can awaken us to a higher state of being. Charles Muir coined the term "sacred spot massage," which is the stimulation of the G-spot in the vaginal wall that can bring a woman into a high orgasmic state to ejaculate her amrita, the nectar of immortality. In the everyday sex world, that would be called squirting.

When we started dating, I gave him *The Art of Conscious Loving* as a gift, writing on the inside cover in gold ink, "A bedside read. It's more for me – so I can share with you the secrets I've learned." I wanted to be the best lover. I wanted to master the art and science of love making. Clearly, we never ended up practicing anything from the book, and as you know, it took a blow to my head, the crushing of my heart, the annihilation of my ego, and a torrential rainfall of tears before I could revisit Tantra and master my sexuality and my sexual magic.

I pulled the book from my bookshelf and decided to play the role of Dakini as part of my project, the representation of the sensual, feminine divine in ancient Buddhist, Taoist, and Hindu societies. She was known to have the ability to move energy and liberate the soul. She transformed through bliss to get to wisdom and enlightenment. She was more the representation of the natural sensual universe, than sex practitioner. Her skills in the sensual and sexual arts both increased the level of erotic pleasure for the participants by helping them focus on a non-physical state of spiritual joy and the physical pleasure of sex at the same time. I could do that, I thought. I had a book! Plus, my charts said I was supposed to have the talents of a Dakini.

The special thing about Dakini energy is that she is part Goddess, part nurturer, part sexpert. She pulls from the energy of her yoni, which is another word for the female sexual organs, through to her heart and out to her hands and body. The energy flows in an infinity loop so she can serve sexually with loving energy.

I wore all white, put a bindi crown in my hair, I even put on clip-in extensions (I highly recommend hair extensions!). I wore all the gold fake jewelry that I had once used for one of the Fundraisers at my son's school, a Bollywood theme. I had a few Bollywood movement moves already, and all the accoutrements for my outfit. I used gold fake tattoos all over my body to resemble henna painting. I loved this look, it made me feel really elevated. I typically run around like the Energizer Bunny, as if I was stuck in yesterday trying to catch up to today, but the Dakini had me walking around as if I was floating. My movements were graceful and I did everything with conscious awareness. I received a lot of attention that day. At first I was self-conscious about it, I didn't want to stand out. I thought I might take something away from another person if I walked around in a generously loving and sensual way. But I soon came to notice the kind smiles, the nods of appreciation, and even a little gratitude. Namaste, I'd say over and over.

The energy in my house that afternoon was calm. Maybe there is something that shifts the perspective of others when they see white. What I realized is that it takes calm energy grounded into the earth to anchor a tranquil quality in those around you. All I did when my kids came home, was drop my pelvic floor and fill it with love energy and I allowed myself to radiate with love. There were snacks out, ready for them. When I asked how their day was, they gave the typical "good." All my friends with boys say that the one-word conversation is normal. They put their backpacks down, had a snack and immediately did homework.

The dinner table was decorated with a hundred candles, I wanted to give the feeling of Diwali, the Hindu Festival of Lights, to represent lightness over dark, good over evil, and hope over despair. I put red rose petals out. Everything I did, I did with love. Even the dinner I prepared, I prepared like I was writing a love poem to my family. Full disclaimer here, I did not make everything from scratch.

That evening, I moved all the candles and petals to the bedroom and recreated the scene, only I added more candles and a trail of rose petals. I did not let my husband enter the bedroom until much later. He would have to use our small hallway bathroom that the cats adopted as their own, with a large cat litter box that took up most of the floor space. I told him he could change into the robe I left him in the cats' bathroom.

When all of our nightly chores were done and the kids were off to their bedrooms, I let him enter. Our bedroom was dimly lit with beautiful sparkles of light. I guided him to the bed, and had him sit in lotus position. That wasn't a good idea because he didn't have the flexibility in his hips to sit like that. No problem, I had him sit on his knees. Then I sat on top of his legs and we looked into each other's eyes for a really long time.

The first time I had tried to do this with him deliberately, he made a joke of it which hurt my feelings. I had just come back from an event called Seduction of the Spirit, where we had to move in a concentric circle to look in the eyes of all the participants. There were over 200 people, so I had to look into the eyes of at least 100. Every person I shared a glance with was different, I felt like I could really read into the truth of their souls. Some were filled with joy at that moment, some had tears swell up, some seemed so lonely, some were just happy to be seen. I had no idea that I rarely looked people in the eyes. And I didn't realize how rarely my husband and I looked at each other in the eyes in such a deep way. So when I got back from that event, I told him my epiphany and asked him to participate in an eye gazing exercise with me. It failed. He thought I was boring into him and he said I looked *Fatal Attraction-y*. Perhaps it was because he had just gotten home from work, and I didn't give him the context or the "Visiting Dignitary" treatment. I think it was partly because we had managed to become so distant with each other that eye gazing was too intimate a thing for us at the time. It upset me to be able to connect with a 100 strangers, but not the man I was living with.

This time would be different. I had more command of my body, my energy, and my intentions. There was no sex in that group of eye gazers, but I knew the Dakini used her sexuality to help awaken others. So I would start out our eye gazing practice with all the sexy love I had in me. I would make him see me, see himself. He struggled at first because it was an intentional practice that brought keen awareness to our hearts and souls. I didn't budge with my loving energy, my eyes telling him that it was okay. He tried to play around by making funny expressions, but I did not let that bother me. After a few minutes, I knew it was time to change tactics. It is unfair to push people in a direction they can't go to at any given moment, baby steps are key.

So that is when I turned up the sexual energy. As we sat, yap yum position, I moved my gaze to his lips. I stared at them deliciously. I slowly moved my lips close to his, he gestured to kiss me, but I pulled back just a little, telling him that I was in charge. With my arms still around his neck, I touched his lips lightly with mine. I barely brushed my lips over his, then pulled back again. My body followed my slow deep breaths as it rose and fell, taking my hips back and forth in the same rhythm. I once again brought my lips close to his as he closed his eyes and opened his mouth. When my opened mouth was close to his, I sucked in air, as if I was sucking a piece of his soul into my body. That surprised him a bit, but I could tell it interested him. Then I took a deep breath, put my lips to his and blew in. I silently told him that he could have a piece of my soul. Then I just allowed myself to move on top of him, following my breath.

I pulled off his robe from the shoulders, and slipped off his body and had him lay down flat on his back. I took warmed coconut oil, and dripped it into the hollow space of his throat. I gave him a massage up and down his body. Then I took his lingam, or wand of light in Sanskrit, which is also code word for penis, and performed the "never ending yoni massage." I am making up this name, because I can't remember what the teacher called it during a very short afternoon Tantra lesson, where the teacher used a banana in place of a cock.

I kept my loving intention on my husband, and I felt honor for his lingam as any good Dakini would do. I softly stimulated his perineum with my fingers, and then gently cupped his testicles in my palm. To help wake up his lingam, I gave the bottom portion a little pressure massage with my thumb and index finger starting at the bottom of his shaft slowly making my way up the full length of his penis. Then I began the downward strokes. I held the tip of his wand in my hand and gently and slowly rubbed in a screwdriver motion down the shaft, but before I let go, my other hand embraced the tip and massaged down in spiral motion too. I continuously stroked without ever letting his penis free from my touch – the never ending yoni. I took him to the edge of orgasm, and then slowed down so he would not ejaculate. I held tightly, then started up again. I would move from slow to fast, and then I used just one hand to massage the top in circular motions until he got into to a rhythm where he would almost let go again. This was not torture, this was worship.

In ancient sexual practices, refraining from ejaculation was said to lead to enlightenment. I am not sure if my husband had reached enlightenment in that way, but he did awaken. I'm now learning how to take him out of his tenth gate, a practice that requires simultaneous orgasm, eye gazing, and placing the tongue at the roof of your mouth.

LESSON: Eye gazing, synchronized breath and love making can open spiritual portals.

I AM NOT YOUR GURU

There's a documentary film called *I Am Not Your Guru,* featuring the self-help motivational speaker Tony Robbins. The film follows his weeklong, uplifting "Date with Destiny" workshop, which helps guide participants to discover their purpose in life. Tony Robbins makes it clear in the film that his goal is to help the participants to take charge of their own wellbeing, that he is not a guru. Still, so many consider him their guru. If you watch the film, be sure to keep a keen eye out for me, I am in it for about fifteen seconds of fame.

Tony Robbins has a personality and dynamism that is larger than life; he got me and a few thousand other people to walk on fire. I even brought one of my kids to walk across the burning embers when he got a little older. I'm sure Tony enjoys being on stage, and I can see why people consider him their guru. But I believe it when he says, "I am not your guru."

There are three types of disciples in the self-help world, the first being one that needs a guru. They will zealously follow the one person they have projected all of their needs, desires, and hopes on. They are the ones who refuse to own their own power.

The second type of disciple is the one (where I fit in), who is pretty much an information whore. I will go to every teacher I feel called to, and try to find the essence of truth in what they are teaching. That includes teachers I get a bad vibe from, I'll take the class or workshop anyway, just to see if my intuition was right or wrong. This second group either branches out on their own to co-create with the Universe (me), or they keep searching for the answers outside of themselves.

The third type of disciple is repulsed by the word disciple. They are the skeptics that think self-help is bullshit. Since I'm admitting to my heavy "sleeping around" with the self-help world, I do have something to say about the gurus out there.

Beware of the guru who says they are the only ones that can help you. No one can activate or create or unleash your power, but you. The only thing guides, inspirational leaders, or gurus can help you with is showing you *a* way, not the *only* way; they can create safe and sacred containers for you to explore in, they can be there as support while you journey through your own metamorphosis. It is important to take heed, the teacher who has not done the work to embody what they are teaching. Many experts gain intellectual knowledge through institutions, books, and classes, which is a must of course. However, full embodiment, heart intelligence, conscious feeling, in addition to the brainy stuff is the only way to really transmit information that has to do with the body's awakening. You can't *think* into feeling sexy, or overcoming betrayal, or reigniting the fire in a relationship, or embody the roles with authenticity without the energetic and somatic sensations of experience. All types of healing and awakening and growing require energy and body-based sensations that cannot be practiced with the head alone.

There were a few "gurus" that I have experienced that made me feel uncomfortable, and I later realized that they were doing the work because they were looking to heal themselves. For the record, the Bodanskys know what they are doing. At the time of my first meeting with them, I was the one closed down to the various ways of teaching. They have a unique relationship that breaks most conventional ideas of love. Vera now has dementia, and Steve is brilliantly taking care of her and loving her. He uses sexuality to keep their situation playful and endurable. They are a beautiful love story.

But, there are dangerous people out there that call themselves sexperts who you need to watch out for. It is important for you to use your intuition to know who they are. To me, they are the relationship coaches who share a cookie cutter system, but have really shitty relationships themselves, don't have the relationship you aspire to have, or they are perpetual singles that can't practice what they preach.

There are embodiment teachers who are brilliant with sharing intellectual concepts, but are not embodied themselves. Watch them, do they look and feel comfortable in their own skin? Can you tell if they are cut off at the waist? It is not about how "good they look," it is about their level of confidence in, and command of, their body presence that is essential to teaching body presence. There are men teachers of feminine embodiment trying to turn you into the type of woman they are comfortable with, and women teachers who do the same with men. Energetically, the male body has centers that are polar opposite than the female body, so a man cannot teach a woman what it means to *really* feel and be sexy or orgasmic or nurturing, because they simply don't have the same organs or energetic composition as women do. A lion cannot teach a bunch of bunnies to be better bunnies. When you are deciding to work in such an intimate area, such as owning your own body (which is really what being sexy is all about), simply be aware that there is nothing wrong with you. The guidance you seek is to help *reveal* the most authentic and most potent aspects of who you already are, not to change you into someone you aren't.

The Tantra circles might be the most difficult arenas to navigate. Much of the Tantra out there has been demoted from being a spiritual practice that reflects the electric and magnetic creative pulse in the universe and in all divine beings, to glamorized prostitution. The problem I found when I was searching for a legitimate Tantra practitioner was that most of the Dakas and Dakinis who call themselves healers, were not fully healed themselves, nor did they do enough shadow work to hold a strong container for their clients. In this often polyamorous and sexually open group of "pros", I've witnessed neediness, blame, and those just trying to validate their own sexuality. It is a pretty gross feeling. But, do not worry, there are gems out there that have helped me to awaken my body and see sexuality as something more sacred. Just know what you are getting into.

Even in the B.D.S.M. world, you will find teachers who teach power *over*, which is a false sense of power. Or they are teaching dominance without the heart. Sometimes they teach the student to be dominant when she clearly wants to surrender. And, many are just reading a script and wielding a whip.

To truly awaken to your sexy, soulful, shapeshifter self is to be fully embodied. That means know that stirring, moving, ethereal thing deep inside you that animates your physical body, I call it the soul. It can be felt through breath sometimes. It also means awakening and using all of the senses in all parts of your body: touch, sight, smell, taste, sound. This is what it means to be sensual, to be alive in your body from the inside out. And then of course there is the heart and mind, energetic ideas that we can't really articulate. Using the mind to stimulate and serve the body through imagination, intuition, and intention, while using the intelligence of the heart to make better choices and proactively relate to the world around you. Finally, there's the energetic body, which I'm encompassing all the other "bodies" we cannot see; the emotional body, the etheric body, the astral body and the causal or spiritual body. This is the path of the sexy woman who has self-love and can share it with another without any shame, but curiosity and joy to having an affair with life itself. No one can resist a pillar of loving, sensual, joyful, all-encompassing light.

LESSON: You are the real guru of you.

14. Queen of Reclamation

CROWNED

After being thirty different women in thirty days, I just wanted to be me. I left an envelope for my husband on his dresser drawer with the handwritten letters saying, "Meet me Saturday night on the top deck at eight p.m." We have this miniature roof deck on top of our home where we can see the Bay Bridge and the San Francisco skyline. He kept asking what it was about, and I just winked at him.

That Saturday evening, I met him in my sweatpants and a sweatshirt. That is me sometimes. I had him sit across from me. It seemed eerily similar to the day I asked him to tell me the truth. We just looked into each other's eyes.

I grabbed his hands in mine and said, "I'm sorry for turning my back on you. I'm sorry for not trusting you. I'm sorry for not appreciating how much it took to provide for us. I'm sorry I didn't give you enough attention. Please forgive me. I love you."

This was from the Hawaiian practice of forgiveness, called Ho'oponopono. I'm sure I did it wrong, but my intentions were pure. As Bob the therapist so wisely suggested, I just wanted to take ownership of my role in the demise of our relationship. I was really pissed off at them for ganging up on me then, but now I can appreciate the power in taking full responsibility of everything that happens in my life. I could change what I do, I can't change what anyone else does. So, I felt empowered to rid myself of any more bad karma between us and just truly forgive. My husband looked at me with remorse and apology, maybe there was a tiny bit of moisture in his eyes.

"I have no idea what happens next, but I so appreciate you," I paused. "You are the maker of kings and queens, in the way you have forced me to rise up."

He didn't quite understand.

"I mean this in the best possible way," I said. "I would have remained asleep all my life, and you had to do what you did because it was the *only* way. I know this in my bones. I feel like I've been crowned a queen."

He remained silent. He didn't want to talk about the past, and I understood that. So, I finished with my speech and said, "All I want to do now is cuddle."

He pulled me into his arms and whispered, "I love you."

"I love you too," I whispered back.

LESSON: Forgiveness is courage and compassion is sourced from the center of our wounds.

KEYS TO YOUR QUEENDOM

I have never met Amma, the hugging nun whose mere presence is said to heal. But there are people in my life that offered me that same energetic exchange of gracious, no strings attached, pure love. This story, my story, is an offering of that same sort of energetic healing and wisdom, where you subliminally download an initiation to the sovereignty of your own being. Consider this book a transmission of sorts.

I said to myself during one of my many moments of despair, that there had to be a bigger purpose for all the betrayals in my life, an obvious karmic lesson I had to master. If the problem is the solution, I was supposed to learn the lessons of betrayal. I needed to learn how to forgive, how to trust, how to be grateful, and to know faithfulness and devotion in something even greater than me and what was.

I was to learn this for *me*, within *me*. I had to forgive myself for disassociating with the parts of me that felt fear and shame. I had to trust my heart, my needs, my desires. I had to know that I am enough. I had to be faithful and devoted to the "thing" that was greater than me, and my marriage. I had to become love, in order to know love and be in love. Only then could I forgive my husband, and feel absolute gratitude for his gift of awakening me to the path of coming home to myself, to meeting the sovereign of my own being.

The path of the sexy, soulful shapeshifter is an awakening of your multifaceted self. This is a journey full of twists and turns. There is no true linear process when it comes to activating the divine within. To know your erotic self, to get a felt sense of your greatest power, to radiate your inner most beauty, and to own the truth that you are the most special, and complete, and unbetrayable ruler of your own queendom is the woman you truly are.

Becoming the Queen of Reclamation, I understood that I came into this world for a purpose. We all do. We all wrote the epic stories of our lives from somewhere up in the ether, and are currently in the middle of it. To experience my situation this way, helped me to rise above the minutia of pain and see the glorious lessons. Accepting the idea that my betrayals, pitfalls, blocks, and tragedies were simply trying to wake me up to the rest of my journey. This was my first step onto a road less traveled.

My inner Sleeping Beauty was the metaphor for that first kiss that awakened me to the truth of my frozen heart. Without this "kiss," I may have never been able to experience my soul's yearning to be alive. The blow of betrayal wasn't exactly the type of kiss I'd prefer, but it did wake me the fuck up. I was forced to see what I hadn't seen before, and this changed everything for the better. I see that my punch in the gut kiss was my opportunity to make some really needed changes in my life, which allowed me to see clearly the magnificent castle on the hill. I had a new destination toward a realm that held my desires. I had to ask myself what I really, really, really wanted from myself and my relationship. What are your dreams?

After I woke up, I started on a path of seeking (in stilettos of course) to find the fragmented pieces of myself. I found many resources that helped, I stumbled a few times, fell into mud pits, got addicted to self-help, and laughed quite a bit. It was comforting for me to know that many of us have wounds and we are all on a path to revealing who we really are. I also realized that in order for me to really heal, I needed to do something courageous that would break the habitual patterns of our relating. Are you willing to try something new?

There was still plenty of old characters that I was accustomed to playing, like the martyr, the victim, and the desperate housewife who was stuck in a role that served everyone but myself. I had to be willing to break free from the box of shame, the prison of right and wrong, the chains of convention and control that society, religion, and my upbringing tied me to. I realized that I had been doing things for other people for so long, that I didn't know who I was. I didn't know that I was running on empty. Even though my husband and I resonated in so many ways, we lost our fire and all the juice that sustains the spark of passion for each other. Is there a role that you are stuck in?

After I woke up from my deep slumber, I stepped onto the path of awakening, and released the outdated roles that held me back from being radiant. I needed to find my inner goddess. It was time for me to nourish myself. Self-care was what would unleash my inner Venus who was simply waiting to become love in the flesh. I moved my body to keep her active and healthy, I fed her nourishing food, I took time for myself and meditated, I spent time with nature, I practiced loving myself in the mirror. I needed to accept that the pleasure of self-love is a birthright. And I was willing to dive into the nooks and crannies of my own mysterious caves to get to it. Self-care was my preparation. How can you love and honor yourself even more?

When I decided to create an experiment of my own, to add the much needed variety and spice in my relationship, I did not know that I was revealing parts of myself that were screaming to be expressed, or that I had shy ones that needed to learn a certain skill in loving. I came at it with a beginner's mind, and that's how I would suggest anyone come to it. I made some crazy mistakes, but kept on in the name of research. I tried on the thirty different personas in no particular order. But in hindsight, I would have accessed them in a more grounded and thoughtful way (and give them space!), especially because I was involving an unsuspecting lover. So, I'm sharing this in the order that is appropriate for an authentic expression, versus "acting." I think it is so much harder to do this kind of work with someone you have been living with for so long. We have triggers, habits, and resentments that we can't fake. Understanding where the energies of expression lay in my body, and allowing them to be revealed from that point feels more authentic to me.

So, I start with the heart and that innocent, playful inner child before anyone said, "No, don't do that." Before putting the wild haired adventurer into a box, before the billboards representing only one kind of sexy woman, before the fear of being taken advantage of, before the closing of our hearts. She is the one who sees with wonder, leads from the heart, and just loves love. From the heart space, we find her. What deity lives in your heart chakra? What does she look like? How does she play? What does she like to wear? Of course this project is about adding sexy variety to our love lives, but it feels really good to begin at the beginning. Both my husband and I got to play a game of innocence, which was the erotic theme. I got to be that girl who was never defiled, he got to play that boy who was intrigued by my innocent flirtation. We added flirting back into our repertoire and sometimes that is enough. How can you flirt with life, with yourself, and with your partner a little bit more?

Now that I had opened through my heart, there was still a lot of charge that needed to be released. My Femme Fatale was accessed through my root chakra; she was the protector from the events that made me feel unsafe in this world. I needed an underground assassin who could help me feel secure enough to root back down into mother earth. She grounded me, she knew where she stood in this world, she had nothing to prove. My inner Femme Fatale helped me release the pain and unleashed a pleasure response that coursed through my entire body (alone, but still). Not everyone has the same wounds, but they can be accessed and turned into a sexy Atomic Blond, or the Bond Girl, or the Femme Fatale. I learned how to refine her intense energy and turn it into an erotic tension that is really appealing to my husband, and most men. This energy helps "man up" a man. I know you have badass in you. Do you dare to set her free?

The feeling of releasing tension and using tension, gave me access to the sensations of my body. My inner kitty and her primal urges gave me permission to find sensation not only in my body, but through my surroundings, I was able to move in an effortless, meandering, and natural sexy way. The sacral chakra is said to be an empathic center that allows us to feel others. Our animal instincts allow us to feel the body intimately, to feel others, to feel our surroundings. It is also the source of our sexuality, creativity, and even magic. Your primal body might be feline, like a kitty or a lioness. She might be a fox, or a snake, or all of the above. The point is, we are animals that have not been allowed to know the animalistic impulses of our bodies. When I'm in flow like this, my husband responds to it. We can undulate in the flow of our instinctual bodies, and create intense polarity because our bodies respond to each other naturally. What animal does your body feel like today? Can you try moving and loving like that animal? Will you trust your basic instincts?

I chose to include the Executive at this point, because the prior personas can be played without a partner. I would recommend embodying a few personas before taking it into a relationship, just for practice. The worst thing is to embody a persona in a superficial way that might trigger a habit or a trauma that you aren't prepared for. Practicing being in the energy of, the physicality of, the emotionality of an archetype helps to remedy the superficiality of persona work. The Executive was a commitment to include my lover in this experiment in a fun way. It made him feel like he had a stake in the remaking of our relationship too. My Executive was accessed through my solar plexus, the area of power in the world. Creating a playful contract can be done for the entire relationship, or for a set of scenarios, or for every persona. I've since refined my contract to include many more agreements that I didn't understand I needed then. What do you want to accomplish in your relationship? Write it down and sign on the dotted line.

According to Carl Jung, there are a few archetypes that are universal. Like the prostitute, who represents the collective shadow of "selling our souls." I sold my soul by not communicating my feelings of loneliness to my husband early on. He sold his soul by crossing our boundaries of commitment. How many times have I said yes to something and meant no? Or participated in gossip just to connect with another person? We have all sold out in some ways. The prostitute gave me an opportunity to discover my worth, and illuminated the shame I had about being overtly sexual. I didn't only shut down because I felt unsafe with men, women also portray huge amounts of jealousy and judgment to other women who appear "sexy." On the flip side, I also realized how much my religious upbringing made me feel wrong for just being born a woman. I learned that my husband had a little bit of the Madonna/Whore complex, as many men do. For both men and women, shame is in the sacral chakra of sexuality, one of the biggest shadows there is. I could pull out so many personas sourced from the sacral chakra alone, like I did for my Medusa, my Lap Dancer, and my Devil. The beautiful flip side of the Prostitute is that she can turn into the Lover. How worthy do you feel?

The Mail Order Brides gave me an idea of how we might superficially present ourselves for love and the conditions we have. It also helped to refine what I knew about my husband's preferences. Good to know, he doesn't like the *Fatal Attraction* vibe (thank Goddess). The twins gave us a laugh and made me really appreciate how easy it was for him to adapt to the different roles I did. Even though it wasn't as obvious, his roles changed as my roles did. He responded effortlessly to all the different energies that I offered, and he is the stoic, hold the line, straight as an arrow type of guy. The call and response is that easy; I just had to be clear. And then I got to reminisce with the Geisha and be a devotional kind of love that I had not expressed to him in a very long time. It felt good to give. Giving voice to all these characters in their unique ways is tapping into the throat chakra, your power of expression and your authentic voice. If we have all of these energies inside us, I argue that allowing them to communicate uniquely through you, the synthesis will turn into the poetry that becomes the music that becomes the creative expression of your authentic being. How can you creatively express your loving nature?

My Dominatrix and my inner Mother of Dragons are the power icons that come from the pain of the underworld. They are a dynamic power to be reckoned with. They mark an even more defined polarity of domination and submission, and how these opposites provide intense erotic friction. Unlike the Femme Fatale who protects, and perhaps annihilates with sacred rage, these icons believe it or not, dominate through love. They are sourced from the dark side of the sacral chakra, powered through the solar plexus, delivered with love from heart, and expressed with authoritative words and creative scenarios. These are the transformers who transmute darkness into light, which requires badass, yet loving dominance. How fierce is your love? How much do you surrender in love?

The dakini serves humanity, or at least her partner, by elevating erotic energy from the root chakra through each chakra center in the body to her third eye of intuition. Her devotion to sexual healing of her partner can be so moving that she opens up cosmic portals to new dimensions. This might sound a bit dramatic, but there is a new paradigm for sex, and that is a sacred union between two beings co-creating in love that is not just a physical experience, but a spiritual one. It is simple and pure surrender to the Divine.

We have a diversity of personalities that make up the whole of us, like the diversity of people that make up this world, like the different planets in our solar system, and the galaxies within the Universe. If we decide to love each one of them for how they serve us, protect us, and enliven us, we can begin to feel the ease and flow of our natural rhythms, we can cultivate this unique combination to radiate a light unique to only you, we begin to feel like we have everything we need within us, including sexy, fierce, raw, innocent, flirty and powerful. This is wholeness. When you realize that each facet of your soul has something to offer, you have the keys to your queendom.

LESSON: Integration of your power centers and personas is ownership of your soul.

TO THE GUILLOTINE

As I mentioned before, it was really exhausting trying on thirty different women in thirty days. I don't recommend anyone going to that extreme, unless of course the idea tantalizes you, then go for it with gusto! I am here for you.

For those of you still curious about the potential of the unexpressed sacred power of your own eroticism, I humbly suggest you dip in slowly. One persona per week is how I'm guiding my inner circle of courageous initiates (a.k.a. really good friends) who chose to join me on this sexy, soulful shapeshifter path to know their many expressive flavors too. One persona per week allows us to really get to know the unique personas within each of us, her messages, the lessons she's trying to share, and the talents she has to offer.

This is a never-ending journey that I am enjoying. I can re-experience original personas, and perfect the flow between my true essence, which is simply my purest energy of infinite possibilities, and the various personalities that I use as tools for communication or manifestation. Accessing these different primordial energies helps me during my daily life as well as in the bedroom. Life is full of ups and downs, and I can tap into the right energy to help me through a painful loss, or celebrate a deserving accomplishment.

There are many newer archetypes that continue to come forth through me, just as my charts and the psychics said was my gift in this lifetime. I've got mythical deities, fairytale creatures, and mystical entities from the magic realm, the choices and expressions are endless. I find the discovery of the self through an archetypal lens to be infinitely joyful and enlightening. They have offered me a great tapestry of depth, richness, and flavors from which I live and love in relationship to others, not just my partner.

The icons that I sent to the guillotine for this story are the fillers that I threw in for ease's sake, the hot messes, and ones that require a redo, like my Dominatrix.

In the filler category, I became a Hollywood Diva when I traveled to L.A. for the day to meet my girlfriend Kirsten (the beautiful, blonde, Atherton-American). She is a yoga instructor who also happens to look like a picture-perfect Malibu beachcomber. We were designing and creating cute stretchy dresses that could be used for yoga by day and cocktails by night. Kirsten and I have the same free-spirited and impulsively creative Aquarian energy where we must follow every one of our inspirational whims.

We met in Los Angeles, for fabric shopping and a production meeting in the seedy part of L.A. The warehouse that produced our dresses seemed more like a money laundering operation than sewing outfit, my Hollywood Diva was not having it. I should have come as a gangster, that might have made things more constructive. Kirsten picked me up from the airport in a convertible that was so typical of L.A. She wore bright sunny colors, while I contrasted that with dark glasses and dark everything. I intentionally looked like a famous person staging a paparazzi stand off for publicity's sake, I heard some do that. Kirsten humored my aloof and snobby Hollywood Diva, and happily took photos of me on every corner with my hands in front of my face trying to protect my identity. I'd text them back to my husband just for fun. I never took my sunglasses off all day including at our meeting with the mafia/manager. People either stared at me because they were trying to figure out what movie I was last in, or they just thought I was absurd wearing my sunglasses indoors. It turns out that the mafia/manager didn't like us very much and basically told us he couldn't finish with our production process. I made a note that different personas work for different situations, gangster would have been better.

Another filler was the sexy workout coach. I wore hot pink booty shorts and a matching sports bra. I made my husband do push-ups over me, while giving me kisses each time he lowered himself down. That was a fun filler that lasted about ten push-ups. Although this persona wasn't a "dud" in the perspective of entertainment, it did lack any substance. I was like a smutty adult entertainer trying to get a rise from something outside myself and outside of my husband. I'm not opposed to erotica, it depends on the type and if you and your partner use it as play together, but if over used without conscious awareness, porn suppresses our true emotions and feelings, leaving us with one-dimensional sexual relationships that have no depth or meaning. Beware the superficial stereotypes that don't feel right for you, go for the personas that turn you on. If you are turned on, your partner will be turned on. I'm sure if I was more thoughtful, I could turn my work out coach into someone that was exercising her inner strength, determination and confidence, which is much more attractive to me than someone who only focuses on superficial physical aspects.

I also chose to be a ballerina, White Swan by day and the Black Swan by night. I am far from having ballerina strength or flexibility; I can barely touch my toes. But, my gyrotonic teacher is a former prima ballerina who guides me, and all the dancers who go to her exercise studio have strength and flexibility training. I figured that counted. I was able to play in the duality of light and dark by carrying myself perfectly with virtuous grace all day long, and then tapping into my shadow side for something a bit more sinister and sensual at night. Understandably, my husband preferred the light version. I was inspired to finesse my darker energies so that they would not repel, but intrigue. Since then, my darker energies have become the source of my most erotic experiences in such a loving way.

My hot messes were Medusa and the Devil. As you can imagine, these two icons might not be so much fun for a partner who wants to connect, not be scared away. I was once Medusa for Halloween, and already owned a green wig with toy snakes that I sewed into it. I chose Medusa because I have an affinity for her story.

Medusa is one of the most misunderstood creatures in Greek mythology. She was once a lovely virgin priestess in the temple of Athena, known for her long luscious hair and radiant face. Many men lusted after her and came to Athena's temple just to get a glimpse of her incredible beauty. Athena, although a goddess, was jealous of Medusa's looks. Even Poseidon was wildly impassioned by Medusa, and tried to have his way with her many times. After consistent refusals, Poseidon finally forced himself upon the virgin Medusa. Athena could not discipline a god (which seems so typical of patriarchal rule), so in her envious rage, she punished Medusa instead. Athena turned Medusa's exquisite hair into ferocious snakes, and her face into a hideous monster that turned anyone who looked upon it into stone. This is the ultimate betrayal of women against women, a betrayal that turns beauty and the sensual into something repulsive and feared. I can totally relate. My poor husband, imagine what it was like for him to come home to my swampy outfit, a face painted green, and a head full of green snakes. It wasn't exactly a turn on for him.

My Devil was much more seductive than Medusa, she inspired me to wear slick designer clothes, a sexier take on *The Devil Wears Prada*. I happen to like anything vampire and admit to reading *Twilight*. The story tapped into a core desire of mine, which is to love and be loved for my truest essence, to be wanted for something deeper than the superficial reasons why unconscious relationships are formed; like coming from the right family, wearing the appropriate clothes, looking the part, loneliness, or the security of money. Isn't there a piece in all of us that yearns for something eternal? Plus, I liked the idea of not having to sleep, having sparkly skin, and staying youthful for forever. My devil was pretty vampy, I just didn't know how to translate the erotic nature of someone who enjoys stalking and wants to suck the life out of someone, not because I want to kill them, but because I can love so deeply that I can't help myself. I've mastered my devilish side since then, but I freaked my husband out with my amateur attempts at lascivious and demonic devouring.

The icons that fall into the redo category are ones that I didn't have time to fully play out but felt a hint of potential for. Many men have a "thing" for the teacher role. They are the good little prepubescent boys who were bewitched with teacher crushes during their budding sexual years in grade school. I decided to google "how early are kids exposed to porn?" The articles are depressing, eleven is the average first exposure, while ninety-four percent of kids will see porn by the age of fourteen. The women in porn are the new idealized adult these days. With little real sex education out there (which includes sex positive content, boundary lessons, empowerment, and getting rid of shame at an earlier age), I can see how we project sexual desires onto the people around us. The idea of hanging out with a favorite teacher in detention or having to get extra lessons to get a good grade was an erotic boyhood fantasy I would honor. If Van Halen's smash hit "Hot for Teacher" could make it on *Glee* and a *South Park* episode, you know there must be something to this teacher-student fetish.

I purchased a skimpy little skirt from a boutique called Felicity's Fetiche. Felicity's Fetiche did not carry fine French lingerie as the name might suggest; it was a shop for exotic dancers, Burners, and the daring crowd. To my horror, when I came down from the shop there was a father from my kids' school staring into the window. I had to duck behind one of the displays, hoping he didn't see me. Unfortunately, he stayed for much longer than an innocent passerby would.

Three things popped into my mind then. The first was he saw me and wanted confirmation that it was me, so he could spread some good gossip. That seemed legitimate; I might have done the same thing. My second thought was he has a secret shoe fetish, and stopped by the window from time to time yearning for the variety of stripper shoes he was too ashamed to buy. That thought made me sad for him. He and his wife were *very* into the social scene of San Francisco, and hobnobbed with creators of big high tech industries like Sales Force and Facebook. I doubt any of his friends would understand that particular fetish. My third thought was he did *not* recognize me, but assumed I was a call girl and was prepared to proposition me. At that time, I was still untrustworthy of men in general. I thought they all wanted a noncommittal side dish. I'll never know why he hung out so long.

I told the sales person that I was uncomfortable with the guy lingering outside, so she went out and asked him to leave. I waited a few more minutes before I made a mad dash outside to my car. I should have just walked out, said hi and told the truth, "I'm just shopping for the Teacher persona I'm going to try out tonight." In the safety of my car, I sent my husband a text telling him I needed to talk about his grades, and would he please meet me in my office after school. When he got home, I had a report card waiting for him with a bunch of B's and B minuses. He is an over-achiever, F's would not have worked well for his ego. I added a sticky note telling him that he had an opportunity to get an A+ if he wanted to. When he came in to meet me, I was wearing my new little skirt and a white button down blouse with a tie. I told him not to consider this detention, but a learning opportunity.

Another time, I wore a low cut silk red dress, red lipstick, and curled my hair in soft waves that I parted on the side. I took a picture in various sexy poses and texted them to my husband with the words, "Move over Jessica Rabbit." That icon lasted the amount of time it took me to get ready, put on the lipstick and dress, and send a text. We had an emergency plumbing issue, my boys have yet to learn not to waste toilet paper *and* to flush the toilet! I didn't want the plumber to get the wrong impression, so I changed into sweatpants. My husband did not seem to notice the evening was free of an icon, nor did he ask any questions. I'm sure he was probably exhausted too. Jessica Rabbit is the ideal seductress who deserves a redo.

Still new to the feminine, sensual flow that I practice at my dance classes, I pretty much made up the moves for the Lap Dancer icon I played. Plus, I wanted to make up for the time I chickened out years before. By then, my husband accepted whatever I wanted to try on him, the ones that failed were only because I didn't believe in myself. I had to be careful with this one, I intuited that this overt and sexually forward icon might also bring up memories of his affair for me and him. My husband didn't like me reminding him or being reminded of it, he still felt really guilty. In my heartbroken days, I'd listen to songs, or send him songs, that expressed how angry or unhappy I felt because I had no words for my pain and disappointment.

The song mattered, I couldn't use anything too raunchy that might make my conservative husband (who potentially had the Madonna/Whore complex) feel uncomfortable. I spent half the morning trying to find the perfect song that was sexy and stripper worthy, but not overly hardcore. I went old school and found a Tina Turner version of "Whole Lotta Love" which was perfect.

I put on layers and layers of clothing that I would strip off slowly. The rules were no touching the dancer, besides putting dollar bills (preferably no less than twenty dollars) in my straps. Even if I sat on him or climbed on the chair, he was not to do any fondling. The tension of (my attempt at) erotic dance and not being able to do any touching was fun. This icon requires a consistent redo because I am so much better at sensual movement now thanks to my dance classes, and it is so much fun to do.

Finally, my free loving hippy chick was an exploration in carefree living, flowers in my hair, and yes a little bit of marijuana. I did my grocery shopping at Gus' and picked up a few pints of ice cream at the Ben & Jerry's store, both on Haight Street. I felt at home with the all the shops filled with tie-dyed t-shirts and smoke trappings. Months before, my doctor had given me a prescription for medical marijuana for a persistent lower back injury that wouldn't go away. I don't even like taking Aspirin, so I never ended up opening any of the items I purchased from the dispensary. I forgot where I had hidden the illegal (at the time) substances, but when I decided to be a hippy for the day, I searched my bathroom for the Sativa and Indica blend of fruit flavored gummies. Just before everyone got home, I decided to micro-dose by taking just half of the gummy while I did some writing. The package did say something about creativity. But when the medicine finally kicked in, I was the opposite of creative and felt completely wasted. I had to call my kids an Uber to get home from school. All I wanted to do was eat the Ben & Jerry's ice cream, and that is what I was doing when my family got home. I had such a fun time making and serving dinner. I thought to myself that maybe I should have a half a gummy every time I went out to dinner with the in-laws. Before bed, I did take another quarter of the gummy. I noticed that my body completely relaxed and moved more fluidly. I felt every yummy sensation. It was the first time where I didn't need extended amounts of foreplay and mental stimulation. I was entirely out of my head, and fully embodied in the most delicious sensual way. The sex was amazing.

LESSON: Not all the icons will be smash hits.

PROS AND CONS

I hope you try the Kinky Vanilla Love Project; it is such a fun experiment. I also want to caution the things that can go wrong. There are superficial personas you *think* your partner would be interested in but might not be a right fit for the moment. Unfortunately, we often try to be something that we are not in order to please another person, and it can feel yucky and wrong. This experiment is for *you*, and the more you find out about which authentic personalities or archetypes want to be expressed through you, the more fulfilled you will be, the more wholeness you feel, the more you can share love with your partner. You don't want to be a bad actress.

Believe and trust that each persona that comes forth is who she is. Faking it isn't the end of the world, I faked a few before I was conscious about it. We do it all the time during Halloween, and it can be fun, but to try and awaken a new part of yourself and have your partner respond in an authentic and meaningful way, faking it until we make it might not work. I had to believe in myself and be vulnerable enough to share my most tender parts; vulnerability is what makes us who we are. My inner Venus challenged me and continues to challenge me to love myself deeply. When I share in a way that is not begging for a compliment, but shows my shyness or insecurities, I know that it can open the heart of my partner.

A bad actress is guarded and sterile, she doesn't expose her raw emotionality. I had to get to know my naked truth, which was to express the most hidden parts of myself. That means the places where I felt mean, petty, jealous and ugly toward myself and others. My inner Femme Fatale showed me how much rage I had, and she taught me how I can turn that fury into sexual passion. My inner whore gave me a look into my lack of self-worth, but also taught me how to be an awakened lover. Finding the naked truth in each persona I embodied chipped away at my really good presentational skills that served others, but not me.

Use each authentic persona to actively listen. It was so obvious when my husband and I unconsciously played our typical roles. We both exercised listening as just waiting for our turn to talk. The words that finally came out had nothing to do with the present moment, but everything to do with a past failure. I learned to find that perfect persona that will listen with love, and it is worth spending the time to find her before any argument. I use my flirtatious ingénue whenever I feel like my husband is in a bad mood. We both have intense personalities when it comes to what we believe in, I found that my Femme Fatale, Medusa, Hollywood Diva are not so effective when we disagree. My inner executive, my queen, even my ingénue work better in these situations.

Being self-conscious, meaning worrying about what your partner thinks about your authentic truth, leads to robotic interactions. You don't want to show up and just say your lines. Speaking and moving in expressive ways helped me be truthful with love. I called in my inner kitty, my seductive Jessica Rabbit, my hippy, and my lap dancer when I found myself in a rigid thinking mode and needed to get back into my body.

Another thing you want to be aware of is timing. You can do this alone if you want to know yourself, but if you are exploring in partnership, you want to be hyper in tune with your energy, your partner's energy, and what is going on in both of your lives. My husband was a 100 percent willing participant because I communicated with him every step of the way. Moving forward, I can easily refine the vibration of a persona that wants to come forth and works for both of us. It would be unfair of me to throw a different persona onto my partner and then be disappointed in the way he responds. I had to be extremely open and fluid with my experimenting, and promised myself that I would try my best not project any of my past wounds onto my partner in the future.

Remember that it is "and not or" when it comes to discovering the various personas within you. It is not just how you style yourself. Dressing the part is just one way to get to know your personas, but it is the most superficial part. I am a master at dressing the part, but when I don't feel it fully, I look like I am a little girl in my mother's clothing – cute but unbelievable. It's not just how you move, you can fake moving in a sexy way, I did that on the beach in Kauai. Only when I really started feeling sexy in my body, did my body move with more grace and freedom. It is not only about the expressions either, fake orgasms I had perfected if you recall, and the slimy salesperson has perfected the perfect words that will bullshit you into buying a timeshare if you don't want one. Your personas need to come from a deep authentic part of your individual soul, then connect to the archetypal collective energy that I'll call spirit, and then be expressed through your body in movement, voice, expression, and from there dress her up. Yes, it helps to have witnesses and guides for styling and movement and communication, and I highly recommend it. Just remember that no one but you can tap into your most authentic self, and only you can get to your deepest knowing.

Another thing that might happen in this world of exploring the various personas that lie dormant in your soul is the awakening of a spiritual path that might be different from your partners. Before I did this experiment, my husband and I were at the same vibrational selfish level, only thinking about what wasn't working in our relationship. This experiment 100 percent rekindled our passion, enhanced our romance, and amplified the way we love and made love. I did transform my betrayal into bliss. We did reach a beautiful place of forgiveness, respect, and ultimate gratitude for each other. I want this for everyone in my same position.

As I continue down this path of knowing myself intimately, I have awakened to an energy of supreme consciousness, and I surrender to a path of divine inquiry that lies even deeper within me and outside of me. I have to include a reminder here that I am a soul seeker (in stilettos) that is also a self-help addict. While my husband's path remains on the material plane, mine is a spiritual path that seems like a constant spiral into knowing myself. This persona work seems even more important in this realm, as my sexuality now includes a more sacred power, and my soul has found a cosmic bliss that can be incredibly intense at times, some call this Kundalini Rising or the Ascension of the Soul. This is new territory for us, and I trust that we both have the tools to navigate this terrain with even more honor and reverence for each other. It's a continuing process of revealing the self.

LESSON: There are pros and cons to everything.

SELF-SOVEREIGNTY

One of my journal entries just days after I found out about my husband's affair was, "I am reclaiming my beauty, my emotions, my essence. I'm stripping naked my body, my mind, my heart, my soul. Exposing my deepest fears, my most sensual desires, and my most absolute truths. I need to be aroused and awakened to the whole of me. I take back my light. I need to find that safe place where I will never feel shame or humiliation. Where I can open up and blossom completely, where I can fill myself up and explode in love."

I have managed to reclaim all of me, I have become the Queen of Reclamation that has mastered self-sovereignty. The Queen persona was for me and only me. I could not inspire a King in my husband, until I stepped into my Queen. My journey and this project may have started out as a desperate need to feel sexy so my husband wouldn't cheat on me again. It was also an attempt to see if I could be the type of woman who was alluring enough to have a wild affair with. Infidelity for us, was the lack of connection through intimacy, so in my head this project started out with just sex in mind.

Instead, my journey turned out to be a revelation of who I really am. I fell in love with me, which made all the difference in how I felt, how I presented myself, and how I lived in the world. This epic love story, is a love story about reclaiming all parts of me. I learned that I have to love me first, choose me first, be married to me first. From this point of self-awareness and self-love, I can love a partner as much as his mind, body, heart and soul can manage. We all have to do our own inner work of healing and improvement before we can ever expect it in others. It is not my place to force anyone to accept *all* of me, although I know my husband will. All I can do is be love, act through love, and spread love as much as I can. My heart has opened to bliss.

It was my intention to be the sacrificial lamb of some really great gossip, and share the details of my story so you don't feel alone in your own experiences whether they be a slight yearning for something more, or the devastation of ending a relationship. I am unbetrayable. To be betrayed, I'd have to be a victim; I'd have to feel like someone did something to me, which means I'd have no control. I don't need saving, I'm the one who wields my own power. I realize now that the "betrayer" only betrays himself. I forgave my father and am grateful for the templating of raw power and rage for me. To really forgive someone is to find the gratitude of the gifts the experience gave you, and understand that the other is hurting too. I forgave my husband, he forgave me, and we fell in love again. Even if our relationship were to end after all this, I would never consider us a failure. We have learned so much together, and I now have the ability let go of control with the upmost gratitude, compassion, integrity and forgiveness.

I am aligned, I am open in every way, yet I have the boundaries I need to hold myself accountable. I married my inner King with my inner Queen and am energetically complete. This project did elevate my marriage, and saved it from disaster. It allowed me to be fully present to my needs and his needs, it opened our minds to seeing each other for the first time again and again. It allowed us to play in a sexual arena that is natural and playful. My Kinky Vanilla Love Project gave my long term monotonous marriage the juice, variety, and security it so desperately needed.

Maybe this journey will help those of you in long term monogamous marriages to reignite the fire. If you can't decide if you want to leave your marriage, maybe this will offer a full understanding of self, to make the right choices from a place of power. At the very least, this project is a hell of a lot of fun.

LESSON: We are all on a journey of reclamation. You can reclaim your sovereignty now.

Crazy Cosmic Love

You have journeyed with me into my most intimate of secrets, my biggest wounds, and my deepest fears. You are witness to my pains and my pleasures, my betrayal and my bliss. This was good enough gossip for any tabloid, but now that it is out in the open, it is just truth. I'm not sure how this will land for everyone, but I hope through my story you could take the sexy, soulful journey from betrayal to bliss. I hope it was healing and transforming to you in some way. At the very least, I hope it was entertaining.

I gave my husband an experience beyond any man's wildest dreams, which was not the point. I really created this experiment because I wanted to know how to be everything for him, and wanted permission to be more for me. My Kinky Vanilla Love Project not only added spice to our sex life, but it saved my marriage from ending, empowered me sexually, put me into this law of attraction vortex that called in the wisdom of ancient tantric rituals, esoteric philosophies, modern teachers on archetypal energies, and astrological theories that support my tried and true experimentation. I even manifested a soul family who accepts me for who I am, understands me, believes in me, supports and loves me at a deep level. I am on the right path if there is any truth to the ideology that we are all here for a purpose, that everything happens for a reason, that the constellations we were born under have some influence on our personalities and our journeys, and that my psychic is really talented.

Monogamy can lead to monotony, long term relationships can lead to complacency, and it's really hard to keep the spark going, to create the mystery, to feel the tension of polarity in our traditional marriages and vanilla relationships. We're so used to rejecting anything that doesn't resemble missionary style sex or the mundane.

While I was in the midst of experimenting with personas and trying to reignite our sex life, I didn't realize that I was tapping into a kinky world that has existed for ages. I was using my many personas to curate techniques that would add spice to my vanilla relationship, but not take me too far into a lifestyle that I couldn't maintain. Unknowingly, I was working with a set of guidelines that balanced the dangerously exciting world of kink, with the safe and comfort of my vanilla life. What I had inadvertently created was something perfectly in between for us.

If you prefer monogamy but not monotony, and want variety, mystery and fun with just *one* man, and rather go deep instead of wide, then maybe becoming a sexy soulful shapeshifter is for you too. Actually, if you've stuck with me this far (thank you, by the way), then for sure you are ready to attract the love you desire in this way.

No first date is going to share that she has an inner Medusa, or that he has an inner Incredible Hulk. We find these things out over time. The key is to know that everyone has variety of personalities within them, and to try and understand these various energies. We are all human's prone to make mistakes. In my most tender and nurturing roles, I could see the wounds in my husband that he couldn't (or can't) admit to himself. Needing more motherly love, affection, and attention. Afraid to fail or disappoint his loved ones. Maybe we all have that general fear of not being fully accepted for who we are, but only for what we do "right." Maybe we are all ashamed of a primal sexual nature that is feared and shamed in today's climate. My husband may have the collective wound of neglect, just as I have the collective would of betrayal. We are working it out together.

Marriage is a crucible where we learn the many facets of love; the romantic, the nurturing, the sexy, and even the painful parts. I know that my journey was not only to awaken sexually, or to only experience the sensations of my body. I know that I am also to learn the difference between conditional and unconditional love.

My husband and I have probably lived many lifetimes together, our lessons having to do with betrayal, control, and finding our own freedom. I've seen some of them, and they are lessons worth diving into. I have also seen the future, and know our story, and my story, is still in its unfolding and creation. I now have the tools to navigate the many twists and turns to come, and appreciate the bliss. My next phase involves more magic, ascension, amplifying love and serving in love. I get to use my vortex to travel into the next dimension of this new paradigm I call crazy cosmic love.

LESSON: The story never ends.

Acknowledgments

I'd like to first and foremost thank my incredible husband: a rock star, a hero, and a lover all rolled into one. For better, for worse, and for everything in between, he has given me the impetus to rise up from a diminished self, the strength to fight for myself, the vulnerability to forgive our human mistakes, and the boundless support to share our deepest, darkest secrets so that other women might be inspired to reignite the love and passion within themselves, and then share it with their partners. I'd like to thank my kids, who are forbidden to read this book, for putting up with their parents and for being so mature and accepting of our truth; they understand that this redemption story is shared in service to a higher form of love.

I have to thank my siblings for a shared experience, and my parents for giving me life and doing the best they could under circumstances that were hard to cope with; they are brilliant souls providing me with the best lessons in life. I love my special friends Patty and Tracy, who served as surrogate parents, big sisters, and tireless warrioresses. They have supported me throughout my trials and tribulation since the beginning of my journey. Natalie and Vero, soul sisters in my witch coven, are sorceresses of love who encouraged me through the fear and doubt of sharing my wisdom. My coach Anne Davin, who has a mythical, magical way of words that helped heal my soul and emboldened me to see how my experiences and transformations are divine gifts that I should use to pay it forward to guide women on their own journeys.

I am grateful for my very first teacher on the path of embodiment, Sheila Kelley, who is a witness to my evolution, for Regena Thomashauer who provided me with the container to create this project in the first place. I'm grateful for my psychic Diane, my astrologist Tashi, Moriah Howell for her editing prowess, and Dr. Angela Lauria at The Author Incubator who has helped revolutionize the publishing industry and assist unknown writers like me to share our wisdom. I also want to recognize a bit of stardust who floated into my life and inspired my heart with the passion and impulse to write my truth. And I can't forget my dog Boomer, who kept me company during some of my late nights on the computer.

About the Author

Lord Coltrane believes that every woman deserves to feel, taste, smell, see, and hear the naked truth of her multidimensional being. This encompasses the electricity of her radiance, the pull of her magnetic core, the tender, fierce, sacred, compassionate, sensual, wild, yearning, and loving facets of her heart. She believes that at the center of the soul is exquisite beauty, sacred power, raw and primal love – that when unleashed, a woman becomes whole.

Lord Coltrane is a Beauty Illuminator, Persona Provocateur, Archetype Guru, Soul Seductress, Couture Creatrix, Sacred Rebel, Light Brigade Pioneer, and Shapeshifter. Translated into layman's terms, she is an accomplished photographer, archetype and persona consultant, empath, couture designer, certified Ayurvedic educator, esoteric philosopher, and polarity coach. Lord Coltrane uses her considerable knowledge and visionary creativity to inspire and assist women in awakening to their fullest potential and essential selves, unleashing their own dormant feminine powers, discovering their multidimensional souls, and ultimately in attaining radical self-love. She is an excellent guide for women to know their fullness of being and to get to the essence of their souls.

A self-described self-help addict, Lord Coltrane started on her journey of awakening as she faced the pains of betrayal, the body shame instilled in her by societal norms, and the impact from a traumatic childhood. She is heavily influenced by and integrates the works of Joseph Campbell, Carl Jung, Jean Houston, Peter Levine, and the ancient wisdom of the Vedas. Her theological teachers include: Deepak Chopra, Caroline Myss, Lynda Caesara, Neale Donald Walsh and many more.

Coltrane fuses her photography and design expertise, her innate magic, and her knowledge of mystic rituals to create an illuminating experience where women can uncover their multi-dimensional souls and their sexiest selves. She loves to share her knowledge with other women and guide them through their own individual awakenings. Her supreme goal in life is to amplify love on this planet.

When Coltrane is not working, she can be found in soup kitchens serving the homeless, traveling the globe for cultural experiences, curled up reading trashy novels (and non-trashy reads!), dancing in the moonlight, accessing her inner mermaid while swimming in the ocean, loving mother nature, spending quiet time with her family, meditating, and never missing an opportunity to learn something new.

Thank You!

Hello Beautiful,

Thank you so much for reading *The Kinky Vanilla Love Project* and joining me on this sexy, soulful journey from betrayal to bliss!

From the bottom of my heart to the tips of my stiletto shoes, I want you to know that you are a magnificent, multifaceted being worthy of the greatest love affair ... with your partner, with life, and with your *whole* self.

Since you've come this far, I imagine your soul is bursting with the desire to unleash her sexy, soulful, shapeshifter self. I support that!

To learn more about how to amplify love, tap into archetypal wisdom, become unbetrayable, and awaken to all your shapeshifter superpowers, visit me at www.lordcoltrane.com to get the golden ticket, the secret passcode, the undiscovered roadmap, the mysterious magic spell, and the powerful compass that will help you navigate your own Shapeshifter's Journey. Or, just stop by to say hi! I love it when souls connect.

Hugs & Kisses.